Europe and the United States

EUROPE

AND THE

UNITED STATES

Vera Micheles Dean

RESEARCH DIRECTOR,
FOREIGN POLICY ASSOCIATION

ALFRED · A · KNOPF
NEW YORK
1950

THIS IS A BORZOI BOOK,
PUBLISHED BY ALFRED A. KNOPF, INC.

FIRST EDITION

To the memory of

RAYMOND LESLIE BUELL

a great teacher

and a generous friend

FOREWORD

This book makes no pretense of being an exhaustive study of the postwar situation in Europe and of Europe's postwar relations with the United States. Many books on these subjects, some of them by former American and European officials who are much closer to the inner core of international negotiations than any layman can hope to be, have already been published; more will be written in the years ahead. The layman, no matter how well informed on contemporary events, sees only the top of the iceberg. What lies under water sometimes cannot be revealed until a new generation of historians has come upon the scene. Nor can any responsible person lay claim to omniscience about a period so overcast with unresolved and fateful conflicts.

What I have tried to do is to set down my own understanding of the forces at work in Europe today; the historical background to which they can be traced, their impact on the United States, and our impact, in turn, on Europe. In discussing world affairs with many different kinds of audiences in this country and abroad, I could not but become aware, like others with similar experience, of the misconceptions Europe and the United States have about each other. These misconceptions, based on ignorance of history, on wishful thinking, on apprehensions and hopes that have little or no basis in reality, are at best disturbing. But they become dangerous when, on both sides of the Atlantic, they are invoked by political leaders, by the press, or by private individuals as justification for this or that course of action.

The kind of blindman's buff that sometimes seems to be played even by nations so seemingly "like-minded" as Britain and the United States is particularly alarming in an age when all accepted values are being revalued—but at a different pace and according to different scales from country to country. No one can yet predict just what values will survive, what way of life will in our times prove most practicable or most desirable for any given people. This is no cause for pessimism. As the late Cardinal Suhard, Archbishop of Paris, wrote two years after the war: "The present uneasiness is neither a sickness nor a decadence of the world: it is a crisis of growth. This fragile and impetuous adolescence is a crucial moment, for it involves the delicate substitution of new values for structures hitherto valid. What is dying? What will live?" This very uncertainty should caution both us and our friends in Europe to keep an open mind and not assume that we alone have all the answers to problems with which mankind has been wrestling for centuries. Nor is it appropriate for the United States, which was brought into existence by men and women who had the courage not to conform to the pattern of their age and place, to insist on conformity by other peoples with the standards we have found to be satisfactory for ourselves.

Modern life is so rushed that there is little time to think, and even less time to write. I am therefore deeply grateful to Mills College, where two summer sessions, 1948 and 1949, afforded me the opportunity of teaching and writing in an atmosphere of peace and intellectual stimulation unrivaled in my experience. The intoxicating fragrance of the Mills eucalyptus trees on luminous afternoons comes back, among the noise and haste of New York, to haunt me, like the memory of a lost paradise. San Francisco, and the Bay area, have cast a spell over me—a spell that I hope will never be broken. Anyone who doubts the future of the American people should go forthwith to northern California, where the pioneering tradition is sturdily alive and it seems physically impossible to be a reactionary. There, looking seaward from sunlit hills to the gray distances of the Pacific Ocean, one realizes with ever renewed humility that, rich as has been the achievement of the Western nations, it is only a segment of the world's civilization.

I owe a debt I can never repay to many California friends who in difficult years infused me with their own courage, optimism, and sense of perspective—especially to Professor Laurence Sears and President Lynn White, Jr., of Mills College; Professor Harold H. Fisher, director of the Hoover Library at Stanford University, and Mary and Arthur Wright of Stanford; President Paul Leonard of San Francisco State College; and Emma McLaughlin, Persis Coleman, Martha Gerbode, and Georgiana Stevens of San Francisco.

To my children I am grateful, as always, for their cheerful co-operation and their unfailing sense of humor, which gently puts me in my place.

VERA MICHELES DEAN

NEW YORK,
MARCH 1, 1950

CONTENTS

PART I

The Present Seen through the Past

Chapter I

FROM NATION-STATES TO
UNITED NATIONS

Paris, Frankfort, Berlin, Prague, Warsaw, London—all
within one or two days' flight from New York. Yet a home-
ward bound American realizes with a shock that he returns
from far places, distant from us not in air-mileage but in the
mileage of experience the inhabitants of these cities traversed
during the war and postwar years.

Europe since the war is like a human being who has suffered a grievous personal loss. The United States acts as a
sympathetic friend, eager to help but somewhat bewildered
by the magnitude of a disaster of which we have no first-hand
knowledge. Like any bereaved person, Europe listens pa-
tiently, and even gratefully, to our well-meant attempts at
consolation. It genuinely appreciates our economic aid, which
has greatly eased its physical hardships. But, deep inside,
Europeans know that some losses are beyond repair and that
no amount of material comforts can remedy inner desolation.

Yet, like a person bereaved, Europe has two advantages
over us who have known no comparable calamity. It believes,
perhaps with unjustified optimism, that in this generation at
least it has given all possible hostages to fortune and cannot
suffer quite so deeply again. And it finds joy and sustenance
in the small things of life that an actively happy individual
or nation is apt to take for granted.

What, it may be asked, is there to enjoy under the British
system of austerity, what sustenance for the spirit can be
found among the ruins of Warsaw? Contrary to what one
might expect, there is an air of serenity on the faces of many

3

Europeans—the kind of other-world serenity that must have illumined the face of Lazarus when he returned from the tomb. Just to be alive is a miracle—just to have escaped the blitz in London, to have returned from the charnel-houses of Dachau and Auschwitz, from war prisoners' camps in Russia, from the ordeal of underground resistance in all conquered countries.

Survival in itself may not bring contentment, may in fact be fraught with disillusionment and new anxieties. It is heartrending to see the extent to which the fine ardors, the poignant hopes, that inspired many of those who resisted Nazism have flickered out in the gray dawn of postwar "stabilization." Again and again one wishes that the spiritual quality of Europe's underground fighters could have been captured and distilled for future draughts. Instead, it has been largely dissipated—partly because of the reaction that usually sets in after the great exertions of wars and revolutions; partly because of the sense of frustration engendered by Moscow's postwar policies among non-Communists who in resistance movements had been fired by the fervor of Communist comrades-in-arms; and partly, too, because of lack of sympathy on the part of Britain and the United States for the determined men and women whose very anti-Nazism, for example among Italian partisans, seemed to augur postwar unrest. In this period of revaluation, fraught with self-questioning and ambiguities, communism for Europeans west of the Oder has seemed a dead end, and even in the east non-Russian Communists like Wladyslaw Gomulka of Poland and Marshal Tito of Yugoslavia have scrutinized Russian Communist theories and practices with a skepticism that in the eyes of the Kremlin is tantamount to heresy. This does not mean, however, that the American way of life is viewed by Europe as the only way to salvation. Political dictatorship and suppression of opposition are repugnant to all Europeans who have had knowledge of the humanistic tradition and experience with freedom. But so are the emphasis on material achievements, the racial discriminations, and the growing intolerance of nonconformist opinion that many Europeans regard as characteristic of the United States.

Dark though the world outlook may seem to the peoples of Europe, they seem curiously less apprehensive than we are. Perhaps this is because men and women who faced incalculable risks and underwent untold sufferings to preserve their own lives and those of others can never again take the mere act of living for granted. They are almost painfully conscious of the sense, the color, the happiness or sorrow of every passing moment. They have had, in life, the taste of death; and this liberates them from fear, makes them inwardly strong, capable of accepting without surprise or tremor changes that to us sound revolutionary. The Europeans who during the war had to remain where they were, limited for the most part to resistance on the spot, are the ones who through inner travail journeyed to far places. We who were at liberty to move about, who in our war efforts encircled the globe, are the ones who by comparison seem to have stood still. It is we, not they, who are most afraid of the forces unleashed by two world wars, for we have yet to experience their full impact. Nor do the inhabitants of Coventry and Darmstadt, of Berlin and Warsaw, who saw lives and material possessions destroyed by ordinary bombings from the air or by artillery fire, feel the same anxiety about atomic or hydrogen bombs as the inhabitants of New York, Chicago, or San Francisco, who for the first time are gripped by the realization that we, too, are vulnerable to attack. But while the Europeans are not discouraged, they lack physical vigor and the optimism physical well-being generates. Two world wars have taken a terrible toll of material and moral resources. Centuries of disastrous strife and hard work have made Europeans skeptical about courting risks or embarking on new adventures. They long for safeguards against the two great scourges of modern times: global warfare and unemployment. The desire for security, both military and economic, dominates the thinking of the man and woman in the street. This makes Europeans more cautious, more ready to accept economic and social regulation, than is true of us who have not shared their tragedies and have but an inkling of their perplexities.

Not that there is a lack of cheerful sights in Europe. In the spring fountains play and daffodils bloom in Grosvenor Square, where Franklin Delano Roosevelt strides forward, cloak thrown back, with the familiar look of confidence and determination that made him the best-loved American in Europe. Soap-box orators again denounce and exhort their good-humored fellow citizens in Hyde Park, while little girls skip rope unconcernedly in the sun. Barrows of primroses and violets tempt the passer-by in Oxford Street. Violets also are sold by kerchiefed old women in Warsaw at the entrance to a demolished church, soon to be rebuilt, where worshippers crowd into underground catacombs for Sunday Masses. Warsaw's Belvedere Park, spared by the Germans who were quartered in that district, is abloom with pastel-colored baby-buggies from which smile seemingly innumerable infants warmly wrapped in wool and fur. Even in the ghetto, razed to the ground by the Germans, where one faces in all its nakedness the unrelieved horror of the utter cruelty man can wreak on man, the nobly tragic monument erected by the Jewish people to "its fighters and martyrs" lifts one's spirits from the uttermost depths.

No one who has known Paris in days of youth can ever look without emotion on the enchanting vistas of the Tuileries and of the Seine bathed in that incredibly tender light which falls like a blessing on gray roofs, and chimneypots, and streets that might be a part of a stage set by Christian Bérard. But perhaps the most moving sight of all in the spring of 1949 was the Bovril sign in Piccadilly Circus. Throngs poured into that world-famous thoroughfare night after night just to see the bright lights made possible by reduced use of electricity in summertime, and to display this sight to children brought up in a decade of blackouts. The most insensitive person must have felt moved to tears, realizing, with fresh poignancy, the tenacious will to live of human beings and the modesty of the claims they make on life.

But even after being put through the crucible of two world wars and the weary grind of two attempts at recovery, Europe appears outwardly unaltered. On this continent, rent during many centuries by conflicts between nations, between religions, between classes, the physical landscape, by some miracle, remains essentially the same, stirring the memory to recollections of the many phases of its turbulent history. Such change as can be observed is in the figures traversing the landscape. In spite of great losses of manpower—through wars, revolutions, emigration—which might have irremediably depleted another area, Europe has rallied again and again, nurturing civilizations that, carried far afield, have in turn fertilized and given spiritual sustenance to other continents. Today the spotlight swings to other regions—the United States, Asia, the Near and Middle East. But wherever it focuses, it reveals the imprint of European ideas and movements that only now are beginning to shape the destinies of non-Europeans. Among these the most significant are nationalism; expansion overseas, whether we call it colonialism or imperialism; the Industrial Revolution; and, most recently, the trend toward socialism and economic planning.

It is an unpleasant surprise for Americans to realize that in Europe nationalism, far from ebbing, is still at floodtide. The "nation," as Ernest Renan made it clear in his essay *"Qu'est ce qu'une nation?"* is not primarily a material substance that can be identified with territory, language, race, religion, or even the homogeneity of a given group. The Swiss are a nation, even though they speak three languages —German, French, and Italian—and practice two religions, Catholicism and Protestantism. The Poles, partitioned three times in the eighteenth century, dispersed between the German, Russian, and Austro-Hungarian empires, retained the

sense of being a nation and, after repeated uprisings, succeeded in 1918 in achieving national reunion within the
framework of a recognized state—only to be split up again
in 1939. The Jews, scattered all over the world, both those
who became assimilated into existing nations and those who
felt eternal wanderers on the face of the earth, were inspired
by a common desire to bring the Jewish nation together in
its own "homeland" of Israel. Among leading Zionists were
found not only leaders guided by a common religious faith,
but also agnostics who thought of the Jewish people in terms
not of religion, but of an organized community possessing the
rights and responsibilities of a nation-state. Peoples from the
four corners of the earth, of many racial origins, religions,
traditions, and stages of development, found it possible to become fused here into the American nation. In Russia some
one hundred and sixty different nationalities, even more
disparate than those that form the United States, have been
cemented in times of crisis—in 1941 as in 1812—by the
feeling of having a common fatherland. Nationalism is a
powerful spiritual force compounded of sentiments, experiences, traditions shared by a given group of human beings—
an immaterial substance that can exist without material
nourishment, like those Chinese flowers that subsist without
water. Common danger, a struggle for survival, far from
weakening nationalism, increase its strength a thousandfold,
as we saw during World War II when even peoples like the
Dutch, the Belgians, the Norwegians, who had matured beyond the stage of blatant nationalism, found in love of nation a unifying element for resistance movements drawn
from all social groups and many shades of opinion.

Far from being obsolete, nationalism still plays a dominant
part in shaping contemporary Europe. If we could for a moment be transported back to Europe as it was before the
French Revolution, we might discover there signs of the
unity many of us wish could be achieved today. For in spite of
many wars, Europe for centuries had been spurred toward

unity by the Roman Empire, by the Roman Catholic Church, and by the Holy Roman Empire. Like ocean tides each of these unifying influences swept across the continent, but each ebbed away as it neared eastern Europe. Neither the Roman concepts of law and administration, nor the religious and cultural influence of the Roman Catholic Church, nor the sway of the Holy Roman Empire, left lasting imprints on peoples east of the Vistula, the Oder, and the Danube. Nor is it mere coincidence that European thinkers who are now trying to find some practicable basis for a union of Europe turn almost instinctively, like Arnold Toynbee, to the idea of "a world universal church" or, like Robert Hutchins and Professor C. A. Borgese, look back with nostalgia at the common fund of ideas available in the Middle Ages.

Feudalism, too, with its elaborate tradition of knightly conduct, was a cohesive element before 1789. The crusades linked Christianity and feudalism in what was in essence an international campaign against "infidels" alien not only to Christian beliefs but also to the then accepted traditions of European civilization. Yet similarity of traditions and of institutions in prerevolutionary Europe did not prevent the continent from being torn by wars and religious strife. Those of us who today believe that the creation of "One World" will of itself automatically eliminate all conflicts might bear in mind the cruelties of the Hundred Years' War between England and France, the brutal methods by which, in the sixteenth century, secular princes sought to destroy the universal power of the Church, and the wrath that the Church then turned on all "heretics" who questioned its authority.

Within this seemingly united community of western and southern Europe the rise to power of the king, subjugating his fellow lords, challenged both feudalism and the universal authority of the Church. The king, by invoking the Deity in support of his claims and policies, by asserting his "divine right," emerged as the "sovereign," the individual designated by God to rule over his subjects and act as their spokesman in spiritual as well as secular matters. Louis XIV gave epigrammatic expression to this new concept when he, *"Le Roi Soleil,"* the King-Sun around whom lesser men revolved like satellites, proclaimed: *"L'État, c'est moi"* ("The state, it is I"). For four centuries, from 1400 to 1800, the canvas of Europe's history is crowded with figures of powerful kings and queens—Henry VIII, Queen Elizabeth, Louis XIV— against a dim background of undifferentiated human beings, serfs, and even freemen. Not only were the rulers of that period building the political framework of national states, thus breaking up the outwardly unified structure of feudal society. They also shattered the unity imposed by the Roman Catholic Church, insisting on the establishment of national churches politically independent of the Vatican. When Maxwell Anderson's play about Henry VIII and Anne Boleyn— *Anne of the Thousand Days*—was on the New York stage during the trial of Cardinal Mindszenty in Hungary, it was difficult to escape its connotations for our times. For it showed a shrewd and ruthless monarch starting out four hundred years ago on the road to separation of church and state— deposing Cardinal Wolsey, expropriating the Church, and overriding the opposition of idealists like Sir Thomas More. This is but one of dozens of examples that might be cited of the time-lag in the development of eastern, as compared with western, Europe. Just as the Roman Empire, the Roman Catholic Church, the Holy Roman Empire, had failed to make much of a dent on the East, so, too, the East was little affected by the Renaissance and the Reformation, which played such an important part in shaping the civilization of the West, including that of the New World. Thus in the past the world has known not one integrated Europe, homogeneous in traditions and aspirations, but two Europes—west and east.

But even though western Europe before 1789 had been fragmented into national states, there still remained a community of ideas that cut across national boundaries and gave the philosophy, literature, and arts of that period a "European" rather than a national character. Voltaire was read not only in France, but also by Catherine the Great in Russia, and in Prussia by Frederick the Great. The concepts of the French Encyclopedists, of Locke and Paine, kept on detonating like a trail of dynamite in the eighteenth century and into the early decades of the nineteenth. The most distinguished spokesmen of the prerevolutionary years displayed a tolerance that seems extraordinary in our intolerant times. Voltaire's famous phrase: "I disapprove of what you say, but I will defend to the death your right to say it," illustrates the extent to which Europe had progressed in an era that seems to us materially backward, and makes one wonder whether material progress has not been blighted, in our times, by intellectual regression. Goethe, who had little influence on the thought of the German people, wrote not as a German but as what would now be called a "cosmopolitan," a man capable of rising above national passions and prejudices and of thinking in universal terms. National hatreds, he contended, would vanish into thin air once mankind had reached a plane from which "one as it were looks down upon the nations, and feels the weal or woe of a neighboring people as intimately as if it were one's own." Such sentiments would sound out of place not only in Nazi Germany or in the U.S.S.R., where since 1945 "cosmopolitanism," admiration for or even interest in cultural values other than those sanctioned by the Soviet government, are regarded as tantamount to treason, but even here in the United States; for fear of Russia and of communism has caused some of us to feel it is "un-American" to study Marxism.

The notable effort made by a few American intellectual leaders, on the occasion of Goethe's bicentenary, to revive the cult of the German poet, like the recent interest in Thomas Aquinas, represents in part at least an attempt to recapture the common fund of ideas both have come to symbolize for a generation rent asunder by doubts and conflicts. In Goethe's time, however, this fund of ideas was accessible only to a small circle, an élite—the aristocracy of Europe, which was linked across the continent by ties of intermarriage, by comparable traditions and education, by similar interests and aspirations. This aristocracy, like the ruling groups of other periods, could afford to overlook and even defy the prejudices and conventions of what they regarded as the lower orders of society. The British writer George Catlin has pointed this out well. "When, therefore," he writes, "we say that Goethe fought, in a struggle which immensely concerns us today, for the preservation of threatened values against insurgent barbarism and malevolent despotism, we must not forget that Goethe regarded a limited 'cultural' circle as the natural custodians and interpreters, even as against the *profanum vulgus* of their own land, of these values."

The aristocratic attitude toward a given civilization is not limited to any one national group, but rather is characteristic of a stage of development in the life of all nations. The plantation-owners of our own South had a polished mode of existence that they regarded as a prerogative not to be shared with other social groups, least of all with Negro slaves. Even today one meets in Southern cities highly educated men and women who regret the disappearance of a slave economy that once sustained the standard of life enjoyed by the few and gave them leisure to practice the arts of learning and of statesmanship. In Russia, too, before 1917 a small élite, for the most part big landowners like the aristocracy of our South, not only savored the cultural pleasures of their epoch, from literature to ballet, but frequently traveled abroad and felt themselves citizens of Europe—without giving much thought to the conditions in which lived the peasant serfs who made their cultivated existence possible. It is true that the Russian aristocracy displayed interest in the rising intelligentsia, drawn largely from the lower strata of the population—as the aristocracy of France, and the kings and emperors, had been interested during the eighteenth century in the works of Voltaire, Montesquieu, the Encyclopedists, or Goethe. But the intelligentsia remained on sufferance, having little opportunity to play an active part in the momentous decisions of their times.

Whenever intellectuals are excluded from political life, they tend to question the basic premises of society and are inclined to join revolutionary movements, which they either lead or give voice to in literature, art, or music. This was true of western Europe in the century of the French Revolution; in Russia between the Decembrist coup of 1825 and the Bolshevik Revolution of November 1917; in Asia, especially in China, in our own day. Great as is the need for the establishment of a new world order, for harmonization of disparate and clashing ideas, this need cannot be filled merely by placing the cultural values of the twentieth century in the custody of a new élite, however designated or recruited. The time for this has passed in nations where the majority of the population have acquired even the rudiments of literacy and education.

It is not altogether surprising that the current nostalgia for a period that, compared with ours, was remarkably free of nationalism should have antidemocratic overtones; for the birth of nationalism at the time of the French Revolution coincided with the birth of democracy. As kings had once challenged feudalism and the universal Church, so in 1789 the "third estate," the rising middle class of thriving towns, challenged the divine right of kings. With the constitutional limitation of monarchy, as in England, or its bloody overthrow, as in France, sovereignty—the supreme authority to make decisions on behalf of the state—was transferred from the monarch to "the people"; and the people became identified with "the nation," the group held together by common traditions, experience, and sentiments. "The people," having ended the rule of monarchy and aristocracy, asserted the right to rule themselves, gradually developing in the course of the nineteenth century institutions of self-government to which in the Western World we have given the name of "democracy."

The development of self-government, which proceeded at a faster or slower pace according to the special circumstances of each nation, was confined for the most part to western Europe, directly affected by the ideas of the French Revolution, which Napoleon's armies subsequently carried to many parts of the continent. Again eastern Europe remained outside the mainstream of these ideas until the middle of the century; while the Germans and Italians, although in contact with the concepts of both nationalism and democracy, did not proceed beyond the stage of local loyalties to cities or regions until their unification into nation-states, between 1860 and 1870. Like a delayed explosion, the influence of the French and American revolutions, fused with that of the Industrial Revolution, affected many peoples in the remoter areas of Europe and then on other continents. Today, nearly two centuries after the initial upsurge, nationalism and democracy are ideas to conjure with in India and Palestine, in Indonesia and the republics of Latin America, and even among the most backward dwellers of Africa.

From the outset nationalism was identified with the ringing ideals of 1789—"liberty, equality, fraternity"—although these ideals were then thought of primarily as applicable to Europe. Not until the twentieth century did they seem to have relevance for the peoples of areas conquered and settled by European colonists. "The popular will," according to Rousseau, was to prevail, no longer the will of the individual ruler, however benevolent he might be. Since 1789, philosophers and politicians the world over have wrestled with the problem of discovering just how the popular will could be translated into effective and relatively rapid action without degenerating into demagogy. From self-government there was but a step to self-determination. First slowly, then with the gathering momentum of a tidal wave, every group that felt it had a national identity began to insist on the right to determine its own existence and rule its own destiny. In western Europe, where more or less homogeneous communities had already developed within more or less clearly defined territorial boundaries, the growing-pains of nationalism were relatively brief. True, a few burning issues concerning the exact administrative ties of some disputed populations have survived into the twentieth century. Northern Ireland, claimed by Ireland against determined opposition by Britain; Alsace-Lorraine, rich in strategic raw materials, which twice since 1870 has changed hands between France and Germany; Schleswig, bone of contention between Germans and Danes; a few small enclaves in the Alps, important because of their hydroelectric resources, which France after World War II insisted on wresting from Italy; Trieste, principal outlet for the trade of the Balkan hinterland, but peopled by a mixed citizenry of Italians and Slavs; Carinthia, a section of Austria containing a considerable Slovenian minority, which Yugoslavia contends must be included in its borders—these continue to plague peace negotiators.

But they now seem relatively minor problems when compared with the hazards and obstacles encountered by nationalism in the territorially ill-defined areas of Europe east of the Vistula, the Oder, and the Danube, where mighty migrations of many centuries had left residues of countless peoples, like layers of silt after many floods, inextricably mixed beyond the point where boundary demarcations satisfactory to all can be permanently fixed. Not only did it prove difficult in eastern Europe to make nation coincide with state, but in the nineteenth century the self-rule connotations of nationalism ran head-on into the authoritarian concepts and practices of the kingdoms and empires of that area whose rulers had been frightened, but not shaken, by the French Revolution and were determined to defend autocracy at all costs against the onslaughts of democracy. The national aspirations of Poles, partitioned in the eighteenth century between Prussia, Russia, and Austria, broke out again and again into insurrections ruthlessly subdued by the Russian czars, or found expression in sullen resistance. The national aspirations of Hungarians, Italians, Croats, Czechs, threatened disruption of the multinational Austro-Hungarian Empire, which in 1848 called on Russia for aid in suppressing rebellions that spread like forest fires. The Slavs of the Balkans rose up against the Ottoman Empire; and Russia, eager to promote Pan-Slavism and to drive the Turks as far as possible from the Dardanelles and the mouths of the Danube, supported their revolts. But elsewhere antinationalism and antidemocracy joined forces in trying to keep nationalism and democracy at bay. For several decades Metternich succeeded in holding together the Holy Alliance of monarchs who had encompassed the defeat of Napoleon and, they thought, of the French Revolution. But eventually the great empires of Germans, Austro-Hungarians, and Russians were shattered by national groups that took advantage of the disorder precipitated by World War I to assert their independence.

A powerful lever in bringing about the downfall of these empires was the slogan of "self-determination of nations" proclaimed by Woodrow Wilson and embodied in the peace treaties of 1919–20. The Poles were reunited in a national state; the Czechs and Slovaks, breaking away from the Austro-Hungarian Empire, formed a binational state of their own; the Croats, rid of Vienna's rule, joined Serbs, Montenegrins, and Slovenians in creating the state of the South Slavs, Yugoslavia. Finland, and the Baltic states—Estonia, Latvia, Lithuania—obtained recognition of their national independence in 1917 from the provisional government in Russia that had succeeded Czar Nicholas II. Nor is this process of national assertion by any means at an end. New demands are being made for self-determination—demands to which Hitler catered when, in 1939, he encouraged the Slovaks to establish a puppet government headed by a Catholic leader, Monsignor Tiso. Erstwhile empires are seeking to bring back within their administrative structure areas that had gained independence after World War I. The U.S.S.R. in 1940 reintegrated the Baltic states and eastern Poland into the confines of what was once Imperial Russia; in 1945 it obtained from Prague cession of the mountain area of Ruthenia, inhabited by people of Ukrainian origin, which had once formed part of Austria-Hungry.

Within the U.S.S.R. itself national aspirations to self-government have been vigorously pressed, notably in the Ukraine, which with the addition of the Ukrainian populations of eastern Poland, claimed as "blood-brethren" by Moscow in 1940, and Ruthenia, now has forty million people, equal to the population of France or Italy, and greater than that of post-1945 Poland. The Nazis, inspired by their determination to make nation synonymous with race, demanded for the Third Reich all German "blood-brethren" living in other areas—particularly the 3,500,000 Germans of Sudetenland, a part of Czechoslovakia. Hitler had hoped to bring back into the German fold not only people of German origin, but also the territories on which they lived as well as their material possessions, thus using racial nationalism as an instrument of expansion to increase the patrimony of the German nation. By a reversal worthy of Greek tragedy, the nations of eastern Europe Hitler had hoped to cripple or destroy decided, after his downfall, to expel all but a handful of their citizens of German origin to Germany—but shorn of their lands and possessions—and to retain only technicians and other particularly valuable experts. From the areas of Germany assigned at Potsdam to Poland, from Hungary, from Yugoslavia, from Sudetenland, some eleven million German "expellees" who had been slated to act as outposts of Germanism in eastern Europe poured into what many of them had once proudly called their *"Vaterland"*—only to discover that their German "blood-brethren," themselves struggling to rebuild life among ruins, felt less than pleased at their arrival, fearing the newcomers would rob them of jobs. The U.S.S.R., meanwhile, sought to extend its influence over the countries of that no man's land from the Baltic to the Black Sea for control of which great powers have fought over many centuries. The Kremlin, however, made its influence felt not by outwardly nationalist attempts to russify neighboring peoples, but by spreading among them the ideas of communism, which claims international allegiance.

Then, by another ironic turn of events, communism in eastern Europe became identified with nationalism, as in 1789 nationalism had been identified with democracy. Although the Kremlin invoked principles it regarded as universal, the very fact that in lands along Russia's borders communism was fostered by men and women trained in Moscow, imbued with loyalties to Russia and eager to transplant to their own countries the ideas and practices developed in the U.S.S.R., made their efforts appear to be merely a new method of extending the sway of the Russian nation. Not only did nationalists in Poland and Yugoslavia, in Czechoslovakia and Bulgaria, rebel against the prospect that their newly emerging nations might again be subjected to the dictates of a great power, but many native Communist leaders felt disappointed when they found that they would not enjoy the latitude they had hoped for in adapting Russian Communist ideas and practices to the conditions, often vastly different, of their own countries. When Marshal Tito in 1948 defied the Kremlin, he did so not as an opponent of communism, but as a nationalist opposed to dictation by Stalin, who, in his opinion, was using communism to advance Russia's national ambitions. Tito insisted on applying what he considered to be the true doctrines of communism as he thought best for the national interests of Yugoslavia. Thus again nationalism, as in the nineteenth century, has become a rallying-point in a struggle against great-power domination and for self-rule—even when this self-rule takes the form of Communist dictatorship.

At its best, nationalism is a creative force, making a people keenly aware of the spiritual ties that bind it, firing its imagination, inspiring it to eloquent expression both of its past traditions and of its hopes for the future. Fichte, Mazzini, Kossuth, Palacky, Chopin, Liszt, Paderewski—these and many others, through their political activities or their contributions to the arts of their respective nations, crystallized emotions that captivated intellectual leaders in nations already formed, like England and France. Byron's devotion to the Greek struggle for independence, French sympathy for the Polish insurrectionists, entwined with admiration for the music of Chopin, reflected the emotions aroused by national groups aspiring to liberation from foreign rule. The most comparable episode in our times was the passionate concern felt by people in many lands over the struggle of the Spanish Republicans, which more than any other single incident of this century's war and civil strife came to symbolize revolt against fascism.

It was only later, when the electrifying memories of the 1848 barricades and Garibaldi's Red Shirt march on Rome had grown faded and tattered like worn banners, that nationalism began to lose some of its pristine glory. By 1870, as the German nation coalesced into a Reich, which Bismarck cemented with "blood and iron," it became evident that nationalism was not always synonymous with democracy, but on the contrary might become a dangerous vehicle for authoritarianism and militarism. This danger grew more acute as German leaders, finding in the works of Gobineau and Houston Stewart Chamberlain confirmation for their belief in Teuton superiority, openly identified nation with race, and consciously twisted the term "Aryan," used to describe a group of languages (Latin, Greek, Sanskrit), into a label of racial purity applicable above all to the Germans. Ruthless emphasis on "blood" as the test of national unity led with horrifying logic to rejection of all elements deemed unworthy of being part of the German nation, and to their physical extirpation, notably in the case of the Jews, who, as J. J. Saunders points out in *The Age of Revolution,* were guilty of the supreme sin of being "nationless," of partaking of other cultures besides that of the Germans, of being "cosmopolitan," as Soviet spokesmen would put it.

Yet shocking as Nazi brutalities appeared to the rest of the world, it is only fair to realize that German nationalism was but a terrible caricature of what the nationalism of every people could become if carried to comparable excesses. In the days of the czars the Russians, too, had confined Jews to a ghetto, the "Jewish Pale," forbidding them to settle in large cities like Moscow and St. Petersburg, depriving them of opportunities for university education, condemning them to third-class citizenship. What this treatment did to sensitive and thoughtful Jews has seldom been recorded with greater poignancy than in *Trial and Error,* where Dr. Chaim Weizmann, first President of Israel, recounts the tragic experiences of his childhood and adolescence in the Jewish Pale. Even the French, who are commendably free of racial prejudices, revealed during the Dreyfus affair at the end of the nineteenth century the unreasoning frenzy to which any people can at least momentarily descend when passions over race have been aroused. And in this country, in spite of notable strides toward larger civil liberties for Negroes and other minorities, in moments of stress such movements as the Ku Klux Klan emerge out of the darkness of our lowest motives to remind us that no national group, however well versed in the technical skills of modern civilization, is immune from the inhuman tendencies that, to salve our own consciences, we have attributed primarily to the Germans. In fact, there is a lesson to be learned from the unexpectedly friendly treatment that many Germans, in spite of Hitler's indoctrination about the evils of close relations between different races, accorded to Negroes in the American occupation forces. In *The Last of the Conquerors* a young American novelist recounts how in

Germany, where white women did not show contempt or repugnance for black soldiers, some Negroes, without expressing bitterness about the United States, decided that they would be happier to remain in a war-torn country where a living is hard to earn rather than try to pick up the threads of their lives in Alabama or Georgia.[1]

From the 1860's on, the aggressive nationalism of the Germans was translated into military preparations and programs of colonial expansion both overseas and in eastern Europe under the slogan of *Drang nach Osten*—at a time when the more advanced nations of western Europe had already gone through many wars, had had time to win and lose colonial empires, and asked for nothing better than to enjoy in peace the fruits of their past achievements. German nationalism exacerbated the latent nationalisms of neighboring peoples— the French, the Russians, the Italians. Pan-Germanism, which, long before Hitler, preached the unification of all Germans within one Reich, strengthened France's determination to have its *revanche* for the Prussian victory of 1870. It consolidated Pan-Slavism, the political movement that expressed the Russians' desire to unite all Slav peoples under the national and religious leadership of a Third Rome, with its center in Moscow. Much earlier, and before national unification movements had emerged in Europe, the United States, by proclaiming the Monroe Doctrine, had drawn a line around the Western Hemisphere which non-American nations could cross only at their peril, had undertaken to defend the nations of this hemisphere against all comers, and had laid the basis for Pan-Americanism—even though the nations founded in Latin America by Spanish and Portuguese conquistadors or the French settlers of Quebec had little in common with the descendants of English colonists. In our own times the Japanese proclaimed a doctrine of exclusion, "Asia

---

[1] William Gardner Smith: *The Last of the Conquerors* (New York: Farrar, Straus & Co., 1948).

for the Asiatics," which, by raising a hue and cry against white nations, greatly strengthened the demand of the peoples of southeast Asia for termination of Western rule.

Thus nationalism, raised to the nth degree of potency by assertion of racial principles, became a factor of cohesion for entire geographic regions, threatening to isolate them from other regions. Instead of unifying national groups of a given area into a regional union or federation on a basis of equality, nationalism all too frequently became an instrument for domination by a great power over its neighbors, as the Nazis sought to dominate Europe, and the Japanese Asia. These attempts at nation-race hegemony were the bitter dregs of the once heady wine of nationalism—all the more bitter because meanwhile the nations of western Europe that were the first to emerge as nation-states (British, French, Belgians, Dutch) proved slow to understand the national aspirations of the colonial peoples whom they had come to rule. Even today Westerners are inclined to believe that Asia's nationalist movements are the work of a few fanatical leaders, usually labeled Communists whether or not they support communism, and fail to detect the deep-running currents of desire for self-rule with which Europe's own experience in the past century should have made us familiar. Britain, which in Europe led the way in limiting the power of the monarchy, creating institutions of self-government, making effective use of the Industrial Revolution, and broadening the franchise to include more and still more layers of citizens, blazed the trail also in Asia (aided by our example in the Philippines) when it granted independence to India in 1947 before its hand had been forced. The Dutch and the French were either less responsive to the new winds of opinion blowing in the colonies or less flexible. After the war they promised Indonesian and Indo-Chinese nationalists a transitional period of association with the mother countries in more or less loose unions, on the plea that colonial peoples are not yet prepared for independence—without recalling how unacceptable similar proposals would have seemed to them when their own nationalism was reaching its high-water mark in the eighteenth and nineteenth centuries. In 1949 the Netherlands, at the urging of the United Nations, transferred sovereignty to the United States of Indonesia, but the French, in early 1950, were still struggling to suppress the nationalist movement in Indo-China, after having granted limited autonomy to Emperor Bao-Dai.

The colonial powers of western Europe may justifiably contend that nationalism has dangerous aspects in an unsettled world—that it threatens to atomize societies long held in relative security and prosperity under colonial rule, and would leave many small, weak, unsheltered national groups at the mercy of any predatory great power or group, by which they mean Russia and native Communists. A comparable criticism has been made about nationalism in Europe, which by encouraging self-determination of nations produced, after World War II, many small, weak, unsheltered nations—for example, the Baltic states, with populations averaging between one and two million—which found it impossible to withstand the economic pressures and military assaults of their great neighbors, Germany and the U.S.S.R. It is obvious that mere assertion of national identity gives no guarantee of viability or security. And it can be cogently argued that perhaps Hungarians, Austrians, Czechs, and Croats were relatively better off, both politically and economically, when they jostled each other in the Austro-Hungarian Empire than after they had achieved the national independence they coveted. It can be argued, too, that India might have enjoyed greater internal order and prosperity under continued British rule than when it had to rely on its own unaided efforts. Yet the fact remains that, since 1789, national groups in an ever widening geographic circle have sought to liberate themselves from the rule of others and have fought and bled to be able to govern themselves, even if their own rulers turned out to be less humane or less capable than foreign overlords. The Indonesian leader Sjarafuddin is reported to have said to the Dutch: "You governed us well, but you governed us!" This sentiment has inspired nationalists in colonial areas as it once inspired Poles and Hungarians, Italians and Czechs, who preferred the risks and difficulties of independence to the relative security and prosperity of the Austro-Hungarian Empire. Every national group is bound sooner or later to pass through the stage of national self-assertiveness, comparable to the stage of adolescence in the life of the individual, before it can proceed to maturity, to more advanced forms of relations with other nations.

The great nationalist leaders of the nineteenth century did not view the formation of nations as a final step, after which all national groups would freeze into a *status quo*. On the contrary, some of them, notably Mazzini, were convinced, as J. J. Saunders has well put it, that "once the multi-national absolute monarchies were destroyed, a federation of free and independent Nation-States would establish a system of the fullest economic cooperation, which would do away with tariff barriers and trade monopolies, permit the free export and import of food, capital, raw materials and manufactured goods, and thus stimulate the production and increase the prosperity of the world." Their dream of "One World" was not very different from that cherished in our century by men and women of many lands who, in the wake of two grueling world wars, are now striving to build permanent bridges between nations and to erect the structure of an effective international organization.

Once the Roman Empire, under the impact of barbarian invasions, had broken up into fragments, the peoples of Europe who had been held together within its framework struggled with one another for territory and power, long before they coalesced into distinct nations. For centuries Europe was threatened by invasions from Africa and Asia. The Moors were checked at the Pyrenees by the forces of Charlemagne (what western European can forget the haunting and desperate call of Roland's horn at Roncevaux?). The Asiatic hordes of Tamburlaine and Genghis Khan repeatedly swept across the steppes of Russia; Tatars defeated Russian princes in epic combats recorded in legends about Prince Igor that are as eloquent as the *Song of Roland,* and ruled over the Russians for two centuries; and the Turks laid siege to Vienna as late as 1683.

The English, having withstood after Hastings all attempts of continental peoples to invade their island home, waged bitter wars with the French on the soil of France (what European schoolboy can forget Agincourt, or the burning of Joan of Arc?), and later, as both peoples set out to build empires overseas, in the New World also. Spain challenged England on the seas, only to go down to defeat when its Armada was routed by Elizabeth's captains. The peoples of the Low Countries overthrew the tyranny of Spanish viceroys and formed the two nations of Belgium and the Netherlands. As the French became consolidated into a nation under the strong centralized rule of able kings, France assumed the leadership in Europe, reaching the peak of its power under Louis XIV in the seventeenth century. After the bloody interval of the French Revolution, when France was invaded by foreign armies that hoped to achieve the twofold aim of defeating the Revolution and bringing the French nation to its knees, the French under the generalship of Napoleon carried French ideas and practices as far as Moscow in Europe and Cairo in Africa. Crushed at Waterloo by a coalition with Britain and Russia at the head, France did not recover its military and political primacy except for a brief period under Napoleon III in the 1860's, although it not only maintained, but actually expanded, its cultural influence on the continent and in the rest of the world.

As France declined, Britain, armed with the production facilities of the Industrial Revolution, rose to dominance, its

naval power unchallenged on the seven seas. The British were
not concerned to establish political domination over Europe.
What they wanted was to prevent the formation on the continent of any coalition that might threaten their security, and
to prevent Russia from acquiring outlets to open seas. They
combined a balance-of-power policy toward the nations of
western Europe with a policy of "containment" toward Russia. Britain joined Russia in defeating Napoleon, but it co-
operated with France and Turkey to prevent Russia from
gaining control of the Dardanelles and the mouths of
the Danube. Britain's "containment" policy reached its
nineteenth-century climax with the Crimean War of 1856,
in which Russia suffered a disastrous defeat, and twenty-two
years later at the Berlin Congress of 1878, at which Russia
was deprived of the gains it had reaped in the Balkans by its
victory over Turkey in support of the southern Slavs.

By that time the German people, belatedly consolidated
into a nation, had challenged France on land in the Franco-
Prussian War of 1870, disastrous for the French, and was later to challenge Britain on the high seas; for Imperial Germany aspired to become both the dominant nation on the
continent and a great naval power with overseas colonies. Germany sought the support of the multinational Empire of
Austria-Hungary, as well as Italy, also recently come to nationhood and, like Germany, eager to acquire colonial possessions. Russia, outwardly linked to the Germans by a re-
insurance treaty, forerunner of the Nazi-Soviet non-aggression
pact of 1939, was fundamentally in conflict with Austria-
Hungary, which held Slav peoples—Croats, Czechs, and Slovaks—under its rule. While Britain still sought to "contain" Russia and found itself in conflict with the Czarist Empire in new areas—Persia, Afghanistan, and India—it swung
back to its traditional balance-of-power policy on the continent once the ambitions of the German Reich became clearly
discernible. At the turn of the century the Triple Alliance of
Germany, Austria-Hungary, and Italy was confronted with

the Triple Entente of Britain, France, and Russia, for the
sake of which the British had reached sphere-of-influence
compromises with the French in 1899 on Africa, and with
the Russians in 1907 on the Middle East.

A seemingly isolated incident at Sarajevo unleashed the
long-gathering storm. World War I began as a European conflict, but soon nations of the New World, Asia, and Africa
were sucked into the maelstrom. When the smoke of battle
cleared, Europe emerged greatly diminished in economic
wealth, in military strength, and in moral influence, while
the United States rapidly waxed in industrial might and
the U.S.S.R. began to exercise far-reaching ideological influence through propagation of communism. World War II
completed this process of transfer of power from Europe to
other regions of the world. With the defeat of Germany and
Italy and the further weakening of Britain and France, the
United States and the U.S.S.R. emerged as the two great
powers, or rather superpowers, of the twentieth century. It
was then that the Europeans, realizing their continent's relative decline from its centuries-old position as center of the
universe, began to wonder whether they might find new
strength through a unity they had not known since the Roman Empire and the Middle Ages.

Meanwhile, partial attempts had been made to create various forms of limited supranational organizations. In 1949 the
British Commonwealth of Nations, which had cemented the
loyalties of British-settled communities overseas—Canada,
Australia, New Zealand, the Union of South Africa—by the
symbol of a common monarch, by common tradition, and by
common economic interests, found it possible, through a verbal device, to gather into its fold non-English and non-white
peoples only recently come to nationhood and independence
—India, Pakistan, and Ceylon. The Union of Soviet Socialist Republics, which within its administrative structure
holds some hundred and sixty national groups, is the only
multinational state to survive the political upheavals of the

nineteenth and early twentieth centuries. The bond that
links the disparate elements of the U.S.S.R. is principally a
common ideology imposed by a strict dictatorship, although
the peoples of the Soviet Union have many cultural experiences and economic interests in common. The United
States has been pre-eminently successful in blending peoples
of diverse national origins, religious beliefs, and stages of development into a great nation, "one and indivisible," without having to resort to force. Our unique experience could
be of inestimable value in the development of an international organization that will rise above clashing nationalisms
only if it assures variety within unity.

The United Nations, forged during World War II as successor to the League of Nations, is still in the process of de-
fining the scope of its responsibilities and the range of its effective authority. During this transition period, marked by a
sharpening test of strength between West and East, it has
seemed to many Americans and Europeans that a regional
grouping of "like-minded" countries should be formed in
western Europe along the Atlantic seaboard, linked across
the Atlantic with the United States and Canada. Such a
grouping, it has been argued, would achieve two main objectives: it would provide a larger area of free trade for its
members (although American proposals for western European union usually envisage the lowering or complete abolition of tariffs only among the European nations, not on the
part of the United States); and it would give the participating
countries military security against possible aggression by the
U.S.S.R., which shortly after 1945 drew the nations of eastern
Europe and the Balkans into its orbit and started to form an
economic and security bloc of its own.

The concept of a European federation, which under modern conditions would restore in part at least the unity that existed on the continent before 1789, has strongly appealed to
many distinguished European leaders, especially in France
and Italy, from Aristide Briand, who pleaded eloquently for

European union after World War I, to Count Carlo Sforza, Italian Foreign Minister, who urged it after World War II. The first step in formulating plans for a European union, however, is to arrive at a geographical definition that would win general acceptance. Should Britain be included in a European union? The British have always been actively interested in the affairs of the continent, but in their island fastness they do not regard themselves as part of the mainland, even now that air warfare, and the threat of atomic bombs in future wars, have demonstrated that no area is immune from attack and destruction. Britain is both a European and an extra-European power. Through its balance-of-power policy it has consistently sought to prevent the formation on the continent of any coalition that might endanger its existence. Whenever such a coalition seemed to be in the making Britain has rallied other European nations to fight against it, as it did in the days of Napoleon, Kaiser Wilhelm, and Hitler. At the same time Britain has strong ties of strategic necessity, economic interest, and sentimental attachment with the dominions and with its colonial possessions scattered all over the globe. It is constantly faced with the task of harmonizing its regional balance-of-power policy with its effort to maintain a world-wide balance between its European concerns and its overseas commitments. Many Europeans, especially the French, fear that Britain will never wholeheartedly become an active member of a European union. Nor, meanwhile, will it permit the organization of any continental grouping that in its opinion might sooner or later assume the character of an anti-British coalition.

Is the U.S.S.R. part of Europe? What would be its role in a European union? Like Britain, the U.S.S.R. is both a European and a non-European power; and like Britain it has oscillated between isolation from and intervention in the continent's affairs. Its interests are divided between Europe and Asia and, whatever its form of government, it must always look both west and east. Unlike Britain, it is a physical part of the European continent and is directly concerned in continental developments. Like Britain, it is fearful of any coalition that might assume a hostile character; and it is not mere coincidence that the two countries had fought side by side against attempts at hegemony by Napoleonic France and by Imperial and Nazi Germany. It is inconceivable that the U.S.S.R. could accept the formation of a European union from which it was excluded. Yet if it is included, its two hundred million fervently indoctrinated people would so overbalance the rest of Europe, especially if Britain remains lukewarm toward union, as to fill non-Russian Europeans with mortal fear of being dominated by Russia and by communism.

If, by an unlikely combination of events, it should prove possible to exclude both Britain and the U.S.S.R. from a European union, what should be done about Germany? Even after a war in which it lost approximately seven million people, the German nation, counting the expellees who have found a haven in its confines, numbers about 70 million—considerably in excess of the other principal continental nations: France with 40, Italy with 42, Poland with 24 million. If Germany, its four zones ruled until 1949 by the four Allies, were to enter a European union reunited into a single state, it would overshadow the rest of Europe not only by the size of its population, but also by the technical skills which have made the Germans the leading industrial nation on the continent. Yet to leave out Germany would be to disregard the realities of the European situation, and to nurture among the Germans a resentment that sooner or later would lead to another explosion. That is why some French leaders, foremost among them Foreign Minister Robert Schuman, whose Alsatian origin has given him a keen perception of the issues at stake and a strong desire to overcome Franco-German antagonisms, have looked with favor on the possibility of including in a European union western Germany alone. The West German state has a population of 45 million, which closely corresponds to the present-day populations of France and Italy. It is doubtful, however, whether such an arrangement could be regarded by fervent German nationalists as more than a stopgap solution, pending the eventual unification of the German nation, which is the ultimate objective of all political parties.

The two nations that have most vigorously advocated European union—France and Italy, both Latin—see in union not only a safeguard against undue domination by Teutons and Slavs, but also an opportunity to exercise the ideological leadership they enjoyed in their heyday but gradually lost when other countries outdistanced them in the race for industrial power, prerequisite of modern military might. But even in France and Italy it is recognized that western European union would not solve the problems of the European economy, which, in the past, has depended on exchange of the West's manufactured products for the foodstuffs and raw materials of the East and of overseas possessions. In the long run the Latin nations believe it will prove necessary to bridge the existing gap between west and east in Europe and to seek unity not merely within a region, but on the continent as a whole.

Is it possible in any case today to maintain a standard of living regarded as adequate or to enjoy a modicum of security conducive to a "good life" through membership in a regional or even a continental grouping—no matter how technically advanced and politically skilled that grouping might be? We may have overleaped the stage of regional or continental unions and federations, and passed without transition from nation-states to the United Nations—just as the peoples of Latin America and China, overleaping the age of railways, jumped without transition from primitive transportation by burro or coolie to transportation by plane. If this is true, then efforts to create regional groupings, whether as temporary substitutes for international organization or as armed coalitions may represent a step backward.

Nationalism, clearly, is not dead. On the contrary, two world wars that caused peoples to become painfully aware of their national identity, and the spread of nationalist sentiment to areas hitherto little affected—the Near and Middle East, Asia, and Africa—have given nationalism a new lease of life. Meanwhile, as the paramount influence exercised by Europe—specifically the western European nations—has gradually declined and nations of other continents have come to play an increasing part in world affairs, the stage has been set for a genuine international community in which all national groups, without distinction of race, color, or religion, could actively participate. Then nationalism, recapturing its once creative character, could become a rich contribution by each nation to a common fund of ideas and practices, a universal—and no longer purely European—heritage on which, in turn, all nations could draw for such ideas and practices as are best adapted to their particular conditions at a given stage of development. But before this transmutation of nationalism into an internationalism enriched by the traditions, ideals, and policies of all nations can be achieved, Europe and, in lesser measure, the United States will have to alter fundamentally their attitude toward non-white peoples—an attitude that in the past had led the Western World to assert, both consciously and unconsciously, the racial superiority toward non-whites that we have deplored when displayed by the Germans toward other Europeans. This attitude left a deep, but it must be hoped not an indelible, imprint on the course followed by European nations in their colonies. Today "imperialism," even though greatly moderated and modified, and in some areas—India, Pakistan, Burma, Ceylon, and the Philippines—actually abandoned, still creates grave psychological obstacles to the establishment of relations of mutual trust between the West and colonial peoples. It also furnishes one of the most effective weapons of Russian and native Communist propaganda against "capitalist powers."

Chapter II

FROM IMPERIALISM TO
COMMONWEAL

At no time in its history has Europe existed as a continent
unto itself. To use the words of John Donne, it has always
been "a part of the main." From earliest days the seafaring
peoples along its periphery—from Greek and Phœnician sea-
men, and Roman legionnaires crossing the Mediterranean to
conquer Carthage, through the Vikings, the traders of Venice
and Genoa, and explorers setting out from the ports of Italy,
Spain, Portugal, France, and England to discover new worlds
—have sought adventure, financial profit, and political power
in other continents. Some went overland like Alexander the
Great or Marco Polo; others, explorers or Pilgrims, braved the
dangers of uncharted seas. Early European discoveries often
proved to be hit-and-run affairs. The treasures of newly
opened lands—gold, silver, spices, and silks—were gathered up
greedily, with no hesitation to use force, and shipped back to
Europe, where they went to enrich the ruling groups of the
times, both secular and religious. In other instances European
conquerors extended political control over the territories they
had discovered, claiming social and economic privileges superior to those of native peoples. By the eighteenth century
Spain and Portugal, France and England had brought rich
overseas territories under their domination and developed
with them the "colonial" relationship. The mother country
provided the administrative machinery, operated by its political representatives and backed by its military force. The
natives worked in mines and on plantations to produce the
raw materials and foodstuffs that western Europe came to

33

need more and more as it stepped up the tempo of industrial production.

But by the time the Industrial Revolution went into full swing, some of the nations once in the van of colonial conquest had lost many of their overseas possessions. The thirteen American colonies revolted against Britain's attempt to maintain trade monopolies and to prevent them from developing their own manufactures. Asserting their independence from the mother country, with its mercantilist policy, they opened up the American continent, creating here a great industrial nation in what was once a wilderness. In the course of bitter colonial wars between France and England during the eighteenth century, France lost its settlements in Canada, whose French-speaking population are now Canadian citizens. British communities in Canada, Australia, and New Zealand had already started on the road toward independent existence, and a century later achieved dominion status. Britain, having been forced by the American revolution to abandon its principal colonies in the New World, had no desire to see Spain become the leading European colonial power in the Western Hemisphere. When it appeared in the 1820's that Spain might attempt to suppress revolts in its overseas colonies, which were struggling to become independent republics, Britain's Prime Minister, George Canning, "called in the New World to redress the balance of the Old," and appealed for intervention by the United States. At Britain's behest the young American Republic proclaimed in the Monroe Doctrine of 1823 that it would oppose any attempt by a European nation to interfere in the affairs of the Western Hemisphere. Although at that time the United States possessed no military might comparable to Spain's, British naval power served to enforce the Monroe Doctrine. In contrast to the Europeans, we have had few colonies, and gave independence to the Philippine Islands in 1946, less than fifty years after acquiring them from Spain. Through the Monroe Doctrine, however, the United States demarcated for itself a

sphere of influence in which other great powers could intervene politically only at their own risk; and this sphere of influence happened to be an entire continent.

Barred after 1823 from establishing colonies in the New
World, the European nations still retained rich possessions in
Asia—Britain in India, France in Indo-China, the Netherlands in the Dutch East Indies. The colonial powers not only
proceeded to develop their Asian colonies, but sought special
rights and privileges in long-established national states of the
Far East, China and Japan, which could not be claimed as
colonial areas. They also acquired colonies in then barely
developed Africa, so little known except for its Mediterranean coastline in the north, already familiar to the Romans,
and the Union of South Africa in the south, that it was called
the "Dark Continent." By 1900 Europe had become the focal
center of the world, from which intellectual influence, political control, and economic domination radiated to all other
continents. The United States retained, unchallenged, its controlling position in the Western Hemisphere, where no other
great power emerged; but the nations of Latin America continued to depend on Spain, and even more on France, for
their cultural traditions, and later turned to Germany for
technical and military training. The leaders of India, deeply
as they resented British rule, which they strove to overthrow,
acquired their ideas of political democracy at Oxford and
Cambridge; the future nationalist leaders of the Dutch East
Indies aspired to complete their studies in the Netherlands;
and the native rulers of French colonies in Africa and Indo-
China were trained to adopt the political and cultural patterns of France.

In their relations with colonial peoples the western European powers combined a genuine philanthropic impulse with
a frank desire to make profits. As late as the twentieth century the expansion of colonial rule was justified by two slogans that reflected this ambivalent approach. Westerners ag-
gressively contended that their nations—first Britain, France,

and Belgium, after 1860 Germany and Italy—needed "a place in the sun"; at the same time they wistfully pointed to the obligation of shouldering "the white man's burden." Many Europeans sincerely believed they were helping the natives and felt bewildered or angry when they found that their colonial subjects wanted to go their own way, free of tutelage by white masters. This situation is not unknown in our South, where old families find it difficult to understand why Negro servants to whom they have been "so good" should want to move North, where they may have to face less favorable conditions.

It is neither fair nor accurate, however, to say, as many critics both Marxist and non-Marxist have done for decades, that European "imperialism" was wholly bad. Missionaries, teachers, doctors, engineers, traders, administrators from mother countries made an impressive contribution to the development of backward and dependent peoples. They alleviated cruelty, reduced illiteracy, introduced modern standards of sanitation, nutrition, and health, built roads, ports, and railways, fostered irrigation, encouraged the exchange of colonial foodstuffs and raw materials for previously unobtainable Western manufactured goods, and strove to maintain order and dispense justice.

In fact, Europeans, and more recently Americans, brought about revolutions in colonial areas long before the Communists began to preach revolt against imperialism. Christian missionaries broke up established family patterns and weakened the foundations of deeply rooted religions by trying to make converts of natives. Doctors, engineers, and teachers encouraged natives to develop professional skills and demand better opportunities for education. Traders acquainted the colonies with higher standards of living. The natives, once they had learned that other peoples lived far better than they did, became susceptible to the propaganda of political leaders who assured them they too could enjoy Western comforts once they had overthrown colonial rulers and could do their own selling and buying in world markets. Administrators who showed what democratic self-government could mean in Western terms created a desire among natives to end corruption among their ruling groups, and to achieve political independence from the colonial powers. The more advanced and enlightened a Western colonial nation, the more likely it was to hasten termination of its own rule, for eventual liberation of colonial peoples offered the only policy that could be reconciled with the concepts of political liberty and economic freedom which, according to Western administrators, constituted the essence of democracy. Once imperialism had been linked with democratic ideas, it proclaimed itself to be a self-liquidating undertaking; or, to put it another way, democracy could not be indefinitely compatible with imperialism. After World War I the fundamental issue with respect to the colonies was no longer whether they should be given independence, but when and under what conditions transfer of authority from the mother country to native governments would take place. The first carriers of revolution in the colonial areas were not Russia and native Communists, but all Europeans and Americans who genuinely believed in the potentialities of democracy implemented by industrialization.

Yet it proved difficult for colonial powers to surrender their control of overseas territories whose resources and markets had become an integral part of their national economies. Not that the colonial economic relationship was entirely one-sided, with the mother country obtaining all the benefits while the colonial peoples did all the work. Far from it. Trade did not by any means always follow the flag. Political control did not assure economic predominance for the mother country, except under conditions of rigid mercantilism, which invariably proved self-defeating, as shown by the experience of the American colonies and the case of Britain's cotton exports to India. The expenditures of colonial powers on administration and military defense of their colonies and on naval protection of trade routes far exceeded the returns they received on colonial trade. And such profits as were derived from the colonies were reaped by a small number of traders and bankers, not by the population of the mother country as a whole. It can be convincingly argued that each of the Western powers lost far more than it gained by acquiring colonies—unless one takes into account the intangible benefit of improvement in its strategic position as against other colonial powers. For the Western nations made substantial investments of capital as well as technical and administrative skills in their colonies—investments that deserve our study now that we are weighing the possibilities of a technical-aid program for backward areas. Long before President Truman announced "Point Four" in 1949, the western European nations had recognized the need to develop colonial resources if these resources were to be made available for their own economies or the rest of the world. By these substantial investments overseas the western European powers may have deprived their own domestic economies of capital and skills that would have brought them farther along the road to modern industrialization than they had come in this century when they were outdistanced by the United States and Germany, neither of which had important colonial possessions.

The economic development of the colonies, however, was determined not by the interests of the native populations, or by the carefully considered needs of the non-colonial world, but by the possibilities of profit-making as calculated by merchants and bankers of the mother countries. Even today most of the colonial economies depend on intensive output of one or two products—oil and rubber in the Dutch East Indies, tin and rubber in Malaya, rice in Indo-China.

This dependence makes them highly vulnerable to sharp declines in commodity prices; and they possess few industries, having hitherto received from the mother countries such manufactured goods as they could afford to purchase. Moreover the funds expended by the mother countries in the colonies, whether in the form of investments or outright payment for goods, usually went not to the people, either directly or as indirect social and economic benefits, but to native rulers, rajahs or tribal chiefs, who thereby enhanced their own wealth and prestige and, not unnaturally, favored perpetuation of the colonial system.

As the native peoples began to grasp the rudimentary facts about their political status and economic situation, the growing demand for national independence from foreign rule became identified with hostility toward "capitalism," both foreign and native. Had nationalism developed in colonial territories during the nineteenth century, it might conceivably have become linked with democratic concepts, as in western Europe after the French Revolution. But nationalism in Asia, in the Near and Middle East, in Latin America and Africa, emerged a hundred or more years after it had reached its peak in western Europe, at a time when the capitalist system had become strongly entrenched in the mother countries—Britain, France, Belgium, and the Netherlands. In Europe itself capitalism, after the 1850's, was challenged first by socialism, then by communism. Colonial nationalism developed close ties with Communist ideology. And since the white representatives of the mother countries in the colonies often viewed peoples of another color with contempt, and in some instances—notably the English—held aloof from them socially, nationalism and anticolonialism became deeply tinged with antiforeignism on lines of color.

With the rapid industrialization of western Europe, the advanced industrial nations wanted colonies primarily not as homes for their populations (some of them were still at the stage when they could use all available labor power in their new factories), but as sources of food and raw materials and as markets for manufactured goods. One need not be a Marxist to realize that the industries of the West required more and more cotton, tin, oil, rubber, copper, and other products that could be readily and cheaply obtained in colonial areas; and that the colonies offered promising outlets for textiles, ironware, tools, and various consumer goods. Trade became more important than political control—although traders wanted the protection of the flag, and demanded extraterritorial rights, notably in China and Turkey. Some of the Europeans, particularly the French, understood and appreciated the highly developed cultures of the colonial peoples. Others were insensitive to native art and philosophy, quick to criticize ways of living that seemed alien to them, and brash in their "master-race" treatment of peoples they regarded as "lower breeds without the law." They were interested only in what they could get out of the colonies, not in what they could both give and obtain through mutual relations on a basis of equality. Between the two world wars, however, great strides were made by the colonial powers to correct the more glaring abuses of colonial administration. Today Communist critics continue to berate the Western nations for their "exploitation" of colonial peoples in spite of the fact that many measures have already been taken to improve or abandon the colonial relationship.

Not that Russia itself has abstained from old-fashioned imperialism. While the Western seafaring peoples of the Mediterranean and the Atlantic journeyed across the seas to found new settlements and new centers of trade, spreading their ideas and their way of life along the way, Russian pioneers, traders, and administrators trekked overland, opening up vast areas of the Far East fronting on the Pacific and of central Asia bordering on China. They, too, established colonies and demanded special rights and privileges—particularly from the Chinese in 1896 when the Czarist government, taking advantage of China's defeat by Japan, obtained leaseholds at Port Arthur and Dairen and concessions to build railways in Manchuria. The Russians, like the Western nations, wanted trade, and also sought to obtain Pacific ice-free ports from China and Korea. Like the Westerners they considered themselves more advanced than the peoples of Asia in whose territories they hoped to carve out spheres of influence.

In 1917, however, Lenin declared that Russia itself was a colonial nation, supplying food and raw materials to advanced industrial powers in return for manufactured goods it had no facilities to produce. Russia, he contended, was an object of "imperialist exploitation," just like the colonies of Asia. It could achieve independence only through large-scale industrialization, which in turn required electrification. He denounced all Czarist treaties that had given Russia special rights and privileges in less advanced "colonial" areas, declared that Russia's fate was linked to that of colonial peoples oppressed by "imperialist capitalist" powers, and started to formulate a program designed to transform Russia from a relatively backward agrarian nation then in the early stages of the Industrial Revolution into an advanced industrial state—a program subsequently embodied in a series of five-year plans. This pattern of development—political independence from the West through substitution of an industrial economy for an economy based primarily on the output of food and raw materials—exerted a strong influence on colonial peoples who, even if they had no desire to accept a dictatorship like that of the Kremlin or to come within the orbit of the U.S.S.R., nevertheless found valuable guideposts in Russia's evolution under Soviet rule.

As long as the Soviet government followed the policy set by Lenin of linking its interests with those of colonial peoples and avoiding outright demands for special rights and privileges, the U.S.S.R. could persuade its neighbors that, unlike the great powers of the West, it had sincerely forsworn imperialism. But when Stalin, at the Yalta conference, demanded some of the special advantages in China which had once been enjoyed by the Czarist government, Russia's conduct began to belie Communist propaganda. Many people in colonial areas still believe that the Russians understand their needs and aspirations better than the Western powers, and that the less advanced nations of Asia and the Middle East may benefit by Russia's experience. Russian communism,

however, is no longer regarded as incompatible with imperialism, even though it may take forms different from those
of Western colonial rule.

The turning-point in the relationship between advanced
industrial nations and backward colonial areas had actually
come before World War I and the Bolshevik Revolution of
1917 altered the position of the Western powers, as well as
Russia, toward colonialism. Japan, which in 1854 had been
forced by the United States to open its doors to Westerners,
had since then painstakingly copied the political, economic,
and military institutions that, in Tokyo's opinion, had made
Western conquest of Asia possible. Having adopted some of
the ways of the West, Japan in 1904–5 inflicted a disastrous
defeat on Russia, thereby demonstrating to all Asians that,
once they had acquired modern techniques, they too could
stand up successfully to European powers. This impression
was strengthened by the political and economic decline of
Europe after World War I when the three great white empires of Germany, Austria-Hungary, and Russia collapsed.
The blow Japan inflicted on Russia at Port Arthur in 1904
was paralleled by the Japanese attack of 1941 on the United
States at Pearl Harbor. And even Japan's defeat by American
forces could not wipe out the memories of the humiliations
that the Japanese had inflicted on Englishmen, Americans,
and Dutchmen during their sweeping campaign into southeast Asia, or destroy the appeal of Tokyo's slogan: "Asia for
the Asiatics." The backward peoples of the Far East have
been thrown into ferment by new ideas from both the West
and the U.S.S.R. But neither Westerners nor Russians, no
matter how much they may want to, can effectively guide or
dominate the independence movements fermenting throughout the colonial world. Over the long run the forces that will
mold the future of Asia, and other backward continents, will
be generated by the native peoples themselves. Nor, as India's
Prime Minister Nehru has pointed out, must we expect that

former colonies will merely duplicate the institutions of either Russia or the United States.

Both the West and the U.S.S.R., however, may find it possible to prolong, perhaps for decades, the many ties Europe developed with colonial areas in the heyday of imperialism. New administrative arrangements that would wipe out the colonial relationship might give peoples now achieving or aspiring to nationhood a feeling of equality, or at least genuine autonomy. The British have already broadened the structure of the Commonwealth of Nations, hitherto composed of white peoples most of whom are of English descent, to include the non-white dominions of India, Pakistan, and Ceylon. With the accession of Ceylon, India and Pakistan, the Commonwealth, which once comprised 80 million persons, now has a combined population of more than 500 million. More than three fifths of these are Hindus and Moslems, putting the Christians and Europeans in a definite minority. France has proclaimed the formation of the French Union *(Union Française)* in which all colonies would be united with, not subject to, France, and would have representatives in the parliament of the mother country. But the French have not yet subdued guerrilla warfare in Indo-China, nor has French-sponsored Emperor Bao-Dai won over the followers of the Viet-Nam leader, Communist Ho Chi-minh. On behalf of the Netherlands, Queen Wilhelmina in 1942 announced that "colonialism" is dead and that the Dutch colonies would be invited to enter into a federation with the mother country. Seven years later, in November 1949, Dutch representatives at the Hague Round Table conference ended three hundred years of Netherlands rule over their rich East Indies colonies when they signed the Statute of the Netherlands Indonesian Union, transferring sovereignty "unconditionally and irrevocably" to the United States of Indonesia. The U.S.S.R. exercises strict political, economic, and ideological control over its non-white populations, but since 1917 has encouraged among them a considerable measure of cultural autonomy. It has the psychological advantage, which, at the same time, creates difficult administrative problems, of being the only great power whose colonials live within its boundaries and participate on an equal basis, narrow as it may seem to Westerners, in the union's political and economic activities. Meanwhile Russia's Communist-governed neighbors in eastern Europe and the Balkans, which believed that under Communist leadership the U.S.S.R. would abstain from "imperialist" actions, have begun to feel uneasy about Moscow's attempts to monopolize their resources of food and raw materials, and Marshal Tito has openly accused the Kremlin of "imperialism" at the expense of nations more backward than Russia. The future will show whether relations between advanced and colonial nations can be stabilized at the level of commonwealth, union, or federation or will have to be adjusted in the larger framework of the United Nations.

Both the Western powers and the U.S.S.R. have an opportunity to foster goodwill among colonial peoples by sharing with them the industrial experience that is urgently needed by backward nations now straining to advance as rapidly as possible. In this respect we have the distinct advantage of being far more technically advanced than the Russians. But we will have to overcome the suspicion, still widely prevalent among non-Europeans and non-Americans, that our aid to underdeveloped areas is intended to salvage the economy of Europe and the United States rather than to promote the welfare of colonial peoples.

In the twentieth century industrialization has become for Asia, Africa, and Latin America the lodestar it was for western Europe a hundred and fifty years ago. The test of Western, as well as Russian, influence will be not only the efficacy of our respective techniques, but also the use to which we ultimately put them—conquest or mutual aid, peace or war, the output of goods accessible to a few or improvement in the standard of living of the many. To quote Nehru again, eventual victory as between capitalism and communism will go to the society that "delivers the goods," materially and spiritually.

Chapter III

FROM LAISSEZ-FAIRE TO
WELFARE STATE

The Industrial Revolution did not burst upon Europe fully armed like Athene from the head of Zeus. The changes in technical processes and modes of thinking that around 1800 brought about a revolution in production, distribution, and consumption had been under way for at least two centuries. In agriculture the wheeled plow, crop rotation, and the harnessing of animal power for work in the fields; in manufacturing, the crank, unknown to the Greeks and Romans, had come to be widely used during the Middle Ages. The watermill was quite common, and by the end of the thirteenth century the windmill "had become a typical part of the landscape on the plains of northwestern Europe." From the twelfth and even from the eleventh century there was a rapid replacement of human by non-human energy wherever great quantities of power were needed or where the required motion was so simple and monotonous that a man could be replaced by a mechanism. "The chief glory of the later Middle Ages was not its cathedrals or its epics or its scholasticism: it was the building for the first time in history of a complex civilization which rested not on the backs of sweating slaves or coolies but primarily on non-human power." [1]

Men had long been inquiring into the secrets of the universe and experimenting with various ways of utilizing the forces of nature. The sketches in which Leonardo da Vinci pictured flying machines were but one example of the heights

[1] Lynn White: "Technology and Invention in the Middle Ages," *Speculum*, Vol. XV, No. 2 (April 1940), p. 141.

to which the human mind had soared two centuries before the Industrial Revolution. This new interest in the physical world, this intellectual curiosity, had been tremendously stimulated by, and had contributed to, the breakup of the social order of the Middle Ages—a social order in which feudalism, with its rigid hierarchies of lords and villeins, and the Church, with its rigid enforcement of religious beliefs, did not encourage free thought. In this static, essentially conservative society, peasants challenging feudal barons were treated as rebels, and philosophers challenging the authority of the Church were treated as heretics.

But with the coming of the Renaissance and the Reformation in the sixteenth century and the opening up of new horizons by the great explorers, the atmosphere of Europe underwent a complete change. All issues were reopened, all values became subject to revaluation. Submissive acceptance of authority, whether secular or religious, was no longer an object of admiration. The questioning mind, the mind that would not be satisfied with traditional answers, that rebelled against dogma of any kind and turned to scientific investigation, religious controversy, or exploration of remote corners of the earth—Galileo and Columbus, Luther and Calvin—moved, shocked, or inspired public opinion. Trade and finance, which had been frowned on in an earlier period when knighthood or dedication to the service of the Church was regarded as the only career worthy of men of ability and ambition, and which had been contemptuously left to Jewish "money-lenders," acquired importance and prestige as the wealth of the Indies and the Americas began to pour into Europe. The relatively self-sufficient manor economy, most of whose needs were filled by local peasants and artisans, with only some luxuries such as spices, silks, and ornaments of gold and silver for the feudal lords imported from overseas, yielded place to the increasingly complex economy of the towns. There merchants sold and bought an expanding variety of wares from many lands, financing their transactions through loans or credits obtained from bankers like the Fuggers, whose analyses of business and political conditions of the time are a match for the treatises of twentieth-century economic experts. Kings and emperors, and the lords and ladies of their courts, came to depend more and more on the material assistance of bankers and merchants. Gradually, although not without reluctance, they accepted fuller participation by the rising middle class in the formulation of national policy. The transfer of actual political power from the monarch and the aristocracy to the people, then represented by the "third estate", had been proceeding since the days of Magna Charta in England, and in France had been sealed by the French Revolution. This political transition coincided with a shift from the manor to the town; from the uncomplicated transactions of agriculture and handicrafts to the elaborate economy of industrial cities; and from limited trade over Europe's principal waterways and along its Mediterranean shores to the many-faceted commerce carried across the Atlantic, by which the raw materials and foodstuffs of the New World were exchanged for the manufactured products of western Europe.

As the men of the later Middle Ages turned to the use of non-human power, the importance of the peasant economy, with its combination of tilling of the soil and handicrafts, began to decline, and the drift from the village to the town gained momentum. Deterioration of village life was signalized by the breaking up of the family, with its enforcement of paternalistic authority, and the gradual disappearance of the virtues generally associated with peasant communities as compared with the freer life of the city, which seemed fraught with sinister temptations.

Today communism in Russia or China is telescoping several revolutions into a brief interval and consciously steering them toward the type of society it favors. This, however, should not prevent us from seeing that current changes in backward countries, which are still predominantly agrarian, do not differ in essence from those experienced by western Europe during the early stages of industrialization. Just as the first important industry at that time, in Lancashire and the Low Countries, was the production of textiles, so in the twentieth century the Russians and the Poles, the Chinese and the Indians, started their industrialization with the manufacture of cotton goods. Nor is this surprising. For it is easier to make a transition from the handicrafts of spinning and weaving, of fulling and dyeing, to textile mills, than to pass from an agrarian and artisan economy to mining and use of coal and iron for the manufacture of industrial goods. In nineteenth-century England, as in twentieth-century Russia or China, the first stages of the Industrial Revolution brought about "sweat-shop" conditions, which aroused the workers to revolt against their employers and against politicians who took the employers' side.

Mastery of scientific inventions and of non-human power filled those who witnessed the early years of the Industrial Revolution with boundless optimism, with a sense that man had acquired unlimited capacity to alter his environment, and that the machine could be made to solve all the problems that had plagued humanity since the dawn of history. This optimism, this spirit of supreme self-confidence, so different from the humility and "God's will be done" fatalism of medieval man—left an indelible imprint on western Europe and are still felt today in the United States. The Victorians firmly believed that mankind was destined to progress uninterruptedly from one stage of achievement to the next. Until the end of the century few Westerners had premonitions of possible regressions or anxiety about the future, later voiced in such books as Spengler's *Decline of the West*. By contrast, in Russia, whose backward economy was barely affected by industrial revolution before 1900, reigned a spirit of pessimism, of unrest, of revolt against existing conditions, which found expression in the writings of Turgenev and Dostoyevsky, of Gogol and Tolstoy.

Yet twenty years later, after World War II, when the West began to feel disillusioned about the efficacy of mechanical civilization and to wonder whether mass production might not bring about periods of acute unemployment and distress instead of an ever rising spiral of progress, Russia and other newly industrialized countries took the point of view once held by the West. They hailed the machine, believing it could perform miracles for underdeveloped peoples by liberating them at home from servitude to ruling groups, and abroad from dependence on advanced colonial powers. One of the most effective slogans of Communist propaganda became the promise of full employment, which made a strong appeal to the growing numbers of unemployed in Western countries who did not always realize that newly industrialized economies like that of Russia, where machines are not yet widely used, need all available labor. England, too, had found employment in the early 1800's not only for adults, but even for children. It is only after machine civilization has become solidly established that the problem of knowing what to do with manpower thus released begins to assume importance.

The Industrial Revolution permeated all aspects of European life after 1800, and today its repercussions continue to spread like ripples to the more remote areas of the continent —to Russia and eastern Europe, and farther still to the Near and Middle East, Asia, Latin America, Africa. Like nationalism, the Industrial Revolution is far from having run its course. As its influence reaches hitherto unaffected communities, we see, as if an old film were being run over before our eyes, the same sequence of hardships and abuses that gave the Industrial Revolution a bad name in England and inspired Karl Marx in *Das Kapital*, based primarily on England's experience, to prescribe the drastic remedy of communism.

From Russia to Argentina, from Yugoslavia to China and India, nationalism runs parallel to the demand for industrialization. In the minds of millions of people the desire to achieve a higher standard of living through the use of technical inventions has become linked with the desire for national independence. Today the aspirations of nations newly emerging on the world stage seem to be primarily voiced by Communists. But this is neither inevitable nor actually the case, if one looks at the statements and actions of such diverse non-Communist leaders as Perón in Argentina and Nehru in India. While the Industrial Revolution, like nationalism, is now a living force in countries that had hitherto remained outside its reach, its effects, like those of nationalism, are becoming stabilized in the areas where it first emerged over a century ago—in western Europe and in the United States. The peoples who were in the van of industrialization in the 1800's now have entered the next phase, where they must discover how to harmonize political democracy with the need to share more widely the fruits of industrial production.

Although some branches of manufacturing had been highly developed on the European continent before 1800, especially textiles in France, Germany, and the Netherlands, it was in England that the Industrial Revolution made the most significant strides at the turn of the century and displayed the characeristics, both good and bad, associated with it throughout the world. Nor was this fortuitous. For England, approximately a century before the other nations of western Europe, had achieved constitutional government limiting the arbitrary power of the monarch, and had effected the separation of church and state. The English people were not divided, as the French turned out to be in 1789 and for nearly a century after, by controversies about the nature of their society. The general measure of agreement about political concepts that is necessary for effective functioning of a state had been attained in England, and the ground had thus been cleared for the development of new institutions. Another theory about the emergence of the English people as the first great industrial nation of the world is less flattering. Lewis Mumford contends that England, throughout the Middle

Ages, was one of the backward countries of Europe, "on the outskirts of the great continental civilization," and therefore "the break with the past came more easily, perhaps, because there was less to break with." [1]

Unlike France, which enjoys a fortunate combination of agricultural and industrial resources, Britain must import food and raw materials if it is to give its inhabitants a minimum standard of existence, and even today after valiant efforts to expand agriculture, produces only thirty-five per cent of its food requirements. The British were therefore compelled to find ways and means of paying for their imports, and this they did by transforming imported raw materials into a variety of manufactured goods, which they then exported. True, Britain benefited by its geographic position athwart the newly discovered Atlantic routes, which made it possible for London, crossroads of the flow of commerce between the Old World and the New, to become the principal trading center of that period, a position it maintained until 1914. But Spain and Portugal, too, were Atlantic nations and, like England, had been in contact with the Western Hemisphere. Unlike England, however, Spain and Portugal used the gold and silver of conquered lands to enrich Church and lay dignitaries instead of investing them in productive enterprises. The economies of the two Iberian countries, which under other circumstances might have benefited by the wealth of the New World, remained in a state of arrested development. In our times Spain and Portugal, although physically part of the Western World, are actually more remote from the economic and social developments of the past four centuries than some of the nations of the Balkans and Asia. As a *Christian Science Monitor* correspondent wrote in 1949: "Spain clearly needs a great program of work, of economic rehabilitation, of democratic growth, of integration into the twentieth century. But next to nothing is being done along

[1] Lewis Mumford: *Technics and Civilization* (New York: Harcourt, Brace & Company; 1934).

these lines. . . . The army and the wealthy or noble classes are in complete control and are trying to run Spain as nearly as possible on sixteenth century standards."

Not only were the English driven by sheer necessity to encourage multilateral trade. They were in a condition to take full advantage of the new opportunities opened up by science and invention. Although the English are not averse to sentiment, as their lyric poetry reveals, they are not predisposed to mysticism and superstition. So practical are they, with a strong sense of what is or is not feasible, that they have been described by some of their critics as "a nation of shopkeepers." The dogmas of the Roman Catholic Church, which did not encourage free inquiry or experimentation outside clearly demarcated channels of thought, had not deeply affected the English, who welcomed the rationalism of the eighteenth century—the century of "Enlightenment"—and accepted a materialist view of life without feelings of guilt or anxiety.

Today it is often assumed that doubts about religious dogmas and materialistic rationalism are entirely new phenomena, due to Russian communism, which is denounced, particularly by Catholic spokesmen, for its irreligious or antireligious attitude and its "materialism." Soviet leaders at one time carried their attacks on religious organizations to extremes, mocking religion by crude and shocking exhibits in antireligious museums; but they had had forerunners in the often violent "protestants" of the fifteenth century. The principal target of Communist attack in Russia was not religious sentiment, which many Russians have retained under Soviet rule, but superstition, which had fastened like barnacles on religious faith, and the efforts of the hierarchy to influence affairs of state. Russian priests counseled their flocks, in case of drought, to pray and sprinkle the fields with holy water instead of considering the possibility of crop rotation and irrigation; or to cure diseases by kissing relics of saints instead of establishing clinics where they might have the care of trained doctors and nurses. In twentieth-century

Russia, as in eighteenth-century western Europe, the rejection of superstition was a necessary, although seemingly ruthless, step toward acceptance of rationalism and utilization of science and invention in the development of modern economy. True, Russia, unlike England at a comparable stage of historical development, had not yet attained in 1917 the stage of political maturity at which it might have proved possible to avoid the strains and cruelties of a dictatorship that suppressed all opposition. It is inaccurate, however, to assert that religion in general and the Roman Catholic Church in particular were first challenged by Russia and by communism. England under Henry VIII, as already noted, had defied the Vatican as early as the sixteenth century and had established a national church. The French Revolution attacked the Church as well as the monarchy; and over a century later, in 1903, France officially effected separation of church and state —a step already taken by the United States in 1787. The Western World has thus long practiced the precept of drawing a sharp distinction between the things that are God's and the things that are Cæsar's. But no such distinction had been made in some of the backward countries of Europe and the New World, where in our own times we have seen the Roman Catholic Church challenged in Mexico, Spain, Poland, Hungary, and Czechoslovakia, and the Greek Orthodox Church in Russia. In Russia the Church, deprived of political power but restored to some of its material possessions, has since World War II again become an instrument of the state as it had been in the days of the czars. In eastern European countries Communist governments are intent on breaking off the ties of the Catholic hierarchy with the Vatican, and on creating national Catholic churches, which would then be expected to co-operate with the state.

There is no reason to assume that scientific inquiry is irreconcilable with religious belief; and leading Western scientists have made it clear that ever expanding knowledge of the finite world does not preclude humility and faith about the infinite. But whenever religious organizations assert that poverty or ill health or lack of education are "the will of God," not subject to change, and that the poor, the ill, and the ignorant must rest content with their lot on earth and seek comfort in the next world, such assertions are bound to be questioned in a period when science and invention have made possible many things that would have seemed fantastic in the Middle Ages. If churchmen either accept or defend the *status quo*, Marx's statement that "religion is the opium of the people" will be quoted by others than Lenin. Whenever the churches have kept abreast of the times, and have labored to fulfill the promises of the Industrial Revolution and of political democracy instead of opposing them, as in western Europe and the United States, no problem of antireligiousness has arisen, even among agnostics. But wherever the churches have disregarded the miseries and aspirations of the less fortunate and have allied themselves with reactionary groups—in Spain, in Russia before 1917, in eastern Europe—the struggle against remnants of feudalism, the drive for industrialization, the demand for better standards of living, have coincided with attacks on the Church hierarchy. The Vatican, as early as the *Rerum novarum* encyclical issued by Pope Leo XIII in 1891, had recognized the economic and social issues presented by the modern world and, warning employers against the abuse of their power, had urged reforms to improve the lot of industrial workers. These warnings and appeals have been repeated by the popes after the rise of communism in 1917. Since 1945, however, the Vatican has given the impression that current conflicts between church and state, especially in eastern Europe, are solely conflicts between Rome and communism, disregarding other issues. In the July 13, 1949 decree of the Sacred Congregation of the Holy Office, approved by Pope Pius XII, the Church warned the faithful that Communist leaders, "even though they often proclaim that they do not oppose religion . . . on the contrary both in doctrine and with their activity demonstrate hostility to God and to true religion and to the Church of Christ"; and declared it would excommunicate Catholics who are militant Communists.

The Vatican's attack on the Communists is directed not only against their attitude toward God and religion, but also against the "materialistic" doctrines of communism. The emphasis on material, as contrasted with spiritual, values, however, is not peculiar to communism: it is a distinguishing characteristic of the Industrial Revolution. Materialism has become identified with Marxist doctrine largely because Marx, and after him Lenin, bluntly expressed in unadorned language the materialist views that had gained wide acceptance in nineteenth-century Europe and America. Previous epochs of history had known no such exclusive preoccupation with material values. The Greeks in the age of Pericles were concerned with ideas and with physical beauty. The Romans, more materialistic than the Greeks, had pillaged conquered peoples to enhance their own power and comfort. But while building roads, forums, and aqueducts they had found time for the arts and for intellectual discussions, in sharp contrast to the early stages of the Industrial Revolution, when anything that did not bear directly on production and trade was considered irrelevant. In the Middle Ages feudal lords did not hesitate to improve their own standard of living at the expense of their serfs; and some of the crusaders were less concerned with the defense of Christendom from the infidels than with the establishment of trading posts in the Levant. But the ideology that dominated that period combined respect for knightly deeds with a deep, often mystical faith in God, shared by high and low.

Whenever we in the West talk about the "materialism" of the Russians, it is well to remember that before 1917 leading Russian philosophers rejected Westernism precisely because of what they regarded as the crass materialism of the Industrial Revolution—much as Mahatma Gandhi, and some

Arab leaders, have more recently opposed the introduction of Western customs, contending that the nonmaterial values of Eastern civilization are superior to the material achievements of the West.

Nor does one need to go as far as Russia or Asia for examples of resistance to industrial concepts of a good way of life. There is no lack of people in western Europe who believe that, in our determination to improve living-conditions with bathrooms and launderettes, refrigerators and electric stoves, we have neglected the finer things of life and have developed no appreciation of "culture." In comparing the United States and the U.S.S.R. many Europeans object to the emphasis both great nations give to material achievements. While recognizing the vast difference between democracy and dictatorship, they prefer their own way of life to that of either Detroit or Moscow. This view has been vigorously expressed by British Socialists, who contend that socialism is far less materialistic than capitalism, and far more imbued with moral values. The Socialist, writes Francis Williams, former editor of the Labourite *Daily Herald,* rejects communism, "but he equally rejects capitalism as a means to the good society because he observes that by denying social control over economic power it reduces in practice the effectiveness of the very political liberties it claims to defend." The moral case for socialism, he contends, "rests ultimately . . . on the belief that man is a moral being and not simply an economic being. . . . There is nothing so pitiable as the man who has no standards other than crudely material ones. Yet modern capitalism by its nature, by the credo at the heart of its philosophy, increasingly imposes these standards upon all men." The Socialist, he concludes, works on the assumption "that incentives other than those of private interest can effectively govern economic affairs, that human beings will work together and give what is best in them because they feel themselves members of a social partnership of whose purposes they approve, and that

there is a positive value in cooperation and in human fellow-
ship." [1]

In the wake of the Industrial Revolution Western man became preoccupied with the making of things, with the accumulation of material possessions. Profit-making, hitherto
decried and condemned, came to be regarded as synonymous
with virtue; failure to earn a "decent living" was viewed as a
sign of sloth. Lewis Mumford has succinctly summed up this
process as follows: "Power: the application of power to motion, and the application of motion to production, and of production to money-making, and so the further increase of
power—this was the worthiest object that a mechanical habit
of mind and a mechanical mode of action put before men."
The sovereignty of the monarch had been abolished, but instead of being transferred to "the people" as a whole, sovereignty during the nineteenth century and well into the twentieth proved to be in the hands of those who controlled the
machinery of production. "The divine right of capitalists," as
the British sociologists John and Barbara Hammond put it,
was substituted for the divine right of kings by those who advocated laissez-faire. Today we in the West are still struggling to discover how economic power, hitherto concentrated in the hands of relatively few, can be made as responsive and responsible to the entire body of citizens as political power was intended to be by the leaders of the French
and American revolutions. The prospect of financial gain, of
larger and still larger profits, was the great propulsive force of
the early stages of the Industrial Revolution—as great an incentive as devotion to the Church and attainment of knightly
privileges had been in the Middle Ages, or as adventure,
joined with cupidity, had been in the days of the explorers.
Nor was this a wholly unworthy motive, as it has since been
represented by critics of the profit system. For the traders and

[1] Francis Williams: "The Moral Case for Socialism," *Fortune,* October
1949, p. 1200.

bankers of the 1800's strove by their economic advancement to improve the social position of their families, and thereby helped to make society more flexible, more democratic, than it had been under the parallel hierarchies of Church and feudalism. They were genuinely convinced, moreover, that their private enterprises would benefit not only themselves but society as a whole by making more goods available at lower prices.

When we speak of capitalism, we think of an economic system under which a private individual can accumulate money, whether acquired through wage-earning, inheritance, or other means, and invest it in an enterprise he personally owns, in which he employs workers to produce goods. From the sale of these goods he hopes to obtain profits, but takes the risk that he may fail. In developing private enterprise the man with capital, the "capitalist" of the nineteenth century, wanted to enjoy the greatest possible freedom. As a result, private enterprise became indissolubly linked with the concept of freedom—freedom from interference by the government or by other groups—so that today we usually add the term "free" when we speak of "private" enterprise.

The Liberals of early nineteenth-century England, deeply interested in industrial development (as contrasted with the Conservatives, who represented landowning interests), wanted trade and finance to be untrammeled. In the economic sphere, as their spokesman Adam Smith put it, they advocated a policy of laissez-faire, of "letting nature take its course." They displayed as much faith in the powers of "Nature" to solve the problems of industrial civilization as the people of the Middle Ages had displayed in the powers of God and of monarchs by divine right to settle secular affairs. The distance the Western World has traveled since that time can be measured in current newspaper headlines. In 1949 President Truman declared we could not afford to let "nature take its course", and the leaders of Labour-governed Britain,

Communist-ruled Russia, and fascist-ruled Argentina have sought by various methods of control to ameliorate the economic conditions of their respective nations.

The trend toward qualifying the "natural" right to make profits arose first of all not from the doctrinal assertions of Socialists or Communists, but from a growing feeling that private enterprise for private gain might cause evil as well as good—that while producing more and more material goods it might also have antisocial results. For it soon became evident that private enterprise at its worst recklessly depleted natural resources, created unhealthy slums in green and pleasant land, and transformed relatively independent peasants or handicraftsmen but lately emerged from feudal serfdom into a new kind of serfs—into industrial workers who, as village life deteriorated, flocked into the towns, shorn of personal property, subject to the mercies of factory-owners, and seemingly doomed to work as hard as the machines they tended. Nineteenth-century reformers, earliest of all in England, where the ugly side of the Industrial Revolution first became evident, were particularly shocked by the dependence of industrial production on the labor of groups of the population who were forced to live in subhuman conditions and were regarded by the flourishing middle class, itself recently in revolt against the abuses of monarchy and aristocracy, as destined to know and keep their "station in life." The use of slaves in the British West Indies and in the American South; of children who at the ages of four or five had to work twelve hours a day; of indentured labor, or even of "free" adult workers who were expected to be satisfied with a life limited to working, eating, and sleeping, without even those amusements and leisure activities that slaves had enjoyed in the Roman Empire or serfs in the Middle Ages—these methods of increasing the output of manufactured goods troubled the conscience of Liberals who had previously insisted that production and trade should be free of all restraint.

When we look back to the early days of the Industrial Revolution in England, we realize that respect for the dignity of the human person, which had been a fundamental tenet of Christianity, propagated by Jesuit priests even among backward peoples of Spanish and Portuguese America, was destroyed in the first instance not by the Marxists, but by the early industrial leaders of the Western World. The African Negro, the child forced to work in the factory, the adult worker condemned to live in an ugly and unsanitary slum—all these, as John and Barbara Hammond have pointed out in their brilliant studies on the rise of modern English industry, were regarded not as human beings "but as so much labor power to be used in the service of a master or a system." In the early nineteenth century, they conclude, "the workers, as a class were looked upon as so much labor power to be used at the discretion and under conditions imposed by their masters; not as men and women who are entitled to some voice in the arrangements of their life and work."

Today critics of "the welfare state" contend that government intervention, to quote John Foster Dulles, "makes human beings into mere cogs in a man-made machine," by destroying the individual's incentive to produce and his sense of social responsibility. This would not have been the opinion of the nineteenth-century reformers who saw the Industrial Revolution in all the grimness and griminess of its early stages. To them it seemed that it was the very process of industrialization that, by eliminating the peasant and the artisan and creating large-scale factories, made human beings into mere cogs. The mass-production revolution, as Peter Drucker has well pointed out, divorced the worker from the product and thereby robbed him of the incentive to produce as it existed in the period before the Industrial Revolution. The modern factory worker owns neither the plant where he works nor, usually, the tools he has been trained to use. Most frequently his work consists solely in performing one or two operations on an assembly line, whose beginning and end are not subject to his decision. Nor does he have any control over the myriad factors that may create unemployment and throw him out of work and his family on the dole, as happened in many parts of the world during the great depression of the 1930's. No matter how strong may be the worker's innate sense of social responsibility, he has little or no opportunity to exercise it unless economic processes are far more closely integrated with the processes of politics than has been true of most Western industrial nations, where employers' groups and, more recently, labor unions have developed into states within the state. The modern factory made for collectivism long before anyone thought in terms of "collective" society or "the welfare state."

The conditions denounced by English reformers of the 1830's flourished a hundred years later in the factories of Russia, China, and other backward countries which belatedly felt the impact of industrialization, arousing comparable dissatisfaction and protests. Had these conditions been promptly ameliorated in our time by peaceful means, the Bolshevik Revolution of 1917 in Russia and Communist victories in China might not have occurred, at least not in such violent form. But the ruling group of Russia in the first decade of this century, in China in the 1940's, were no more eager to correct the abuses of the industrial system than their counterparts had been in nineteenth-century England. And even in England, where far greater opportunity existed for the expression of public indignation, and parliamentary machinery was available to translate indignation into effective economic and social reforms, nearly a century elapsed before the conditions that marred the material achievements of industrialism had been alleviated. In 1833 a British critic of the employers and politicians who opposed the passage of a bill providing that children should not work more than ten hours a day said sarcastically that the bill's opponents "had discovered that England's manufacturing supremacy depended on 30,000 little girls."

The resentment of industrial workers against the condi-

tions under which they were forced to live long preceded the
Communist Manifesto and *Das Kapital.* Before Lenin was
even heard of, workers in western Europe, as well as many
far-sighted middle-class leaders, were asking themselves
whether the cost of producing more and more cotton textiles,
coal and iron, steel and copper, and a growing variety of industrial manufactured goods was not too great if it had to be
paid for with the suffering and degradation of human beings.
This rising condemnation of the abuses of the industrial system found expression in many movements of reform in
Britain and the United States, in various proposals antedating
the rise of modern socialism, such as the schemes of Fourier
and Louis Blanc in France, in a succession of local workers'
revolts, usually suppressed by force, and only much later in
the theories of production and distribution that we associate
with socialism and communism.

The *Communist Manifesto,* issued in 1867 by Karl Marx
and his friend and disciple Friedrich Engels, did not open a
new chapter in the social and economic process generated by
the Industrial Revolution. What it did was to bring into focus
the essential features of this process, with no attempt to
palliate the economic and social evils of nineteenth-century
England by references to the institutions of political democracy, in which, in Marx's opinion, propertyless industrial
workers and agricultural laborers who no longer made an
adequate living on the land had no opportunity to participate. Far from minimizing the material achievements of the
Industrial Revolution, Marx expressed admiration for them,
saying: "The bourgeoisie, during its rule of scarce one hundred years, has created more massive and more colossal productive forces than have all the preceding generations together." He listed with relish the achievements of the bourgeois inventors and explorers, merchants and bankers in
harnessing the forces of nature to the machine. What he
resented was that all the advantages made possible by the
Industrial Revolution were accessible only to a small group of

capitalists, who, in his opinion, would continue to hold their workers in subjection. He strongly doubted that the conflict between classes—between capitalists and workers—ample evidence of which he could see in western Europe, could be adjusted by peaceful means. Nor did he foresee that workers, by improving their economic and social position, might eventually acquire at least a modest stake in capitalist society, or that the harsh practices of the early days of the Industrial Revolution could be modified through parliamentary reforms.

He and his followers contended that the "exploitation" of workers by capitalists could be terminated only by a bloody revolution—although at some points in his writings Marx gives the impression that less drastic measures might prove effective. In the proletarian revolution, which Leon Trotsky in the 1920's declared would be a "permanent revolution," the workers of the world were expected to join forces, irrespective of national sentiments or interests, in a concerted attack on capitalism. Once the capitalists had been "liquidated," there would be no further need for administrative machinery and, in the words of Engels, the state would gradually "wither away."

Marx did not anticipate the possibility of a peaceful transition from capitalism to socialism, which occurred in Britain and several other European countries in the twentieth century. He did not dream that his theories would first be put to the test in a backward agricultural country, Russia, where authoritarianism and illiteracy had blocked the development of self-government, and where the autocracy of the czars, with only a brief interval, was succeeded by the autocracy of the Communist Party, itself ruled by an inner group, the Politbureau. Nor did he give sufficient weight to nationalism, which has proved one of the most stubborn obstacles to the world-wide spread of communism. Russian adherents of Marxism were shocked and angered to discover after World War II that Communist-governed nations might resent dictation from Moscow, reject the Russian version of Marxism, and insist on a version of their own. Contrary to Marx's expectations, communism proved particularly strong not in advanced industrial nations, some of which turned to Nazism or fascism when faced by desperate economic problems, or else sought to improve the lot of industrial workers by parliamentary procedures rather than by resort to violence, but in relatively backward countries where the impact of the Industrial Revolution was just beginning to be felt in the twentieth century. In these countries, including Russia, the middle class was small and weak, liberalism had not yet taken root, and Communists felt they had ample justification for their contention that only resort to force could tear down an obsolete social structure that combined the worst features of feudalism and unreformed capitalism. There, too, relatively weak Socialist parties, which on the whole agreed with the Communists about the urgency of fundamental changes, believed that, since parliamentary machinery for orderly reform was either nonexistent or inadequate, it would be for the general good to take short cuts even at the risk of cruelty and suffering.

In backward countries, as we have seen again in China since 1945, the choice was not between democracy and communism, but between two forms of totalitarianism—that of a reactionary autocracy or clique which insisted on maintenance of the *status quo,* and that of the Communists, who promised far-reaching economic and social changes. The assumption, widely held in the United States, that opponents of communism in backward countries were *ipso facto* supporters of Western-style democracy were disproved again and again, from Russia in 1917 to China in 1949. Nor was it possible to find, among populations divided between a small group of wealthy and powerful politicians, feudal lords, or merchants at the top and masses of poor and illiterate peasants at the bottom, the "vital center" that might have been counted on to carry out orderly reforms. In its determination to oppose

Russia and communism the United States repeatedly found itself forced to support, or at least acquiesce in, the policies of antidemocratic reactionary groups. While the Marxists underestimated the potential adaptability of capitalism and democracy, the West greatly overestimated the capacity of peoples who had not experienced political freedom or industrialization to adopt, overnight, the institutions and practices of democracy and free private interprise.

Deep concern with the economic problems created by the Industrial Revolution has not been limited to laymen. Religious groups of all faiths have been wrestling with the fundamental issue of reconciling liberty with economic and social justice. In Europe since 1917, and especially in the wake of World War II, distinguished Catholic leaders, while rejecting the totalitarian methods of communism, have deplored the abuses of capitalism and have urged their correction through far-reaching reforms. Notable among these leaders was Emmanuel Cardinal Suhard, Archbishop of Paris, who died in 1949. The Cardinal vigorously championed the rights of workers, and in his Christmas message of 1947 said: "The workers are sad and discouraged. The Church knows this and is moved. . . . She is not resigned to the proletarian conditions, which she considers the shame of her country." In his pastoral letter issued in February 1949 Cardinal Suhard warned Catholics against allying themselves with Communists. The triumph of the Communist Party, he wrote, "would inevitably produce a marked decline of faith in God . . . an unjust limitation on the rights of the Church, and the recourse to the totalitarian political methods of Marxist theory." He added, however (and for this he was subsequently taken to task by the Vatican organ, *Osservatore Romano*): "Doubtless circumstances may lead Catholics to follow a course paralleling that of the Communists in the pursuit . . . of specific and limited objectives, without being linked essentially with the particular aims of the party. But the Church cannot sanction a close and habitual collaboration."

The Cardinal's own views about the maladjustments of the capitalist system and possible methods of alleviating them were summed up in this pastoral letter, in which he affirmed once more "that the major problem of our times is the suppression of social injustice." He continued:

We sympathize deeply with the just claims and legitimate aspirations of the working class. We understand and deplore the painful conditions in which a large number of workers live. Let no one deceive himself; the Church refuses to ally itself with wealth. Its love and solicitude go first to those who must struggle to better their material lot and safeguard their human dignity. It shows the faithful that it is their duty to work courageously to end the disorders brought about by the present capitalist regime. . . . But even in the face of the injustices that characterize the capitalist system . . . the Church still believes that there are better things to be done than to favor the advent of a totalitarian and atheistic collectivism.

The social reformism of some of Europe's Catholic leaders has brought them close to the position of the Socialists. It has been reflected in the programs and activities of Catholic Action groups and of Catholic parties, often composed of conservative as well as liberal elements, which have increasingly stressed the need for advances in social welfare—among them, since 1945, the *Mouvement Républicain Populaire* in France, the left wing of the German Christian Democrats, led by Karl Arnold, and the Christian Democratic Party of Premier de Gasperi in Italy. The lines of action these parties could follow were indicated by Cardinal Suhard in 1947, when he wrote in a pastoral letter entitled *Growth or Decline?* that the Church today rejects "in social work both the anarchy of economic liberalism which makes struggle the law of progress, and the state socialistic conception in which individual liberty is absorbed to the profit of an anonymous power, in order to orient men towards solutions in which organization is obtained by the cooperation of free wills with respect for the natural societies, families, enterprises, professions, etc." [1] In the Cardinal's view, "one cannot be a saint and live the Gospel we preach without spending himself to provide everyone with the housing, employment, food, leisure, education, etc.—without which life is no longer human."

The Industrial Revolution, however, brought benefits as well as problems. In the political sphere it encouraged greater social mobility than had been possible in the rigid hierarchical society of the Middle Ages. In the economic sphere the machine made large-scale output possible. True, production of manufactured goods in series, on the assembly line, carried with it loss of the qualities the craftsman lovingly embodied in hand-made objects. But it enabled many workers assembled in a factory to produce increasingly larger quantities of goods at lower and still lower prices. Goods were thus brought within reach not only of the powerful and wealthy, but also to some extent of people of lesser means. Large-scale production required ever expanding markets for the output of factories and mechanized farms; hand in hand with it had to go large-scale consumption. Expansion of domestic markets, and of markets overseas, called for a rise in the purchasing power of the poorer groups of the population, the workers and the farmers. Workers' resentment against the low standards of living of the early stages of the Industrial Revolution, and their demand for improvement, pressed on society from one side; realization by enlightened employers that ill-paid workers would not be good customers pressed from the other. Both pressures hastened economic and social reforms that made the stresses and strains of industrialization increasingly tolerable. Sound business sense combined with political considerations and the idealistic desire to advance human welfare to foster extension of the benefits of the Industrial Revolution among wider and still wider circles of the population.

Today advanced industrial nations like the United States, Britain, and some of the continental countries of Western Europe find that their principal economic problem is not how to increase production, but how to assure the distribution of the products of farms and factories in the most equitable way possible, in both home and foreign markets; how to assure a rate of profit that will give the business man an incentive to risk an investment, a rate of wages that will give labor an incentive to work, and a price level that will make the consumer want to buy. It is the advanced industrial nations, not those which are still in the early phases of industrialization, that are most concerned with distribution problems such as that raised by Karl Marx when he said that in a communist society each would contribute according to his ability and would receive according to his need. In the U.S.S.R., where farm and factory production, in spite of considerable strides since 1917, is still far from being able to furnish even the bare necessities of life for a population of two hundred million, the problem is not how to distribute goods so much as it is how to produce enough goods to fill minimum human needs. The Soviet government, which has repeatedly declared that the U.S.S.R. is still at the stage of socialism, has been seeking to make goods available to each, not according to need, but according to ability, according to his or her contribution to society. It has openly offered a wide range of incentives for workers who could produce more than the average quota, and has held out the possibility of obtaining additional material products, including some luxuries, as an inducement to those who displayed particular talents or initiative. In spite of its outward Marxist façade, the economy of the U.S.S.R. has displayed some of the characteristics of economic development familiar to the countries of western Europe a hundred years ago. Unlike the governments of these countries in the nineteenth century, however, the Soviet state, far from limiting its interference to a minimum, is the owner of all basic resources, industries, and banking and credit facilities; it is the sole employer of workers in offices and factories, as well as on state farms; it owns the land, renting it to collective farms, which must pay rent, as well as the cost of using state-operated agricultural machinery like tractors, with a portion of their output; and it plans and regulates the development of the national economy. Russia, which telescoped into a few years the political and economic revolutions that had swept Europe over two centuries, has by-passed the period of large-scale private enterprise for private profit. There, as well as in the countries of eastern Europe and Asia that have been influenced by Russia's example, the Industrial Revolution has been carried out, not by individuals rejecting state intervention, but by the state rejecting individual ownership and control.

Yet when one speaks of "free private enterprise," it should be recalled that in the Western World of the nineteenth century untrammeled freedom was desired by merchants and bankers, and acquiesced in by society, only in the early stages of industrialization. Once industry had swung into large-scale operation, business men began to demand government protection for "infant industries" through tariffs and other trade restrictions on imports from other countries. Thus the very men who insisted on "free competition" proved the first to oppose competition by equally individualistic producers of other countries. Nor were industrialists alone in demanding government intervention on their behalf. In agricultural areas farmers and cattle-raisers opposed with equal vehemence the purchase of grain, meat, wool, and other agrarian products overseas; and labor, when it gained a voice in political life, protested against imports from nations whose lower standard of living permitted the payment of lower wages. American business leaders frequently complain today that a desire for "security" on the part of labor, and of youth, hampers the effective operation of free enterprise economy, where great risks must often be taken to achieve great gains. They tend to forget that industry and farming have long sought to achieve security, too, and to minimize the element of risk, demanding high tariffs and high farm subsidies.

The earlier a nation had developed modern industrialization, the sooner it began to show signs of wanting to consolidate its economy, to achieve stability, to exchange risk for safeguards guaranteed by the state. England, cradle of the Industrial Revolution, had been gradually abandoning the principal tenets of free private enterprise at a time when the Labour Party was not yet a factor in its political life. British industrialists sought to fix prices through cartels, and so did the industrialists of Germany and other continental nations of western Europe—thus sacrificing competition and flexibility, the great advantages of private enterprise, for the security of assured returns on their capital expenditures. After World War II American investors proved less risk-minded than British, French, and other European investors of the nineteenth and early twentieth centuries who had developed the resources of backward regions, and insisted on government guarantees of investments they might make abroad. The growing tendency of western European economy to settle into accepted molds, to rely on various forms of government aid, and to avoid new investments and unexpected risks, which some Americans have associated with socialism, had been under way long before the Labour government took power in England and the continental countries introduced postwar controls and restrictions. One of the principal arguments for the nationalization of British coal mines, which Conservatives no less than Labourites considered to be necessary, was the fact that mine-owners had been reluctant to make new financial outlays for modernization of the mines and improvement of labor conditions in an enterprise where men have been less and less willing to work. Public opinion in western Europe during the past quarter of a century has been divided, not on the issue whether free enterprise should be subjected to social controls, which is not so much in controversy as it is here, but on the areas of free enterprise to which social controls should be applied—some arguing, like Labour in Britain, that all basic large-scale industries, including steel, should be nationalized, others contending, as in France and among British Conservatives, that only a few enterprises having the character of public utilities, such as coal mines, gas and electricity, and railways, were proper objects of nationalization.

The obvious need to conserve natural and human resources, and the urgent desire to avoid breakdowns in the capitalist system such as the world depression of 1929, brought about increasing interest in the possibilities of planned economy. Before World War I, as Professor Seymour Harris of Harvard University has pointed out, planning "existed only in the minds or scribblings of leftward theorists." [1] Today unplanned capitalism is regarded by most Europeans as "a luxury which only a rich country can afford." The planners of the twentieth century are in the fortunate position, to quote Professor Harris, of being able to "capitalize on the early gains made by dynamic capitalism." While Russia's experience with planned economy had a profound effect on the rest of the world, it is regarded by democratic countries with serious misgivings, because the U.S.S.R. has not yet demonstrated that economic planning can coexist with political liberty.

Critics of Russian methods often failed to note, however, that planning in a backward country that had not yet developed the instrumentalities of modern industrialization is a far cry from planning in advanced industrial nations, which do not have to start by first creating the material underpinning of modern economy. It is possible to argue that, had Lenin and Stalin forgone dictatorial methods and allowed unhampered development of the Industrial Revolution in Russia, they would have eventually come out approximately

[1] Seymour Harris: *Economic Planning* (New York: Alfred A. Knopf; 1949).

where the advanced nations of the West are today—with both a modern economic system and political liberty. It is only fair to recall, however, that this process took well over a hundred years in Britain and the United States; while in Germany, which had experienced industrial but not political revolution, it led not to democracy but to Nazi totalitarianism. Moreover, since modern industry is a prerequisite of modern military power, it is not surprising that Soviet leaders, already suspicious of the motives of Western nations, viewed every suggestion that they should slow down their industrialization program as a sinister attempt to perpetuate the relative weakness of Russia as compared with Britain, Germany, the United States, and even Japan. Today no industrial nation, or nation aspiring to industrialization, can be said to have "pure capitalism" in the sense in which it was understood in the early stages of the Industrial Revolution. In his useful volume *Economic Planning* Professor Harris sketches a wide arc of various degrees of planning, from the most limited to the most extensive, ranging from Canada and the United States through India, Australia, the Netherlands, Norway, Argentina, France, Czechoslovakia, Poland, and the U.S.S.R. This arc includes countries with the most diverse political traditions and at the most diverse stages of economic and social development.

Some form of collectivism is inherent in large-scale industrialization. This has become increasingly evident in the twentieth century as large-scale enterprises and cartels have crowded business individualism to the wall. Either capitalism as it was known in the early stages of the Industrial Revolution has reached a stage of stagnation, its machinery being taken over in part at least by socialist governments, as in western Europe and some of the nations of the British Commonwealth; or else vast corporations have gradually squeezed out small individual enterprises, as in the United States. The process that has occurred here has been well described by Adolph A. Berle, who writes: "We have a situation in which, on the capital side, collectivism has arrived without grace of the socialists. . . . You can wonder whether we are halfway along toward inevitable socialism, or whether collectivism in non-statist form slows up capitalism to a point where individuals once more emerge. But you have to face the fact, with all its implications, that modern capitalism is also collectivism. Some administrators of collectivism can send you to jail. Ours can't. In some ways, though, the corporation executive is first cousin to the commissar." [1]

The trend toward socialism has taken various forms, from the still essentially free-enterprise economy of the United States, modified by such socialist features as public education in schools and state universities and regional undertakings for distribution of power and electricity like the Tennessee Valley Authority, through the mixed economy of France, where nationalized and private sectors exist peaceably side by side, and the more stringently nationalized economies of Britain and Norway, to the almost completely controlled economy of the U.S.S.R., planned and directed by a political dictatorship. Greatly as these various degrees of socialism differ in character and motivation, they have in common one feature that sharply distinguishes the economy of the twentieth century from that of the nineteenth. That is the shift in emphasis, sometimes officially proclaimed, as in the U.S.S.R., sometimes only subconsciously felt, as in the United States, from the accumulation of wealth through personal profit-making to growing concern with the development of national, and even international, resources for "the greatest good of the greatest number." Untrammeled freedom for private ownership and exploitation of mines and waterfalls, of fields and forests, which in the early stages of industrialization was regarded as a natural right, has given place to conservation of resources that are considered more and more, not as the personal appanage of private owners, but as the precious heri-

[1] A. A. Berle, Jr.: "Our Collectivized Capitalism," *Reporter*, October 21, 1949, p. 10.

tage of the community as a whole. State protection of forests, state measures to arrest soil erosion and promote irrigation, projects by national and local authorities to substitute for the sprawling, unhealthy, ugly slums inherited from the nineteenth century carefully planned garden cities where fresh air, sunshine, and security against the hazards of modern transportation can be assured to old and young—all these have come to be regarded, not as revolutionary schemes, but as ordinary necessities of twentieth-century life.

And just as there has been a growing consensus on the need to conserve the natural wealth of nations, so there has been increasing concern about the need to conserve and develop their human capital—through opportunities to improve health, nutrition, education, and leisure activities. The acquisition of learning and professional skills, the many pleasures and comforts of life that industrialization had made available, could not indefinitely remain a privilege of the middle class of merchants and bankers who had assumed in the nineteenth and early twentieth centuries the position once occupied by the pre-1789 aristocracy. Industrial and agricultural workers were not satisfied merely to keep body and soul together; they pressed for a chance to enjoy the richer existence promised by the machine. With the spread of literacy came new interest on the part of larger and larger groups of the population in advanced education, in professional training, in art, music, and literature, in the extension of health services to all who might need them. Some might complain that this process resulted in too great popularization of culture, in a spreading of education so thin that the true values of civilization as they had been known to a relatively small minority in past centuries would be obliterated. Yet if the great promises held out by the Industrial Revolution and the accompanying expansion of political action by people freed from the time-consuming burdens of primitive manual economy are to be fulfilled, ever growing opportunities must be offered for the exercise of intellectual and artistic faculties by all citizens. Otherwise the end result of industrialization would be the formation of a rigid stratified society, where the social groups restrained from full participation in all aspects of modern life would be consumed by a resentment that sooner or later would explode in revolution, as happened in other societies that had failed to remain flexible—France in 1789 or Russia in 1917.

Had the debate about the connection between economic freedom and political freedom been limited to the Western World, where both the Industrial Revolution and the political changes precipitated by the French and American revolutions brought about comparable ideas of the role of man in society, it might have been fiery enough, as one can see from the vigorous postwar controversies between Britain and us, as well as among various groups of Americans. This debate was greatly complicated and confused, however, by the emergence of Russia, not only as a great power in Europe and Asia, which it had been for at least two centuries, but also as the fountainhead of world communism. Opponents of any restrictions on economic freedom in the West pointed to the politically repressive dictatorship of the Kremlin as a terrible example of what might happen if western Europe and the United States should depart from laissez-faire and adopt planning and controls in the economic sphere. Soviet spokesmen and their supporters in other countries, for their part, contended that the planlessness of "capitalist" countries, resulting in a sequence of booms and busts, was due to the inadequacies, or worse, of democratic governments, and that the Socialists, by contenting themselves with half-measures, aggravated instead of correcting the evils of capitalism. Fear in the West that Russia as a nation would embark on an aggressive course of expansion became mixed with fear of the impact Communist theories and practices would have on political and economic institutions associated with democracy, capitalism, and reformist socialism; while in the U.S.S.R. the conviction that sooner or later a "capitalist" coalition would turn on Russia fused old apprehensions about the intentions of Britain and Germany, and more recently the United States, to "contain" the Russian nation, with new fears that "capitalism" would seek to destroy the institutions of communism. Rational discussion of the issues at stake became increasingly difficult; and each side gave its ideology the character of a new crusading faith.

In both western Europe and the United States opponents of the "welfare state" contend that the government, which they regard as something apart from the people, should interfere as little as possible with economic activities, and blame Britain's postwar difficulties, for example, on measures adopted by the Labour government, such as nationalization of some industries and a wide range of social services, the most recent of which is the health service introduced in 1948. British Labourites, for their part, point out that socialism is not of recent origin—that many of the social services criticized by Americans were introduced before World War I by the Liberal Party leader, Lloyd George, and that in Imperial Germany Bismarck found it politic to grant an extensive program of reforms in the hope of killing the Socialists with kindness. In the United States spokesmen of the conservative American Federation of Labor contend that the state, far from being an enemy of the people, is its servant; that government in a democratic country, to use Lincoln's phrase, is "a government of the people, by the people, for the people"; that the concept of the welfare state is not new to Americans, since the Constitution provides that the national government shall "promote the general welfare"; and that for nearly a hundred years, beginning with the Homestead Act of 1862, measures have been taken by the government to provide a growing degree of social security.[1]

Critics of the "welfare state" fear that expansion of government intervention, no matter how beneficial it may seem to

[1] Nelson H. Cruikshank, AFL director of Social Insurance Activities: "Welfare State Defined," *New York Times,* July 10, 1949.

the groups receiving state aid, will sooner or later bring about political dictatorship. In their opinion, political freedom in democratic nations has been hitherto safeguarded by the existence of free private enterprise. When the latter goes, so will the former. Socialism, they say, is incompatible with political liberty. Advocates of the "welfare state" retort that political liberty without economic and social security is barren of meaning; that people who cannot make both ends meet at a minimum standard of living, and are harried by anxiety about their own future and that of their families, can hardly prove loyal and stable citizens of a democratic nation. According to them, there is no reason to assume that socialism inevitably results in political dictatorship; on the contrary, by raising the economic and social level of the population, socialism will give new significance and dimension to political liberties.

The concept of the "welfare state" offers as great a challenge to the sovereignty of the producer in an industrialized society as the concept of political democracy offered to the sovereignty of kings in 1789. Its fundamental assumption is that the producer must be responsible to the community, just as the advocates of constitutional monarchy or republican insitutions assumed that government must be responsible to the people. Far from thinking that the government should stand idly by while villages turn into slums, while natural resources are ruthlessly dissipated, while men are thrown out of work through no personal fault of their own, advocates of planned economy and of the "welfare state" take the view that the government has an obligation to alleviate economic and social maladjustments. In its White Paper on Employment Policy, issued during the war, the British coalition government headed by Winston Churchill pledged itself "to accept in future the responsibility for taking action at the earliest possible stage to arrest a threatened slump," and to maintain "a high stable level of employment" after the war.

Nor is this point of view limited to European socialists. The Australians, for example, declare that "the maintenance of conditions which will make full employment possible is an obligation owed to the people of Australia by commonwealth and state government. . . . Unemployment is an evil from the effects of which no class in the community and no state commonwealth can hope to escape, unless concerted action is taken." Canada, which comes closest to the free private-enterprise ideas of the United States, declared in April 1945: "The ultimate aim of all reconstruction policies is the extension of opportunity, welfare and security among the Canadian people. . . . The government has stated unequivocally its adoption of a high and stable level of employment and income and thereby higher standards of living, as a major aim of government policy."

The problems of the next stage have been summed up by the conservative British newspaper the *Observer,* which in April 1949, pointing out that the future of the democratic welfare state was facing its greatest test, said:

The rich prizes of competitive capitalism have largely gone, together with most of its hardships; now the Left-wing hopes of moving on steadily towards a fully equalitarian society, without the compulsions of dictatorship, are seen to be strictly limited. Whence will come the new hopes, the new vision of satisfying goals to be achieved? . . . Our sense of social justice will not allow us to turn back to the rigours of *laissez faire,* with the weaker going to the wall, and our love of freedom rules out the other extreme, totalitarianism. But this "middle" is proving harder than we expected; the enemies lying in wait to destroy it are drabness, dullness, the quenching of ambition, the feeling that no rewards worth working for are to be had.

These enemies are formidable but not invincible; and the party which deserves to win the next election will be the party which gives best promise of dealing with them. The party, that is, which accepts the basic principles of the Welfare State and at the same time shows how it means to provide new incentives, new fields both for co-operative endeavour and for friendly competition, and new openings for the adventurous.

To assert that socialism in western Europe, or communism in less developed areas, is the one and only answer to the problems of the twentieth century is just as dogmatic as to assert that untrammeled private enterprise offers a cure-all for the ills of all nations, no matter what their past traditions or present stage of development. It should be obvious by now that there is no single formula that will fit the vastly diverse needs of the United States and India, of Germany and Yugoslavia, of Britain and the U.S.S.R. Nor has either socialism or communism so far proved less susceptible of being bent to the demands of nationalism than the laissez-faire capitalism of the nineteenth century. In fact, it can be argued that the cartels formed by European industrialists represented an attempt to overcome nationalist barriers to trade by organizing international combinations of a limited character. Such cartels, however, contradicted the whole concept of competition in private enterprise, which has been regarded here as the keystone of modern capitalism. It would be illogical for the United States, which at home combats monopolies in restraint of trade through antitrust legislation, to countenance cartels in Europe, while criticizing economic controls by European governments. Actually, as Europeans become better acquainted with the structure of the American economy and realize that it has retained the flexibility and genuine competitiveness long ago lost in the industrial nations of western Europe, many of them, including socialist economists, have begun to wonder whether antitrust legislation on the American model might not prove more efficacious in restoring healthy circulation in the atrophied economies of their countries than further measures of nationalization. It is entirely conceivable that, while the free-enterprise economy of the United States accepts more and more social responsibilities, as has already happened in Britain and the Scandinavian countries, the European nations, for their part, will find in the revival of competition greater incentives for enlarging production, which in turn can then serve to expand the well-being of the population as a whole.

PART II

Where is Europe Going?

Chapter IV

PATTERNS OF RECOVERY

When one views postwar Europe against the backdrop of its history, out of seeming confusion and conflict emerge four main trends, whose ultimate consequences can as yet be only adumbrated. These trends are economic recovery, which has revived production and restored Europe's material resources but has also created problems of international trade; the growing acceptance of socialism in one form or another, with the "welfare state" and varying degrees of planning no longer a novelty; consolidation of political and social changes wrought by war at a point just left of center; and long-range attempts, so far hampered by resurgent nationalism, to integrate the continent either by regions or in its entirety, and to reweave its ties with the rest of the world.

That Europe is recovering from the nightmare of conquest and war devastation there can be no doubt; and, at differing rates, it is recovering in both east and west. The Western nations owe their recovery to a fortunate combination of two factors: the efforts and endurance of their own peoples; and the aid extended by the United States since the war. This aid, estimated in 1950 at the figure of $23,340,000,000 since 1945, has consisted of supplies furnished by the United Nations Relief and Rehabilitation Administration, seventy-two per cent of whose cost was contributed by this country; millions of dollars' worth of private relief; the 1945 loan of $3,750,000,000 to Britain; Export-Import Bank loans to France, the Netherlands, and other countries; and, beginning in 1948, the Marshall Plan, which promised credits to sixteen countries of about $20,000,000,000 over a period of four years.[1] Without American aid, first in food and fuel, then, as Europe's food and coal production got under way, of raw materials and industrial equipment, western Europe would have recovered sooner or later; but at a cost in material deprivations that might well have jeopardized its hard-won political liberties. Of this informed Europeans are clearly, and for the most part gratefully, aware. But without the hard and unremitting work of the English, French, and other recipients of ERP assistance who courageously grappled with the tasks of reconstruction in spite of physical depletion and moral lassitude, the Marshall Plan would have proved as unfructifying as water poured upon sand. This, for our part, we must never forget.

In contrast to western Europe the nations of the east, at Russia's insistence, rejected the opportunity to share in Marshall Plan aid. This decision was not unwelcome to some western European leaders, who rejoiced that their share of the Marshall Plan funds would thereby be increased. Others wondered whether the American Congress would in any case have approved the ERP if it had included Russia, which by 1947 was regarded as a threat to European recovery and stability. The countries east of Germany had been particularly hard hit by the termination of UNRRA operations in 1946, and complained bitterly about Washington's decision to substitute American financial assistance for international relief and rehabilitation. These countries, for the most part producers of food and raw materials, need to import tools and machinery not only to implement their postwar industrialization programs, but also to rehabilitate and expand the output of their farms and mines. The U.S.S.R., absorbed in the reconstruction of its own severely devastated areas, which included its important prewar industrial centers, is not in a position to provide its neighbors with the tools and ma-

---

[1] On the basis of the budget proposed by President Truman for the fiscal year starting July 1, 1950, the total cost of foreign-aid expenditures is calculated at $29,513,000,000 by the middle of 1951.

chinery they need. Poland and Czechoslovakia, unlike the former Axis satellites—Bulgaria, Hungary, and Rumania—are not under obligation to pay reparations in kind to Russia and, in spite of their rejection of the Marshall Plan, have shown increasing eagerness to trade with western Europe and the United States. But until they have acquired machinery, they cannot increase their exports of food and raw materials, or, in the case of Czechoslovakia, that of manufactured goods.

The countries of eastern Europe and the Balkans actually had no real food export surplus in the past. Before 1939 their sales of foodstuffs abroad were often "hunger exports." Not being able to produce most consumer goods at home, they sacrificed food to purchase abroad urgently needed manufactured products. One of the principal objectives of Communist planners in Russia in 1917, as it is today in eastern Europe, was to terminate this trade relationship, which Lenin characterized as "colonial," and to create diversified economies combining modernized agriculture and newly established industries. This program is determined by political as well as economic considerations, for industrial workers are regarded as more loyal and reliable supporters of communism than the peasants, especially peasants owning individual plots of land. Planners in Prague and Warsaw insist, as Moscow planners did during the interwar years, that trade arrangements with the western nations must fit in with their projects, and contend that Marshall Plan aid, no matter how desirable, would in practice have acted as a brake on their national plans. Yet if the eastern European nations are to finance imports of capital equipment out of their own resources, and achieve capital formation at home, they may have to effect savings, temporarily at least, by reducing living-standards. So far in the east recovery has been achieved at a high cost in human depreciations and in loss of liberties. Meanwhile the western nations, which have facilities to produce the capital equipment and tools required by the east and are urgently looking for additional export outlets, found it necessary to sell as large a quantity of their goods as possible in the dollar area rather than in Europe, so as to finance their purchases of food, raw materials, and machinery in the United States. Moreover, for reasons of security, they followed Washington's lead in curtailing the export to eastern Europe of products that might increase Russia's war potential. Thus, while both west and east have needed to trade with each other, transactions between the two sectors of the continent have been hampered by fear in the west of another war, and in the east by fear of western economic domination. By 1950 the continent remained divided into "two Europes."

There is no question that the seven billion dollars' worth of supplies delivered to western Europe by 1950 under the Marshall Plan gave a great impetus to the rehabilitation of the western nations. Rehabilitation, however, in many instances merely plastered over existing cracks in the economies of the recipient nations without getting to the roots of the continent's major maladjustments. Europe's economic difficulties have been aggravated by communism, but are not in the first instance due to it, or even to the effects of World War II. The emphasis Washington spokesmen have placed on the efficacy of the Marshall Plan as a weapon against Russia and communism has obscured Europe's basic economic problems which would persist even if Russia were to disappear from the map tomorrow. These problems stem from the profound change that has occurred since the nineteenth century in Europe's economic position relative to that of other continents; its lag in new industrial techniques and resulting productivity as compared with the United States; and the need, as yet only dimly recognized, for far-reaching economic changes that could be effected only if political and social conditions were altered within and between European nations.

Such alterations would be tantamount to a revolution. Until recently the United States, apprehensive about proposals for social transformations in Europe, whether urged by Communists or Socialists, has thought in terms of restoration of Europe's economic system rather than of its overhauling. This essentially conservative attitude on our part—conservative in the proper sense of the word, of wanting to conserve the order that existed before 1939—has encouraged those Europeans who opposed change to maintain things pretty much as they have been in the past, on the assumption that this policy will not only suit their own interests but also command the approval and support of the United States. We have thus placed ourselves in an equivocal position. We have urged Europeans to undertake such fundamental changes as the creation of a Marshall Plan economic union and the streamlining of their industrial production by the adoption of American techniques; yet until recently we have discouraged if not openly opposed reforms that might disturb vested interests—such as projects for land redistribution in Italy or labor participation in the planning of German industry—on the ground that reforms would interfere with current reconstruction.

The most favorable aspect of Europe's postwar recovery has been the remarkable increase in industrial production, which in 1948 (outside of the U.S.S.R.) was 16 per cent higher than in 1947 and approached the 1938 level. Contrary to assertions by some Americans that eastern Europe was on the verge of economic collapse, the United Nations Economic Commission for Europe[1] reached the conclusion that in 1948 industrial expansion was as substantial in the countries of the east as in those of the west, and in the U.S.S.R. (according to figures furnished by the Soviet government) was estimated to have risen by 27 per cent as compared with 1938. Western Germany registered a particularly rapid recovery, industrial production there rising from 40 per cent of prewar at the end of 1947 to 64 per cent by the end of

[1] United Nations, Department of Economic Affairs: *Economic Survey of Europe in 1948.* Prepared by the Research and Planning Division, Economic Commission for Europe. (Geneva, 1949.)

1948—an improvement that, welcome as it was to the Germans as well as to American taxpayers, had already begun in 1949 to worry both Germany's western European competitors and eastern European victims of Nazi conquest.

Taking for study a group of fourteen countries of eastern and western Europe (excluding Germany), the United Nations Commission found that the volume of industrial production was 13 per cent above prewar; while in the U.S.S.R. the 1948 industrial output was 18 per cent above the 1940 level. Agriculture did not improve as much as industry, but nevertheless output rose by 12 per cent in Europe outside of the U.S.S.R., where the 1948 and 1949 harvests reached the prewar level. Labor productivity in industry increased, and unemployment remained low except in Italy (2 million unemployed in 1950 out of a population of 40 million), Hungary, Belgium (during the period of readjustment to removal of some government controls), the West German state (nearly 2 million in 1950 out of a population of 45 million), and the Soviet zone of Germany. The rise in production was accompanied by a gradual return to monetary stability. Incentives to work were thus improved in a number of countries, thereby stimulating further output. Better utilization and distribution of fuel resources, especially coal, brought about relaxation in the general fuel shortage, facilitating industrial expansion. A notable rise of over 10 million tons in 1948 took place in steel production, which for western Europe reached close to 50 million net tons in 1949, or above the prewar level.

Europe's industrial progress was largely due to increases in output per man employed in industry (as compared with 1938), which were estimated at 5 per cent between 1946 and 1947, and at 9 per cent between 1947 and 1948—the latter increase being "well in excess of the annual rise in production that can be expected in normal times."[1] Such a notable increase in labor productivity three years after a grueling six-

[1] Ibid., p. 70.

year war should set at rest once and for all allegations often heard in the United States that Europeans "are lying down on the job like WPA workers" and living on American "charity" without trying to make an effort of their own. The United Nations Commission, moreover, believes that the rise in output per man "may be an indication that industrial production will continue to show rapid progress, not only until the pre-war level of output per man is regained, but until productivity in industry reaches the level at which it would stand if progress had continued uninterrupted by the war. In other words, when industry has been able to put into effect the technical improvements which have accumulated during the war and which have not yet been fully exploited, industrial productivity is likely to exceed the pre-war level by something approaching the normal increase that would have taken place had there been no war." Should this prediction prove to be accurate, it is expected that, given the continuance of full employment in Europe, "the rate of progress experienced in 1948 may well continue for a further period of one or two years." [2]

An analysis of European production as a whole shows that the heavy industries—iron and steel, engineering and chemical—continued to rise in advance of other enterprises, with steel in the vanguard. This expansion in heavy-goods industries had by 1948 more than compensated for the postwar decline in German production, "but with the rapid recovery of Germany's heavy industries, there is likely to be a shift to heavy industries in Europe as a whole." By contrast, consumer-goods industries lagged behind. Among them the newer enterprises—electricity, rubber, and rayon—which had shown a high rate of expansion in prewar years have been above prewar levels as compared with the output of older industries, such as cotton and wool, which remained below prewar figures and faced increasing competition outside of Europe. While industry forged ahead, the over-all index for

[2] Ibid., p. 95.

agricultural production in 1948 was still at 85 per cent of prewar, the principal problem being the restoration to prewar levels of war-depleted livestock, which is essential to resumption of pre-1939 standards of food consumption.

These encouraging findings about the rise of Europe's production, visibly reflected in the improved appearance and morale of the European man and woman in the street, are the silver lining of the dark cloud that still hangs over the continent; and the United Nations Commission minced no words and spared no country's sensibilities in analyzing the cloud's storm potential. Anticipated improvements in industrial output over the next five years, or even in the coming decade, are, according to the Commission, not likely to bring about a solution of the continent's basic problem: and that is the severe poverty in which the majority of Europeans live. This problem could be removed only "through revolutionary changes in the technique of production." Yet instead of modernizing existing enterprises, most countries were seeking to achieve greater diversification in their industrial structure in order to reduce their dependence on imports, especially from the United States. This tendency toward economic nationalism threatened loss of the advantages associated with specialization, division of labor, and large-scale production, and creation of watertight economic units. The desire for autarchy shown by all European countries, both west and east, is not due solely, or even chiefly, to exacerbated nationalism. It has been due primarily to the harsh realization that by 1952 Europe must find some substitute source for the one third of its overseas imports that in 1948 was financed with ERP funds. The "dollar-shortage" crisis that developed in Britain and other Marshall Plan countries in the summer of 1949 was not the result of failure by the Europeans to produce or export enough. On the contrary, the unexpectedly rapid recovery had brought the Marshall Plan countries in 1949 to the stage that both Europeans and Americans had not expected would be reached until 1952; the phase of "recovery" was over; and the recipient nations were caught short before they had devised workable alternatives to additional American aid.

To reduce its dependence on the United States, Europe had been striving to increase its exports, which during 1948 rose by thirty per cent in volume, and to reduce its imports from the Western Hemisphere even at the expense of living-standards, particularly in Britain. The principal economic problem faced by western Europe at the end of 1949 was not that of increasing production (Europeans were already talking of "overproduction"), but of selling goods abroad, especially for dollars, so as to be able to continue purchases of American products once ERP aid had come to an end. Further increase in productivity—through modernization of factories, installation of up-to-date labor-saving machinery, and rationalization of techniques—would improve Europe's capacity to export, provided that costs and prices were lowered. The initial cost of modernization, however, would have to be financed either by borrowing funds in the United States, through government or private channels, or by savings at home, which might require further cuts in existing living-standards. For many of the European nations had been forced to liquidate a considerable part of their foreign investments to pay war costs and now lack ready capital.

But even when increased productivity had been achieved, it would not of itself solve the continent's economic problems unless, at the same time, the European nations could find additional outlets for their products. They could do so by reducing tariff and other restrictions on their trade with each other and with countries of Asia, Latin America, and the British Commonwealth, as several of them did after devaluation of the pound sterling in September 1949, which precipitated the devaluation of other currencies. As long as the European nations need American goods, however, their main preoccupation will be to develop adequate markets here, where they can be paid in dollars. It is thus impossible for the United States to expect that the Marshall Plan countries can solve their economic problems by their own actions. We, too, shall have to find answers to these problems in at least two major respects. On the one hand, we shall have to decide whether we can provide investment capital, from either government or private sources, for modernization of the European plant. On the other hand, we shall have to explore possibilities of enlarging our imports of European goods, either through further tariff reductions on specific items such as British woolens, or through re-examination of our customs procedures, or both, to the point where we might absorb at least three billion dollars' worth of imports—the estimated figure of the export gap that will exist between the United States and Europe on termination of the ERP. The most notable gain made at the Washington conference of the United States, Britain, and Canada in September 1949 was that for the first time since the war we recognized the profound change that has occurred in the position of the United States in world economy and, instead of merely devising piecemeal measures of stopgap relief and financial aid, took the bull by the horns and decided to formulate economic policies consonant with our new responsibilities as the greatest creditor, greatest producer, and greatest consumer of the twentieth century.

Many Americans believe that the Marshall Plan countries could solve their difficulties by integrating their national economies into a regional area free of tariff and other barriers, which would become comparable to the United States, by abandoning the various controls adopted before and during the war and thus returning to free enterprise. It is true that in the prewar period intra-European trade represented fifty per cent of the continent's total trade; but this figure included trade between west and east. Creation of a regional union limited to the Marshall Plan countries would not restore the prewar situation unless east-west trade is resumed at least at prewar levels. In spite of Russia's past emphasis on bilateral trade as contrasted with our advocacy of multilateralism, the Soviet government has been gradually adopting the practice of multilateral trade by simultaneous over-all balancing of exports and imports between several countries. For example, Finland sells to the U.S.S.R., which sells to Czechoslovakia, which sells to Finland, and so on, within the region of eastern Europe. It is quite conceivable that, given a prolonged period of peace and at least approximately full employment, multilateral trade might be gradually restored in both west and east, as well as between the two regions. But it is difficult to see how trade between a group of industrial nations alone, as in western Europe, or between primarily backward agrarian nations, as in eastern Europe, would meet their respective needs for food and raw materials in the one case and for tools and machinery in the other.

Nor would the proposed Western European economic union be comparable to the economic situation in the United States. A union of Marshall Plan countries would link together Pittsburghs, Detroits, and Clevelands, but minus the agrarian Kansas, Nebraska, and Iowa that our industrial centers draw on for food and raw materials. At the present time, however, integration of east and west in Europe appears to be remote, because the west fears the possibility of Russian aggression, while Russia is reluctant to let its eastern European neighbors drift into the western orbit. At the same time all European nations, both west and east, are haunted by the possibility of another depression in the United States, which would throw all their calculations out of gear. Consequently they try to safeguard their national economies by a wide range of restrictions that hamper trade expansion.

Would a return to free enterprise improve the chances for trade liberalization? This is a moot question. Many Europeans, while admiring the economic achievements of the United States, point out that at the peak of laissez-faire in the nineteenth century western Europe did not attain the high output and living-standards achieved by us in that period, and the toll in manpower and material resources taken by two world wars has further widened the gap between Europe and this country. To narrow this gap, according to the United Nations Commission, capital equipment and organization of production must be improved to standards comparable with ours. What needs to be done is to discover the political and economic institutions that can most effectively bring about the necessary re-equipment and reorganization instead of merely affirming that this or that system, no matter how feasible and desirable in the United States, offers the only solution for European problems.

We should not be frightened by labels or practices that may seem different from our own, provided the end results we ourselves have achieved here by our particular methods can be attained on the continent. Actually, we have gone much further than France and Italy in redistributing income through taxes, and are more "progressive" in our system of agriculture than many of the Marshall Plan countries. If we could be sure that the advocates of laissez-faire in Europe would in fact carry out basic reforms essential for long-range recovery, we might feel more confident about their return to power. Prewar experience, however, showed that supporters of laissez-faire among industrialists, business men, and landowners wanted to preserve the *status quo* and, far from fostering competition, sought to protect themselves from it at home and abroad by various restrictive devices such as cartels and export and import restrictions. Prewar cartels, formed with the acquiescence of governments, stabilized inefficiency. Through cartels private enterprise achieved integration within nations and even regions; but it was an integration based on higher-cost output kept artificially low. This was in sharp contrast to the economic situation of the United States, which, unlike Europe, enjoyed security from external aggression, maintained competition, and fought industrial combinations in restraint of trade. It is in the light of prewar experience that many responsible Europeans believe some measure of socialization is essential under existing conditions, especially in the wake of war, and that careful planning for the possible utilization of available resources of manpower and materials offers a more promising way out of the present dilemma than return to unrestricted conditions. For vast numbers of people in Britain and on the continent laissez-faire spells not economic progress but black memories of the depression and mass unemployment of the 1930's, repetition of which they want to avoid at all costs.

One of Europe's most serious handicaps is that planning has so far been primarily national in scope, with little or no attempt except on paper to relate the plans of the various nations to plans for a larger area—region, continent, or world. As a result, planning has tended to steer all European nations toward greater autarchy instead of greater co-operation and, according to the United Nations Commission, may "lead to the increased economic isolation" of the individual countries from each other instead of promoting integration of the European economy. The advanced industrial nations of the west have tried to diversify their manufacturing in such a way as to be self-sufficient in case of another war or depression, and have insisted on expanding both their heavy industry and their consumer-goods exports, at the same time refusing to import "nonessentials"—that is, food and consumer goods above the minimum required for subsistence. While threatening each other with cut-throat competition for foreign markets, they were drastically curtailing purchases of each other's output. It is the opinion of the United Nations Commission experts that if Europe is to achieve a higher degree of economic integration and thus a more rational use of its resources, each country will have "to adopt more liberal economic policies or to advance towards more uniform standards of economic planning. A return to economic liberalism might foster the integration of the European economy through the gradual elimination of intra-European trade barriers and the creation of a single interrelated currency system. Conversely, a greater degree of uniformity in the methods of planning might permit a higher degree of integration between the individual planned economies, through the institution of proper agencies for the coordination of plans and the negotiation of long-term contractual arrangements for the development of trade." The danger, as the United Nations Commission saw it in 1949, was "that the nations of Europe will reject the one and shirk the other and will pursue instead half-way solutions, as the result of which their efforts at greater economic integration will prove abortive." Return to liberalism would mean abandonment of the measures of socialization toward which most of Europe, in varying degrees, has been moving since the turn of the century. Greater uniformity of planning presupposes reconciliation, or at least long-term peaceful "coexistence," of the two Europes, west and east.

Is it possible, under socialism, to find the capital necessary for re-equipping Europe and raising its production and living-standards? Critics of socialism contend that heavy taxation, especially on excess profits, discourages incentive and blocks new investment. Yet Britain's experience before 1939 indicates that capital investment in the re-equipment of existing enterprises, notably the coal mines, had been dwindling for a long period. The United Nations Commission estimates that the rate of real capital formation in Europe has actually been increasing at a rapid pace since 1946. In 1948 net investment in fixed capital in Europe as a whole (Germany excluded) was about 5 billion dollars, or half the corresponding figure for the United States, estimated at 10 billion dollars, both in terms of 1938 dollars.[1] Of the continent's total net investment in fixed capital (Germany excluded), Britain and France in 1948 accounted for about one half (Socialist Britain 36 per cent, and mixed-economy France 13 per cent). The largest proportionate increases in capital investment as compared with 1938, however, occurred in both west and east—in France

[1] Ibid., p. 47.

and Sweden, Hungary and Yugoslavia. In all countries a high priority has been given to investment in heavy industries and transportation, with low priorities for consumer goods and agriculture. This pattern of investment, which before 1939 had been regarded as peculiar to the U.S.S.R., has been adopted since 1945 by advanced nations of the west recovering from devastation, as well as by nations of the east striving to overcome their backwardness through industrialization.

Could Europe's emphasis on capital-goods industries at the expense of consumer needs be altered—and should it be altered? One possible approach would be to persuade the countries that are still primarily producers of food and raw materials to reduce or postpone their current industrialization plans and devote more of their resources to modernization and expansion of farms and mines, thereby providing more food and raw materials for the west. Such a proposal, however, would not be favorably received by the U.S.S.R. and its neighbors as long as current international tensions persist, since it would mean continuation for some time to come of the existing disparity in the economic, and hence the military, potential between east and west. But even apart from strategic considerations, the eastern European nations are determined to benefit by Germany's temporary industrial decline to terminate their prewar dependence on German manufactured goods, which made them vulnerable to Nazi opinnomic and military pressures. This objective, in their opinion, can be achieved only if they succeed in creating industrial plants of their own. Another approach would be to have all European countries abandon their present efforts to develop balanced industrial production within their national boundaries and, instead, adopt industrial specialization and regional co-ordination of production and investment. Such coordination, aimed at the balanced development of Europe as a whole rather than of individual national economies, would, according to the United Nations Commission, yield a better return on the continent's capital investment.

What are the prospects for the economic integration of Europe? In spite of vigorous pleas by American spokesmen for the Economic Cooperation Administration and European representatives of the Organization for European Economic Cooperation, all of whom have repeatedly warned that unless Europe achieves economic union by 1952 it is doomed to catastrophe, little has been accomplished so far in the direction of counteracting the marked trend toward autarchy. Even such limited projects as Benelux, which envisages a customs union between Belgium, Luxembourg, and the Netherlands, or the Franco-Italian customs union signed in 1949, are still at the stage of discussion and analysis. Regional co-ordination, however, would involve a far greater degree of planning across frontiers than has yet been contemplated by the governments of European nations, whatever their political complexion. Each country would have to specialize on production and export of the goods in which it has the greatest efficiency, and close down those enterprises in which it is at a disadvantage compared with other countries in the region. Not only would all members of a western European economic union have to make drastic reductions in their tariffs, or even abolish them altogether; they would also have to overhaul antiquated and restrictive methods of production, and retrain workers of shut-down plants and transfer them to other factories, for which increased outlets abroad would have to be found. The many problems of adjustment posed by regional integration alarm governments that are already struggling with unemployment and growing demands for higher standards of living and now find themselves caught in a vicious circle. They realize that improvement in the welfare of their peoples depends on increased productivity, which in turn hinges on "the adoption of superior techniques requiring both more capital equipment and more efficient methods of organization." [1] At the same time they fear that during the transition period, whose duration no one can accurately fore-

[1] Ibid., p. 226.

cast, national economies will be thrown into a state of confusion that would prove fertile ground for extremist movements like fascism or communism.

Can one hope for integration of the economy of the European continent as a whole through the revival of east-west trade? It will be recalled that Secretary Marshall, in his Harvard address, set no geographic limits for American aid to Europe, and in answer to subsequent questions said that such aid would be available to all countries "west of Asia". Actually the original concept of the Marshall Plan supporters went even farther and presupposed the revival of the prewar triangle of trade between Europe, Asia, and the Western Hemisphere, including Latin America. But preoccupation with the tasks of checking Russia and communism on the European continent truncated this concept, with the result that from the outset the ERP developed into a primarily bilateral arrangement between the United States and western Europe—a bilateral arrangement, moreover, that did not even provide for barter of goods, only for a one-way flow of American products to the ERP nations.

By 1947, however, the American Congress, alarmed and irritated by what it considered Russian measures of aggression and non-co-operation, was in no mood to grant substantial financial assistance to the U.S.S.R. and its neighbors. In any case, neither the United States nor western Europe had expected that Russia, itself devastated and impoverished by war, would be in a position to give substantial assistance in the recovery of western Europe—particularly since in the interwar years Russian exports and imports had respectively constituted about one per cent of total world trade. What the west counted on was the possibility, through the resumption of prewar trade with the east, of obtaining such necessary items as food, coal, and timber from Poland; wheat and bauxite from Hungary; oil and wheat from Rumania; timber and various raw materials, among them copper and zinc, from Yugoslavia; sugar, malt, and various industrial and consumer goods from Czechoslovakia. It was the nonparticipation in the Marshall Plan of these countries of eastern Europe and the Balkans, enjoined on them by the Soviet government, that created difficulties for the west; and the subsequent Russian blockade of Berlin in 1948 had the effect of widening the economic split across the continent by cutting off trade between the western and eastern zones of Germany.

What are the reasons for the lag in east-west trade? The western nations say it can be explained by the reluctance of the U.S.S.R. to permit its neighbors' trade with the west, and by Moscow's efforts to milk these countries' resources for the benefit of its own economy. Eastern European spokesmen, especially at sessions of the United Nations Economic Commission for Europe in Geneva, have vehemently denied that the U.S.S.R. imposed restrictions on either the direction or the character of their foreign trade after its own requirements, usually specified in five-year bilateral trade pacts, had been satisfied. Actually conditions have differed from country to country. Bulgaria, Hungary, and Rumania, former Axis satellites, are under obligations to deliver stated quantities of products to the U.S.S.R. as reparations; and some of their principal assets, notably shipping, have been taken over by the Russians as "German assets," the Russians then using such properties as their share of investments in "joint enterprises" —which Yugoslavia, after its break with Moscow, branded as economic "imperialism." Poland and Czechoslovakia have no reparations obligations, and their exports to Russia and other countries of eastern Europe bear a closer resemblance to ordinary commerce.

If it were possible to assemble reliable statistics, it would be interesting to make a more accurate study of the character and quantity of eastern European exports to the U.S.S.R. than is possible at present. The west maintains that after the needs of the bottomless Russian market have been filled, there is in any case little to export westward. The Poles and Czechs answer that this is not so; the Czechs, for example, contend that only thirty-seven per cent of their shoe exports and eighteen per cent of their textile exports go to the U.S.S.R., thereby, incidentally, helping to raise the Russian standard of living. Both the U.S.S.R. and its neighbors have found it difficult to achieve industrialization and to modernize agriculture out of their own relatively undeveloped resources. The eastern countries are not alone in experiencing economic travail. The nations of the west faced serious problems in 1949 when they strove to expand their exports in a buyers' period, vying with each other for export markets. They consequently looked to eastern Europe with growing interest both as a market and as a source of grain, timber, and ores. This trend will become even more pronounced when the West German state recaptures its prewar position as producer and exporter of industrial goods.

From the point of view of the west, and especially of the United States, expansion of east-west trade presents a choice of risks. Should the west, by permitting exports to the east that would strengthen the industrial and agricultural potential of Russia and its neighbors, take the risk of enabling the Soviet government to acquire the necessary production base for eventual military attack on western Europe, but meanwhile help to maintain production and living-standards in the west, thereby averting the resurgence of communism? Or should it continue to bar essential exports to the east, in the hope of thus maintaining an industrial and therefore a military lead over Russia and its neighbors—but meanwhile take the risk that the decline in exports will result in unemployment, falling living-standards, and unrest in western nations, which would further communism, whose influence had been checked although not routed by economic recovery? The decision will depend on two interlocking considerations: estimates as to the vulnerability of western economies, as now operating, to a possible world depression; and estimates as to the capacity of the west, of which the United States is now an integral part, to maintain a long-term lead in production, and thus in military potential, over the countries of eastern Europe. But even assuming that the fear of war diminishes and that east-west trade is expanded in the near future, all of Europe will still need to increase the productivity of industry and agriculture if present standards of living, which in many areas remain at a level we would regard as close to poverty, are to be improved or even maintained.

Can one hope for integration of Europe's economy as a whole through revival of east-west trade? Not all the western European nations are equally interested in trade with the east. So far as France, the Low Countries, and the Scandinavian nations are concerned, they need the food and raw materials of eastern Europe less urgently than eastern Europe needs their tools, machinery, and other manufactured goods. The Atlantic seaboard nations are much more preoccupied with the problem of adjusting their economies to the decline in British imports as compared with 1938, when Britain purchased continental products many of which have been regarded as "nonessential" under its postwar "austerity" program, financing these purchases with overseas earnings now drastically curtailed. By contrast, Britain does need "essential" goods from eastern Europe, and in 1949 it concluded trade agreements with Poland and the U.S.S.R. for imports of food and feedstuffs, with Czechoslovakia for food, manufactured goods, and raw materials, and with Yugoslavia for copper, lead, and zinc.

The key problem of east-west trade relations, however, is that of central Europe—Germany and, to a lesser extent, Austria. It is significant that in 1948 trade between eastern and western Europe (Germany and Austria excluded) reached 63 per cent of the 1938 level; but if Germany and Austria are included, it remained low, only 42 per cent of the prewar level being attained. Nor have the eastern European countries succeeded in substituting trade with the U.S.S.R. for their prewar trade with Germany. The West German state, whose industries are recovering at a rapid pace, will soon be confronted with the serious problem of finding outlets for its exports in competition with those of other western European nations. Germany, which before 1939 was the principal exporter of tools, machinery, and other manufactured goods to eastern Europe and the principal purchaser of its food and raw materials; Austria, whose capital, Vienna, served as the transit center of the Danubian region; and eastern Europe, which needs equipment for economic modernization—all would gain by restoration and expansion of east-west trade. This mutual need gives the Soviet government a trump card in dealing with the Germans, who, much as they may oppose Russia and communism, must soon explore the prospects of finding dependable markets abroad and will probably turn eastward again. At the same time the U.S.S.R., while eager to draw on the industrial resources of the Ruhr, has no interest in seeing Germany restored to its prewar position of strongest industrial nation on the continent unless it can be certain that German industrial potential will be used for peaceful purposes, not for the creation of a new war machine. Nor do the countries of eastern Europe and the Balkans have any desire to become economic satellites of a Fourth Reich.

Aside from the revival of imports by Britain and expansion of the trade of central Europe with the east, what other alternative does Europe have in trying to decrease its dependence on the United States? The two possibilities most often discussed are integration of the economy of western Europe with that of Africa, and normalization of its trade relations with southeast Asia.

Many Europeans are now looking to Africa both as an area for investments that promises more security than Europe, and as a source of strategic raw materials—but not yet as an important market. France with Algeria, Tunisia, Morocco, and Central Africa, Britain with its various possessions in east, west and central Africa, Belgium with its rich colony of the Belgian Congo, which has the unique advantage in the atomic age of possessing sources of the much-coveted uranium, Portugal with territories believed to hold a wealth of strategic raw materials—all these countries of western Europe might conceivably find in their African colonies at least partial substitutes for the products of southeast Asia.

Plans for co-ordinating the economies of western European nations and their colonies, discussed in the Organization for European Economic Cooperation, are also of interest to the Economic Cooperation Administration. For the expansion of raw material and food sources as well as markets in Africa would reduce western Europe's dependence on the United States; and the European Cooperation Act specifically provides for the acquisition by this country of strategic materials in which we are actually or potentially deficient. At the close of 1948, for example, negotiations were pending for the acquisition of certain raw materials in Africa, notably cyanite from Kenya. Among projects approved by the ECA are a British government proposal to expedite geological and topographical surveys in Africa begun in 1946, and the study of certain transportation bottlenecks, particularly in British East Africa, Mozambique, French West Africa, and the Belgian Congo.[1]

The development of African resources, however, even though encouraged by the ECA, will take time. Transportation facilities must be built, tropical diseases, particularly the sleeping sickness carried by the tsetse fly, must be conquered, and native labor must be trained for skilled and semi-skilled tasks. As for southeast Asia, access to the raw materials and markets of Indo-China and Indonesia can be attained only after workable agreements have been concluded between the European colonial powers and the leaders of nationalist movements in these colonies. Meanwhile Europeans find it difficult to understand why, in spite of our opposition to communism, we remain anticolonial and are reluctant to join the colonial nations in a Pacific pact that would obligate the

[1] *Third Report to Congress of the Economic Cooperation Administration,* cited, p. 59.

United States to suppress national movements of independence as a method of resisting both Russia and communism.

But whatever happens about restoration or further development of western Europe's trade with the eastern bloc, southeast Asia, and ultimately Africa, the United States will remain the paramount factor in the continent's economic calculations. While important geographical changes in production occurred in Europe after 1945—the most important being the fall in the relative share of German output, especially in iron and steel, which was made up in considerable part by Britain and Belgium—the most significant geographic change was in the relation of Europe to the rest of the world, particularly to the United States. Here is the key to the recurring crises in the world's postwar economy. Before 1939 the industrial output of Europe had been one third larger than that of the United States. In 1948 it was less than three quarters of our output. This development was not due to the war. It was the end result of long-term trends whose significance had not been fully grasped until 1949. Europe's share of the world's manufacturing production had fallen from 68 per cent in 1870 to 42 per cent in the period of 1925-9, and 35 per cent in 1937. Two years after World War II, in 1947, it was only about 22 per cent, rising to 25 per cent in 1948. Meanwhile, between 1938 and 1947, the United States had roughly doubled its production in relation to Europe. The present disparity, however, may not continue in such sharp form, for during 1947 and 1948 European production showed a greater relative increase than that of the United States, rising by 16 per cent as against a 3-per-cent rise in this country.

Europe's postwar dollar deficit, or, as it can also be described, the dollar surplus of the United States, brought about recurring economic crises, which we tried to meet by shoring up the economy of the western European nations with loans and credits, and finally with the Marshall Plan. By the summer of 1949, however, it became clear that more fundamental methods would have to be found of re-establishing European economy on a stable basis. On the advice of the United States, and much against the wishes of Sir Stafford Cripps, British Chancellor of the Exchequer, Britain in September 1949 sharply devalued the pound sterling—more sharply than had been thought necessary in Washington—from $4.03 to $2.80, a markdown of 30.5 per cent. This rate was regarded as actual undervaluation of the pound, perhaps in anticipation of a further upward movement of British costs and prices. Devaluation of the pound, which, in reverse, represented revaluation of the dollar, brought about similar action in France, Italy, the Netherlands, and countries whose currencies are tied to that of Britain.

The gains Britain was expected to make as a result of the lowering of its export prices were offset, at the start, by the devaluations of its European and other competitors, and by the resulting increase in the prices of the food and raw materials Britain must continue to import. As a result of the increase in import prices, it was at first expected that living-costs in Britain would rise—not only the price of bread, but also the prices of all goods manufactured out of imported materials. Such a rise in living-costs, it was feared, would bring about demands by the trade unions for wage increases. To forestall these demands, the Labour government promptly announced a tax on profits derived from additional dollar exports. This measure was criticized by American officials on the ground that British exporters, who find it much easier to sell in non-dollar markets, where they do not face the same competition as in the United States, would have no incentive to increase their efforts. As a result, it was thought, the expansion of British sales in the American market, recommended by ECA Administrator Paul G. Hoffman as the best method of reducing Britain's dependence on American financial aid, would not take place, and the anticipated benefits of devaluation would be dissipated. Meanwhile, however, Britain as well as other Marshall Plan nations slashed quotas and various restrictions on imports from countries other than the United States and Canada. Thus, while devaluation may not materially increase European exports to this country, it is expected to stimulate Europe's trade with other areas. This will curtail some American exports, but will be at least a step in the direction of the freer multilateral trade long urged by Washington.

In spite of devaluation and other measures, however, the tremendous shift in the relative positions of Europe and the United States cannot be altered solely through European action. It will require the concerted efforts of the two continents. Nor is it enough to denounce the preference Britain and other European countries have shown for bilateralism since the 1930's and to insist on prompt restoration of trade through the International Trade Organization established at the Havana conference of 1948 at the urging of the United States. The transatlantic debate about the relative merits of bilateralism and multilateralism has come to be symbolized by the conflicting views of the United States and Britain—although Nazi Germany under Schacht, and Russia's Communist government, had also practiced bilateral trade. American critics of the Labour government contended that rationing, control of imports, and long-term pacts providing for two-way barter, like the Anglo-Argentine and Anglo-Russian trade treaties of 1949, created new obstacles to international commerce; and that these world-trade bottlenecks, in turn, jeopardized the stabilization of British economy. Labour spokesmen, for their part, took the position that the precarious situation in which Britain was left at the end of World War II, with its overseas investments sharply curtailed and its sources of colonial raw materials depleted or cut off, made it necessary to introduce trade restrictions, sacrifice consumption needs, for the time being at least, to the urgent need of modernizing and rationalizing enterprises like the coal mines, which had been allowed by their private owners to fall into a state of obsolescence, and assure a minimum standard of living for the British people while the nation's economy was being reorganized for ultimately increased production. Americans answered that the British cannot afford the social services they now enjoy, and must learn to cut their coat to fit their cloth, even if this involves some unemployment. To this Britishers retorted that living-standards could not be reduced further without creating serious hardships, and that any attempt to deprive workers of social services would encourage the very kind of Leftist extremism that many Americans had hoped to avert by Marshall Plan aid.

For over a hundred years the United States followed a policy of high protectionist tariffs, in contrast to Britain, which advocated free multilateral trade. Now the roles have been reversed. Britain is no longer able to keep up with the race for expanding industrialization, in which it was once the acknowledged leader. It fears the hazards of competitive multilateral trade and seeks to safeguard its dwindling economic stake by various restrictive devices and equally balanced exchanges of goods with countries that will accept British tools and machinery in payment for the food and raw materials Britain needs. London, once the trading center of the Western World, has lost its commanding position to New York, with the dollar replacing the pound sterling as the yardstick for other currencies. The United States has taken over Britain's role as the world's leading producer and exporter. But unlike Britain, which, because it must import as well as export, found it to its interest to encourage the free flow of world trade, the United States, whose large-scale industrial system can fill most of our needs and still leave a substantial margin for exports, needs relatively few imports with the exception of some luxuries, like French perfumes, British woolens, or German photographic equipment, and certain strategic raw materials, such as rubber, tin, and manganese. When we complain about the effect of socialization on Britain's trade, the British point out that among their chief difficulties have been the continued high cost of American agricultural products, maintained at that level by government subsidies, and our high tariff rates on certain British exports, notably woolens. The British, not without gentle malice, contend that subsidies and tariffs also constitute socialism, and Foreign Secretary Ernest Bevin said in 1949: "The United States is as much a welfare state as we are, only it is in different form."

While many Americans have believed that Britain's restrictive economy was the principal hurdle to the resumption of freer multilateral trade, Britishers, as well as other Europeans, have asked whether the shoe may not be on the other foot; whether it is not the enormous productivity of American economy, which as we saw during World War II is capable of further expansion at short notice, that has been primarily responsible for the postwar disequilibrium in world trade relations. The major factor in the world's disequilibrium, however, is not our supereconomy as such, but rather our failure to integrate it on a lasting basis with that of other countries. It is not enough to talk about interdependence and urge the Marshall Plan countries, or any other regional group, to rationalize their production and distribution, if we remain outside the framework of the proposed integration. Our postwar aid program to Europe, generous as it has seemed to us and to the recipient nations, was only a breathing-spell which gave us time to readjust our internal affairs so that we might effectively fulfill our new responsibilities as the world's greatest economic power. If we are to integrate our economy with that of other countries, we shall have to undergo many of the same internal adjustments we have been recommending to them, such as the shift of production from some sectors to others, specialization in goods in which we have the greatest efficiency, abandonment of relatively inefficient enterprises, retraining of labor, creation of additional purchasing power, perhaps at the sacrifice of savings, and so on.

The transatlantic debate about world trade, however, is so closely linked to the controversy about the relative merits of free private enterprise and socialism that it cannot be considered apart from Europe's trend toward socialized economy.

Chapter V

ECONOMIC AND SOCIAL PATTERNS

Our relations with Europe since World War II have been deeply affected by fundamental differences between our prevailing economic and social concepts and those not only of Europe's Communists but also of its Socialists. The postwar controversy about objectives and methods has consequently proved to be much more than a two-way controversy between west and east, or between the United States and the U.S.S.R. It has been a triangular controversy, in which Americans have found much to question in Russian and Russian-sponsored communism—as have also the Socialists of western Europe—but have questioned, too, the underlying assumptions of socialism, especially as practiced by Britain's Labour government. Those of us who at home oppose government intervention in economic affairs particularly criticized nationalization or socialization and expansion of social services—whether accompanied by political dictatorships and suppression of opposition, as in the U.S.S.R. and the Communist-ruled countries of eastern Europe, or by the preservation of democratic procedures, as in Britain and other western European nations. Some American spokesmen took the view that the United States should make abstention from further measures of nationalization a condition of Marshall Plan aid; and in 1948 Paul G. Hoffman, when appointed director of the Economic Cooperation Administration, declared that he would probably refuse to help Britain develop any industry that its government might subsequently nationalize. Others, however, contended that the United States should not interfere with the internal economic policies of ERP nations. The American Ambassador to Britain, Lewis W. Douglas, for example, warned Congress in 1948 that if the United States urged the Marshall Plan countries to desist from further steps toward public ownership, that would be "too much of an invasion of the right of free people to determine the sort of economic system under which they wanted to live." At that time the State Department reminded Congress that "the Socialists who advocate social planning and economic control, in contrast to competitive private enterprise, nevertheless believe firmly in the democratic process and the fundamental freedoms of speech, press, assembly, and worship, and in the rights and dignity of the individual. They are consequently among the strongest bulwark in Europe against Communism."[1]

In keeping with this view, the ERP agreements concluded by the United States with the sixteen recipient countries in the summer of 1948 contained no reference to the possibility that Washington would expect modification or abandonment of the nationalization or socialization policies adopted by the signatory governments. On the whole, the United States, outwardly at least, refrained from using the lever of financial aid to alter existing economic and social arrangements in the Marshall Plan countries. It is difficult, however, to assess the extent to which American repugnance to socialism has actively helped to entrench in power conservative and even reactionary regimes and to block urgently needed reforms, such as land redistribution in Italy.

As has already been pointed out, in Europe the concept and practice of state ownership or control had long antedated the establishment of a Communist regime in Russia. By 1900, railways were operated by the state in most countries with the exception of Britain and France.[2] Postal service was a

---

[1] Department of State: *The European Recovery Program: Country Studies,* Chapter I—"Introduction" (mimeographed).

[2] This summary of the process of socialization in Europe is based on Herbert H. Heaton: "Socialism in Western Europe," *Headline Series,* Foreign Policy Association, No. 35 (1948).

state undertaking in all countries, and so usually was telegraph service. Telephone systems were for the most part state-owned. When radio broadcasting went into operation it was placed under state control. In many countries the state also took part in the development of public health projects, street railways, water supply, lighting, and housing. Municipal governments often participated in many kinds of enterprises, from hospitals to coal yards, from schools to drugstores, from grocery stores to theaters. Socialists, who did not play an active role in governments until after World War I, advocated socialization as a universal panacea for the ills of the Industrial Revolution. But many non-socialist governments did not hesitate to resort to nationalization when an undertaking was too large or costly to interest private capital, as in the construction of dams or bridges; when competition between private concerns for control of public utilities might prove detrimental to public interest—for example, if several enterprises contended for ownership of gas and electricity; when the government hoped to derive revenues through monopolies over certain widely used consumer goods—salt, tobacco, matches, and alcoholic beverages—or when questions of health or morals were involved.

World War I, which made it necessary for European governments to marshal their national resources for a major military effort and to bring within their control industrial production, agricultural output, transportation, commerce, labor, and other elements of their economies, greatly strengthened the trend toward state intervention in economic life. The war also gave new impetus to the activities of labor groups, both in the professional sphere of union negotiations with employers and in the political sphere. The Social Democrats in Germany, the Labourites, then headed by Ramsay MacDonald, in Britain, the Socialists in France, Belgium, and the Scandinavian countries, either gained an opportunity to take office or at least became important opposition parties whose views affected the formulation of policy. Growing concern with the possibilities as well as the difficulties of state enterprise was encouraged by several factors: the decline of some privately owned major industries, notably coal mines, whose nationalization in Britain was urged by the Labourites; the development of new technical inventions, which in the opinion of many would benefit by being placed under public control, foremost among them radio; the efforts of Europe's new postwar states, particularly in the east, to carry out land reforms and initiate industrialization programs; the effects of the world depression of 1929, which caused many nonsocialists to feel that the government should intervene to check unemployment, help those who had been thrown out of work, and devise measures for restoration of economic life; and the rearmament programs, starting with Germany in 1935, which required increasing state ownership and direction of national resources.

In Britain, where the pattern of government administration of industrial and other enterprises within a democratic framework has probably been most fully developed, control over nationalized undertakings was vested, not in the government directly, but in public corporations. The boards of public corporations are appointed by the government on the basis of ability; they exercise wide powers of self-government, and have to present annual reports on performance of their tasks. During the interwar years the British government appointed the Central Electricity Board in 1926 to administer the network, or "grid," of more than four thousand miles of high-tension wires covering the entire country; the British Broadcasting Company (BBC) in 1927 to administer all phases of broadcasting, which operates without advertisements or sale of radio time; and the London Passenger Transport Board (LPTB) in 1933 to administer all branches of London's transport system. The creation of these three public corporations was supported by both Conservatives and Labourites.

On the continent between 1919 and 1939 Germany, Austria, and France undertook housing projects, and established state or "mixed" enterprises to develop hydroelectric or steam-driven generating plants. The new states of eastern Europe encouraged small-scale agriculture by creating rural credit banks, fertilizer factories, and some processing industries. Professor Herbert Heaton of the University of Minnesota points out that before World War II—before either Socialists or Communists had taken power—the Polish state "owned all or nearly all the plants producing potash, alcohol, tobacco, aircraft, automobiles, and dyestuffs, as well as aviation services, radio, the merchant fleet, the railroads, and fire insurance. In addition, it owned a large part of the smelters, salt works, telephones and banks, and had an interest in machine-tool factories, coal mines, chemical works, and several other industries." France, where the government had had to lend money to the privately operated railways, which were constantly running deficits, nationalized the railways in 1936 when the Popular Front cabinet headed by Socialist Léon Blum was in office, and unified them under a National Railway Company. In Italy, under Mussolini, a public corporation, the Industrial Reconstruction Institute (IRI) was established in the 1930's to avert a banking crisis. The state supplied the IRI with funds to purchase industrial securities held by the banks. As a result of this transaction, the Italian state eventually "became part or sole proprietor of a large slice of the economy—of banks, ships, telephones, radio, iron and steel works, shipyards, chemical plants, and armament industries." [1]

The trend toward state ownership, already noticeable at the turn of the twentieth century and greatly accelerated by World War I and the world depression, spread with lightning speed in the wake of World War II. In the east, Russia's pressure goaded the countries of eastern Europe and the Balkans to nationalize major sectors of their economies and undertake ambitious programs of industrialization. In the west, advanced industrial nations turned to government ownership

[1] Ibid.

and control in order to distribute restricted available resources as equitably as possible through rationing, to coordinate recovery efforts, and to build economic and social dams against a new floodtide of depression and unemployment, which it was feared would otherwise plunge all Europe into communism. The eastern countries, which had initiated some measures of nationalization before 1939, rapidly proceeded to nationalize more and still more sectors of industry, commerce, and transportation. All of them, however, found it difficult to carry out parallel collectivization of agriculture, which was bitterly resisted by the peasants. In Czechoslovakia, to take an outstanding example, the state before 1939 had owned railways, as well as telephone and telegraph services. After World War II, in 1945, the moderate government of President Beneš assigned to the state all properties owned by Germans and by inhabitants of the Sudetenland, and proclaimed nationalization of banks, mines, steel and iron, power plants, armament industries and chemicals, and, in general, enterprises employing more than five hundred workers. Following seizure of power by the Communists in 1948, the Prague government nationalized the food industry, sugar and spirits, building, wholesale trade, foreign trade, transportation, and, in general, all enterprises employing more than fifty workers. Each firm became a "national corporation," operated by a manager (often the former manager or owner), who is directly responsible to the government council or ministry supervising his particular branch of production for technical administration of the firm, while the workers are limited to supervision of wages, hours, and working conditions in the shops and factories. Further nationalization of smaller enterprises was effected during the autumn purge of 1949.

In France, which offers a good example of mixed economy, the state nationalized the northeastern coal mines in 1944, before the war was over. It also confiscated the Renault automobile works and an airplane factory, on the ground that the owners of these enterprises had collaborated with the Germans; and it assumed operation of civilian airlines. By 1946, with general agreement among political parties, the government had nationalized the Bank of France and the four largest commercial banks, holding about four fifths of all bank deposits; the principal insurance companies, handling about two thirds of the country's insurance business; all the gas and electrical industries; and the rest of the coal mines. As of 1949 there was no indication that the French were considering additional measures of nationalization. The nationalized enterprises are operated by central, regional, and local boards containing representatives of the state, the employees, and the consumers. In theory at least, these boards are supposed to be autonomous, free of ministerial or legislative influence. Projects for modernization of the entire French economy and its future development, both in its private and in its nationalized sectors, are formulated within the framework of the Monnet Plan, drawn up in 1946 by Jean Monnet, director of the Plan of Modernization and Equipment Commissariat, who during World War I performed an outstanding job as French member of the Inter-Allied Maritime Commission. Plans for each branch of production are considered and discussed in advance by committees on which the government, employers, workers, and consumers are represented, and the programs agreed upon are carried out on a basis of voluntary co-operation.

In Britain, where the Labourites won an overwhelming victory in the summer of 1945, two months after the end of the war—a victory that took them as well as the rest of the country by surprise—no over-all plan for national economy comparable to the Monnet Plan for France had been announced by 1949. Promptly upon assuming power, the Labour government, headed by Prime Minister Attlee, carried out the program on which it had been elected by nationalizing—with the general agreement of the Conservatives—the

Bank of England and the overseas airlines in 1946, the coal mines in 1947, and inland transportation (railways and buses) in 1948. Since then the Attlee cabinet has also introduced a bill providing for nationalization of the steel industry, which, in contrast with the coal mines, has been flourishing since the war. The steel bill, defended by Labour spokesmen on grounds of strategic necessity rather than industrial efficiency, provoked vigorous opposition not only on the part of the Conservatives, who declared that if they were returned to power after its passage they would wipe it off the books, but also among some Labourites. In the spring of 1949 Labour announced that it would press for nationalization of insurance companies and of sugar, cement, and meat industries. Thus in Britain, as contrasted with France, the process of nationalization is still under way, and its terminal goal has not been set.

The trend toward socialization has been accompanied by a trend toward planning both on a national and on a regional basis. The United Nations European Economic Commission pointed out in 1949 that, with the exception of Finland, Switzerland, and Spain, every country of Europe had some kind of economic plan, ranging in time span from three to six years. At the urgent suggestion of the United States the sixteen Marshall Plan countries, working through the Organization for European Economic Cooperation (OEEC), with headquarters in Paris, undertook to prepare over-all short-term programs for 1948–9, as well as long-term programs for the period 1952–3, but succeeded only in drawing up lists of national needs, which the OEEC had no authority to integrate into a regional plan. The countries of eastern Europe and the Balkans, whose economies had already been linked to that of the U.S.S.R. by a series of postwar bilateral treaties, created in 1949 a regional organization, the Council of Mutual Economic Assistance, which was expected to co-ordinate their respective national plans—the five-year plans of Czechoslovakia, Bulgaria, and Hungary, the six-year plan of Poland,

and shorter-term plans for Rumania, Albania, and the Soviet zone of Germany. By 1950, reports indicated that the east of Europe had been not much more successful than the west in achieving economic integration.

The scope of economic planning and the methods employed to carry it into effect differ from country to country within a given region, as well as between the industrialized west and the still primarily agricultural east. These differences have been summed up by the UN European Economic Commission as follows:

In the countries of Eastern Europe, where manufacturing industry is almost wholly nationalized, the plans extend to the detailed operations of each branch of industry and their execution is controlled both through the allocation of materials and through the supervision of the accounts of individual enterprises. Among the countries of Western Europe, the central direction of economic life is far more restricted in scope and less direct in its influence. The greater part of manufacturing industry is run by private enterprise and continues to be guided by the price mechanism—supplemented to varying degrees by rationing and allocation systems. In comparison with the pre-war situation, however, there is an important difference in that most countries now attempt to formulate a set of consistent objectives for economic policy in quantitative terms and to use their available means of control—the licensing system in foreign trade, controls over raw materials, taxes and subsidies, and controls over credit or the capital market—to further their realization. Hence the published "targets" of the Western European countries, whether they relate to production, manpower, investment, exports or imports, imply generally something more than a mere forecast of prevailing trends, but something very much less than the summarization of a definite operational plan. They are perhaps best regarded as the quantitative expression of the rate and direction of economic change to be fostered by government policy. While the day-to-day running of the economy in the Western European countries is left largely and, it seems, increasingly under the control of market forces, the development of productive resources through capital investment proceeds in most countries under central guidance, if not under central direction.[1]

Socialization of private enterprises has been criticized by its opponents on three principal grounds. It is asserted that nationalized industries are not as productive as private industries; that their cost is excessive, with deficits always present or just around the corner; and that government administration of various business undertakings breeds a bureaucracy that soon becomes intolerable and, by its tendency to regulate the minutiæ of life, could easily, and perhaps unconsciously, develop into a full-blown political dictatorship.

The briefness of the period during which large-scale nationalization has been in effect in postwar Europe, both west and east (the U.S.S.R. excepted), makes it difficult to marshal convincing evidence pro or con on these three points. So far as productivity is concerned, it is a striking fact that throughout Europe today the stress is not only on the benefits of social services in conserving "human capital" and in preventing resort to Right or Left extremism, but also on the cost of socialism. Now that Socialists, no longer playing the relatively easy role of opposition theorists, have had practical experience with government administration, they recognize from London to Prague, that this cost cannot be paid by "squeezing the rich," whose ranks, in any case, have been depleted by the general impoverishment resulting from war, but must be paid by increased effort on the part of all producers, both employers and workers. The 1949 manifesto of the British Labour Party: "Labour Believes in Britain," was a significant chapter in the development of socialism. For it placed the accent not on redistribution of the resources of the rich among the poor, as Socialist declarations used to do in the past, but on higher productivity. "Up with Production," it proclaimed, declaring: "The wealth of Britain is only what we ourselves create. Unless we continue to increase produc-

---

[1] United Nations: *Economic Survey of Europe in 1948* (already cited), Chapter 8.

tion as we have done in the last four years, we cannot improve or even maintain our present standard of living; our people cannot be fed or clothed or rehoused; the social services cannot advance or even survive; and our national freedom and independence cannot continue." There can be no advance, the manifesto added, without effective partnership between government and industry—a slogan to which American business men, as well as British Socialists, might say amen.

The next task of European Socialists will be to convince the rank and file of the trade unions that mere socialization of the instruments of production cannot of itself bring about a new heaven and a new earth; that workers, as well as other groups of the population, must increase their efforts without expectation, for the present at least, of increased pay; and that they must find incentives not in personal profit-making, the principal target of Socialist attacks on capitalism, but in various social services, and in the satisfaction of knowing that they have a proportionate share in such benefits as the national economy, once it has been modernized, is capable of producing, and a voice in its operation. The feeling of satisfaction derived from a sense of economic and social equality may seem intangible to us, who put great stress on material comforts and enjoyments purchasable with increased money wages. Yet it represents an important psychological incentive for men and women who in the past felt resentful because they, and especially their children, could not hope for much improvement in social status and political influence. Whether or not such nonmaterial incentives will prove sufficient to maintain the postwar level of production, which now averages forty per cent above prewar, will be one of the decisive tests of the viability of socialism.

Another, more mundane, test will be its cost. Many Americans, as well as Europeans who are opposed to Socialist ideas and practices, contend that the price of the "socialist experiment" is too high and that socialism should therefore be abandoned. In discussing this point, much depends on one's estimate whether, at the present stage of development of western Europe and in its present condition of war-induced impoverishment, any other economic and social system would have proved less costly or more efficient. It was unquestionably a great misfortune for the British Labour government that it had to carry out its program, not at a time when the country's economy was at its peak, but during its most serious decline in modern times.[1] Labour thus had to fulfill its promises not only when prices and wages were high, but also when world trade was disorganized and when the necessity of sheer survival dictated many restrictions and controls that under more favorable circumstances need not have been identified with socialist practices. To what extent a Conservative government in Britain might have found it possible to avoid the problems faced by socialism, or to overcome them by other means, remains what President Roosevelt called an "iffy" question.

It is also important to ask what we mean by the "cost" of a given economic and social system. Is it cost measured in dollars and cents, pounds and shillings—with constant fear of going into the red and of having government deficits—or cost measured in greater stability of national economy, with greater economic security for all members of the community, including workers, even if measures taken to achieve these objectives may necessitate temporary deficits? On this issue there is a wide difference of opinion not only between Britishers and Americans, but also among leading American economists. The basic question is what system, irrespective of its label, is thought by a given people, within the context of our times, to offer the most satisfactory—not necessarily the least expensive—way of life: "the greatest good for the greatest number." Here, too, socialism—as well as our form of capitalism—still remains to be tested, and no definite answer can yet be offered. It is possible that British socialism will have to

[1] For a British non-Socialist analysis of this point, see "Britain in the Pillory," *Economist* (London), August 13, 1949.

slow down the pace of reforms without abandoning its over-all objectives, while American capitalism will have to intro-duce additional social reforms.

That government administration always presents a danger of bureaucracy is true, but this danger is not limited to social-ism. Bureaucracy has developed under all kinds of govern-ments, both ancient and modern. The type of all-seeing, all-supervising, all-regulating dictatorship that exists in the U.S.S.R., a vast and still relatively backward country, offers little factual basis for judgment as to the kind of government that might emerge in smaller politically and economically ad-vanced and ethnically homogeneous nations like Britain or France, the Netherlands or Norway. No responsible person would want to dismiss as sheer fantasy the grim prophecies of Arthur Koestler or George Orwell about possible socialist governments of the future which, like octopuses, might strangle all individuals in deathly embrace. It is significant, however, that Koestler and Orwell had themselves at one time proved susceptible to the dogmas of communism. While their personal recantations or revulsions provide valuable testimony that deserves to be heeded, there is no reason to be-lieve that their dogmatic repudiation of Marxism will prove any more unassailable than their earlier acceptance of the gospel according to Marx.

Still another question is often asked, both in the United States and in Europe: is contemporary socialism compatible with nineteenth-century liberalism, or are the two so anti-thetical that one must necessarily prove the nemesis of the other? The answer to this question again depends on one's interpretation of liberalism and socialism. Seen in the per-spective of Europe's history over the past two centuries, Eu-ropean socialism, whether it owes its inspiration to Fabian doctrines and the practices of long-established trade unions, as in Britain, or to Marxism, as in the other countries of western Europe, appears to be in direct line of descent from nineteenth-century liberalism, not in conflict with it. As Professor J. Salwyn Schapiro has pointed out:

during the nineteenth century liberalism became the protagonist of political equality, or democracy. In the movement to establish universal, equal suffrage, it was clear to those who favored it, as well as to those who opposed it, that political democracy would become a powerful method for applying the principle of equality to economic matters in the interest of the working class. With the establishment of manhood suffrage in England and in France, a movement began in favor of economic equality. Therein lies the significance of the rapid growth of the socialist and labor parties, which fell heir to the egalitarian principle first proclaimed by liberalism. The many social reforms in the interest of the working class, moderate and halting at first, but comprehensive and far-reaching today, have been so many steps in the direction of economic equality.[1]

Only if European socialism is viewed in terms of this historical background can its true significance be understood and its influence appraised without immediately giving rise to the question: "So you want socialism in the United States?"—which is no more relevant to discussion of the situation in Europe than the famous question "How would you like your daughter to marry a Negro?" is relevant to discussion of the Negro problem in this country. Those societies, whether called capitalist, socialist, or x-ist, which have accepted the necessity of carrying the assumptions of nineteenth-century liberalism to their logical conclusion by practicing democracy in the economic as well as in the political sphere have demonstrated their capacity for flexibility, for adjustment to changing conditions, which is the hallmark of the liberal society as distinguished from any system, whatever its name, that makes a fetish of the *status quo*. Again, to quote Professor Schapiro's analysis:

[1] J. Salwyn Schapiro: *Liberalism and the Challenge to Fascism* (New York: McGraw-Hill Book Company; 1949).

A society constantly in motion had need of a political system that was constantly in motion. The liberal state came into existence in response to this need. Under autocratic rule, the chief function of the state was to freeze the status quo in society established by the caste system. It would not be too much to say that liberalism was the creator of the modern state, of its mechanism no less than of its underlying principles.

Political adaptability, in our times, is measured by the extent to which nations recognize the necessity of enlisting in the making of national policies the active and responsible participation of the large and still growing group of workers of both hand and brain. If workers are forced to remain outside the political forum, they either accept one form of extremism or another (and this extremism, judging by the experience of Germany in the 1930's, may just as easily turn out to be Nazism as communism), or else—what may even be more dangerous for democracy—become indifferent, as many French workers became in 1948, when they turned *away* from the Communists after the politically inspired coal strike, but did not turn *toward* any other political group, feeling that none adequately represented their interests. In a fully functioning democracy active workers' participation is a safeguard, not a threat, and the best bulwark against communism. It is not mere coincidence that British trade unions, with their long experience of organization, their effective educational work, and their admirable sense of civic responsibility, have held the line on wages and avoided large-scale strikes since 1945, in contrast with the strike-overshadowed years after World War I and with the grave coal and steel strikes in the United States. They did this in the knowledge that under the Labour government they had an opportunity to participate on a basis of equality with other social groups in the formulation and implementation of national policies. Nor is it mere coincidence that in Britain both fascism and communism have so far played an insignificant role.

It is sometimes said, with a note of sadness, that as socialism reaches farther and farther into the ranks of industrial workers for political leadership, the level of all forms of expression —especially literature, the press, and the arts—tends to decline, and that the end result will be an oppressive uniformity of mediocre thought. It may be of some comfort to remember that the aristocracy of the nineteenth century felt similar apprehensions about what was considered the sordid mental outlook of the middle class. If it be true—although this is highly debatable—that the intellectual level of workers is not yet comparable to that of the middle class, then is not this situation due less to any inherent lack of qualities in a given group of the population (are there such things as qualities inherent in class or race?) than to the failure of society in the past to provide this group with adequate opportunities for education and development of creative faculties? If that is so, then the remedy is to be sought not in excluding the workers on the ground that their mental equipment is not sufficient to the needs of modern political and economic policy-making, but in throwing facilities for intellectual and artistic development open to all, irrespective of financial status. This, in large measure, has been done in the United States, where free public schools and state universities have offered able boys and girls opportunities undreamed of by the masses of the population in democratic countries of western Europe, even Britain, where until recently certain levels of education, and consequently certain categories of professions, were open primarily to children of small privileged groups. As western European democracy, fulfilling its earlier promise of greater equality, puts into the hands of all citizens facilities for improving their knowledge and skills, current fears that socialism will result in a lowering of intellectual standards may prove as ill-founded as were comparable nineteenth-century fears about the alleged philistinism of the bourgeoisie.

By adapting itself to changing economic and social circumstances, Western liberalism has displayed a vitality unforeseen by Karl Marx, and unsuspected by both Nazis and Communists, whose greatest gains were registered in Europe by very reason of the prevailing expectation that liberalism had run its course and that the world was about to witness "the decline of the West." By the same token any society that, once having come within the orbit of liberalism, then fails to develop sufficient capacity to keep on growing and absorbing new groups into political life—as the liberal society of the nineteenth century absorbed the then new middle class—any such society is in danger of becoming stratified, stunted, a sort of petrified forest where the forms of what once existed can still be seen, but where the sap is no longer running. Germany during the interwar years turned out to be that kind of society; and it may yet re-emerge more or less as it was, the Bonn Constitution and other documents notwithstanding (let us remember that the democratic Weimar Constitution was quite good on paper), unless new blood, new human relationships, can be injected into obsolete forms. When the United States, on this issue at odds with Britain, resists the participation of German trade unions in postwar decisions about the character of the German economy and looks askance at the Social Democrats for fear of encouraging socialism, it is helping to perpetuate the arrested development of German democracy, which has already caused such terrible damage both to the Germans and to their victims in Europe.

Meanwhile what was happening to that "other Europe"— to the nations of the east that had remained for the most part isolated from the main stream of Western civilization during the formative centuries that saw the Renaissance, the Reformation, the Industrial Revolution, and the French and American revolutions? It is, of course, no more possible to generalize about eastern Europe than about Latin America. The Poles and Czechs have had centuries-old relations with the west, sometimes in servitude, sometimes in freedom; so have the Croats in Yugoslavia, who before 1919 had been a part of the Austro-Hungarian Empire; but not the Serbs, who had long lived under Turkish rule. But neither in Russia nor in most of the countries of eastern Europe and the Balkans had liberalism done more than develop a few weak shoots that could easily be uprooted by either fascism or communism. Many of the peoples of this region are centuries behind the western nations, not only because they still use the ancient plow instead of the tractor, but because they are still struggling to overcome political and social obstacles to further growth as the English and the French—and the Americans—once overcame obstacles through revolutions that shook the world of that time.

To the extent that Russia, however revolutionary it seemed a quarter of a century ago when Lenin and Trotsky looked to the overthrow of existing systems by workers united throughout the world, now tends to become petrified, it loses the dynamics that could have assured the survival of communism in its original Russian form. The significance of Marshal Tito's rebellion against Moscow was its revelation that communism, too, might prove capable of adaptation. From the point of view of the Kremlin, Titoism, being a heresy, is far more dangerous than the defiance of unbelievers. But from the point of view of non-Russian Communists it offers promising evidence that communism need not be synonymous with the *status quo*. Tito's insistence on hewing to his own line while asserting his devotion to Communist tenets may have opened the way to future variants (what the Kremlin calls "deviations"), which might make it possible to develop national Communist regimes that would neither conform slavishly to Russian practices nor feel under obligation to accept the foreign policy of the U.S.S.R. as holy writ.

Western European socialism, too, is going through a process of self-reappraisal. Criticism from Right and Left acts as a gadfly on socialist regimes, which are now striving to improve their administration of social services and of the nationalized sectors of economy. The net result will probably be that socialism, born and nurtured among theories that once seemed unrealizable, will come of age in the twentieth century. In the process of assuming increasing responsibilities it will shed some of its illusions, but will retain the core of its aspirations for continued improvement of the lot of mankind—aspirations that it inherited from nineteenth-century liberalism.

With all the differences that still persist between the "two Europes," east and west since the war have considerably modified their respective concepts, in large part as a result of the multiplicity of contacts between them in the United Nations and other international agencies, violent and even bitter as these contacts have often been. In the U.S.S.R. the economist Eugene Varga, demoted in 1948 because of his belief that Western capitalism was undergoing important changes that would prolong its existence, appeared in 1949 to be again in the ascendant as the star of some of his critics, notably Vozhnesensky, declined. Communists leaders in Poland and Czechoslovakia who consider themselves superior as technicians to the Russians and feel irked by Moscow's dogmatic leadership emphasize more and more the need to go slow with agricultural collectivization and intensive industrialization, not to antagonize peasants and workers, to persuade rather than coerce. The western countries, for their part, whether coming to grips with contemporary problems of their own free will or needled into doing it by Communist propaganda and threats of action, no longer view improvements in working conditions, a wide range of social services, participation by workers in political life, and various degrees of national and international economic planning as revolutionary. It seems incredible today that only a little over a decade ago, in 1936, when Léon Blum took office as France's first Socialist Premier, his advent was regarded with apprehension in Britain and the United States, while French industrialists reviled him because he daringly proposed that all workers should have two-weeks vacations with pay. Time has marched on in Europe since 1939, and only the most confirmed pessimist would exclude all possibility of eventually mitigating political, social, and economic differences on the continent.

This does not mean that the west should "appease" the east, or cease to question the practices of Russia and of communism. What we must do is define more precisely than in the past the things we ourselves question or oppose. No one brought up in the tradition of Western liberalism can accept political dictatorship, with its suppression of all opposition, or restrictions on freedom of thought and expression, which obliterate the human person. These must and should be opposed—but always with the realization that they may be the effects, not the causes, of an unhealthy political and social situation, and that they will not be eliminated until the conditions that facilitated their emergence have been brought to an end. At the same time the west must ask with utmost honesty whether it opposes land reform, industrialization of underdeveloped areas, movements for colonial independence, separation of church and state, and other trends that are often attributed solely to the influence of Russia and communism, but in reality had been in the making long before Karl Marx wrote *Das Kapital* or Lenin seized power in Russia. Western liberalism, if it remains true to its original concepts and continues to adapt itself to changing circumstances, promises to be a vital, and vitalizing force. But it will succeed in recruiting new adherents in areas that had been relatively untouched by its influence only if it recognizes the great time-lag in the development of the continent and endeavors to bridge the gap between the two Europes as rapidly as possible. It is doubtful that a political, economic, and military union limited to the nations of western Europe would stabilize that area as long as side by side with it exists a belt of relatively backward nations.

Nor is it realistic to assume that democracy is threatened only from the Left, by communism, when in fact it is also threatened from the Right, by revived forms of Nazism and fascism. Profiting by world-wide concern about the possible expansion of Russia as a nation and of communism as an international movement, various reactionary elements in west-

ern Europe have again emerged from the oblivion to which
they appeared to have been consigned by the military defeats
of Germany and Italy, and are now seeking to band together
under the banner of "liberalism," which in this context usually means opposition to social reforms, in the expectation of
enlisting the support of the United States, regarded by them
as a sworn foe of socialism and communism. The circumstance
that the Vatican, too, is bitterly opposed to Communist theories and has come into conflict with the Communist governments of eastern Europe over their attempts to establish national churches has caused reactionary groups to hope that
they can also count on the aid of the Roman Catholic Church
—in spite of the fact that, beginning with the encyclical
Rerum novarum, the Papacy has criticized certain aspects of
laissez-faire capitalism and has championed economic reforms and social justice. There is consequently genuine danger that fear of Russia and of communism, however legitimate it may be, will consolidate groups essentially hostile to
all liberal ideas and practices, which, by identifying themselves with the United States and the Vatican, would place
the American people and the Catholic Church in the vanguard of a frustrated and embittered struggle against communism, instead of where they should be—in the vanguard of
a constructive and invigorating struggle for democracy.

This is not inevitable. For neither thoughtful European
Catholic leaders nor thoughtful Americans are opposed to
changes in Europe or other parts of the world that would
bring peoples now lagging behind in political, economic, and
social development closer to realization of the promises held
out by Christianity, by Western democracy, and by the Industrial Revolution. It would be nothing short of tragic if apprehension about Russia and communism should cause the
United States to misunderstand the shifts in political forces
that have been under way on the European continent since
World War II and to miscalculate their ultimate direction.

Chapter VI

POLITICAL PATTERNS

Throughout Europe, both west and east, the political changes wrought by two world wars and a great depression are now being gradually consolidated. Parties representing labor—whether they called themselves Labour, or Socialist, or Christian Democrat or Christian Socialist—had been organized in many European countries from the 1860's onward. But nowhere did they play a decisive part before 1914 except as goads to action by governments representing primarily the new business, banking, and professional groups that had inherited the political power once wielded by the aristocracy. The pre-1914 German Socialists appeared stronger than they actually were because of Bismarck's shrewd policy of granting extensive reforms from above in the hope of sidetracking Socialist agitation. The German Socialists consequently had no opportunity to acquire political know-how by fighting for their program through parliamentary channels. The social reforms effected in Britain before World War I were put on the statute books as early as 1909 not by a Labour government, but by a Liberal cabinet headed by Lloyd George. In France so fundamental a change as the separation of church and state in 1903 was effected not by the Socialists, but by the Radical Socialists, who, as one French writer has said, are "neither Radical nor Socialist," but at the turn of the century represented France's liberal middle class.

In contrast with the situation in western Europe, the continent east of the Rhine was governed by autocratic governments of one kind or another—the Kaiser in Germany, whose rule was somewhat qualified by parliamentary institutions; the Habsburg emperors; the Russian Czar. None of the principal countries of that area had had much experience with the democratic institutions of the west. Most of them had no large and active middle class, such as existed before 1914 in Britain, France, the Scandinavian countries, the Netherlands, and Belgium.

Out of the debris of World War I emerged new governments which, however different in form and personnel, had one feature in common: all of them either claimed to represent the workers, or catered to the workers' interests, or at least sought to enlist workers on behalf of their programs. In Britain the Labour Party proved sufficiently strong to form a government in 1924 under Ramsay MacDonald. In France a Popular Front cabinet was organized by the Socialist leader Léon Blum in 1936. Labor parties won office in the Scandinavian countries; the Socialists led by Paul-Henri Spaak and Henri de Man assumed growing influence in Belgium. In Germany and Italy Communist attempts at revolution proved abortive. The German Social Democrats organized the first cabinet of the Weimar Republic, but proved unable to withstand the cumulative impact of renascent nationalism, depression, and reaction and were driven to the wall by Hitler's National Socialist movement. But Hitler, too, played up to the workers, linking social improvements with a nationalism distorted by racialism which had a strong appeal for the German people, who resented their military defeat and yearned to regain their position in Europe. Into the ranks of the Nazis flocked not only the big industrial bourgeoisie, but also white-collar groups, farmers, and industrial workers, including many former Communists. In Italy Mussolini, a former Socialist who had been influenced by the revolutionary syndicalism of the French writer Georges Sorel, presented himself as the country's defender against communism and set up a Fascist regime, which proved to be a mixture of nationalist aspirations for restoration of Rome's ancient glory and efforts to alleviate glaring social and economic maladjustments through the machinery of the "corporative" state, in which capital, labor, and other interests were represented.

In the east, fragments of the three great empires, restored to independent national existence, developed along several different lines. In Poland the government of Marshal Pilsudski, who aspired to creation of a Greater Poland through acquisition of Russian territories, set a pattern for a military-conservative government, which persisted until 1939, when the then Foreign Minister, Colonel Beck, was still trying to come to terms with the German Nazis. In Czechoslovakia the middle-class government of President Thomas Masaryk established democratic political institutions, but carried out in the 1920's an extensive program of social legislation that in the west would have placed it in the category of socialism. Feudal autocracies, masked by a thin façade of parliamentary legislatures, ruled over Hungary with Admiral Horthy, Rumania with King Carol, Bulgaria with King Boris, Yugoslavia with King Alexander, and Greece with King George, who toward the end of the interwar period was dominated by a Nazi sympathizer, General Metaxas. In spite of their autocratic character, most of these governments were more or less clearly aware of the need for economic and social reforms. Some of them carried out extensive programs of land distribution—in Poland, Rumania, and Yugoslavia—and initiated modest steps toward industrialization. In the U.S.S.R. a powerful political dictatorship that claimed to represent workers and peasants replaced the autocracy of the czars, after the brief rule of the provisional government of Prince Lvov, which under more favorable circumstances than those of a major war and widespread economic disorganization might have played the role of Russia's first middle-class parliamentary cabinet. The countries of eastern Europe and the Balkans—always with the exception of Czechoslovakia—lacked the industrial development that in the west had resulted in the rise of a strong, politically experienced, and enlightened middle class. The peasant leaders who in Bulgaria, Rumania, Poland, and Yugoslavia had concentrated their attention on agrarian problems proved no match for the emerging group of city workers led by Socialists and Communists.

World War II, which forced all governments to regiment human and material resources to a degree unknown in modern times, accelerated the political tendencies already visible during the interwar years. In Britain the Labour Party won a resounding victory in 1945, defeating the Conservatives, whose leader, Winston Churchill, more than anyone else had symbolized the wartime determination of the British people. The victory of Labour, led by the seemingly colorless but firm-willed Clement Attlee, who along with several other Labourites had served in Churchill's coalition government, was won with the support of men and women outside trade-union circles who had never before voted the Labour ticket, and revealed the eclipse of the Liberal party, which since then, like the Conservatives whom it otherwise criticizes, has opposed government controls. In the unprecedentedly close elections of February 1950 the Labour Party returned to power with a sharply reduced majority. But even if the Conservatives should win the next round, it is doubtful that they would find it either possible or desirable to set aside the measures adopted by the Attlee government, with the major exception of the as yet uncertain nationalization of the steel industry. In Britain political life has thus become polarized around the Labour Party, which, once in office, displayed moderation and a strong sense of responsibility, and the Conservatives, who, with the notable exception of the fiery Winston Churchill, have also shown understanding of the irreversible changes wrought in Britain's economy since 1914 and have carefully steered away from mere reaction against Labour. It is possible that if the economic situation deteriorates further, the left-wing members of Labour, who on occasion have embarrassed the party, and in certain instances have been actually expelled for public support of left-wing Socialists on the continent, might attempt to form a political group of their own which, without espousing communism, would come close to the position of continental Socialists sympathetic to Communist ideas like the Italian Pietro Nenni.

In western Europe as a whole, the Socialists or Social Democrats, depending on party labels in a given country, have moved into a position that is close to what was called "center" before 1939 and have begun to lose some of their more active members to left-wing socialist groups that are still in the throes of formulating principles and developing organizations. Whether these left-wingers will ultimately cast in their lot with the Communists or form a new party of their own predicated on continuance of democratic procedures remains to be seen. While losing to the Left, the Socialists or Social Democrats have also increasingly come in conflict with the Roman Catholic Church, which in Germany has openly supported the conservative Christian Democrats to an extent that brought a sharp rebuke from Social Democratic leader Kurt Schumacher during the campaign preceding the August 14, 1949 elections; and in Italy has backed the government of Christian Democratic Premier Alcide de Gasperi. To what extent the Socialist parties can avoid a showdown with the Catholic Church, which might then bring them closer to the Communists, is another question that cannot yet be definitely answered. In France, Belgium, Italy, and the West German state, socialism continues to vie for power not only with communism but also with what is currently called neo-liberalism —represented, for example, by Dr. Ludwig Ehrhard in Bonn and Paul Reynaud in France—whose spokesmen urge abandonment of all controls and planning and return to laissez-faire. In many cases this "liberal" opposition to socialism, as Walter Lippmann pointed out in 1949, is "pseudo-liberalism, which is so often the masquerade of reactionary vested interests." It is also to be noted that neo-liberals, for the most part, want complete freedom for the industrialists—including freedom to create controlled systems of cartels—but are reluctant to grant it to trade unions.

Postwar France has succeeded in steering a middle course between the extremes of the Gaullist movement, led by General Charles de Gaulle, and the Communist Party, led by Jacques Duclos, who has been particularly close to Moscow, and Maurice Thorez, regarded as more responsive to France's national interests. In spite of genuine admiration for de Gaulle, who during the war became the symbol of France's resistance, the French have been reluctant to accept a military leader as head of the state, and have felt alarmed by the number of fascist-minded followers whom de Gaulle has attracted to his ranks. Moreover, de Gaulle's seeming indifference to social improvements has alienated industrial workers; while such economic reforms as he has proposed have been so similar to the corporative schemes of Mussolini and Salazar as to alarm neo-liberals who might otherwise have regarded Gaullism as an alternative to socialism. Meanwhile the Communists, who had gained many new adherents during the war by their well-organized and energetic participation in the resistance movement once Germany had invaded Russia in 1941, lost a good deal of influence by their policy of staging political strikes in protest against the Marshall Plan, like the coal strike of 1948, and by their undisguised loyalty to Moscow.

As France's economy recovered, both Gaullists and Communists found less and less opportunity to agitate against the government and to appeal for its overthrow. The cabinet of Premier Henri Queuille, a shrewd and steady country doctor who had served in many governments, usually as Minister of Agriculture, found it possible for over a year, 1948–9, to walk the perilous political tight-rope without major incidents or need to resort to repression. This cabinet, composed of three parties—the Radical Socialists (a moderate bourgeois group), the Socialists, and the Mouvement Républicain Populaire (MRP) combining Catholicism with socialism—was held together by the confidence of all three in the Premier's integrity and by their common fear that a split among them would open the way for a coup by Gaullists or Communists. The Radical Socialists, who had been under a cloud during and after the war because of the weakness shown by their Premier Édouard Daladier at Munich and the alleged wartime collaboration of some of their members, have staged a surprising comeback and now hold the political balance of power. The Socialists may have missed their hour of greatest power opportunity, and have lost their prewar prestige among workers, who regard socialism as too conservative, but continue to play an important role. The MRP, led by Georges Bidault, Queuille's successor as premier, and the eloquent journalist Maurice Schuman, who during the wartime resistance period acted as the radio "Voice of France" from London, has shed some of the ultraconservative and intensely clerical elements that clung to it for safety in the immediate period but subsequently shifted over to de Gaulle. Today the MRP forms a bridge between Catholicism and socialism.

Queuille's three-ply cabinet was able to continue in existence only by avoiding excessive socialist policies that might have alarmed the Radical Socialists; but it also had to avoid abandonment of postwar social reforms for fear of alienating the Socialists, and anticlerical measures for fear of alienating the MRP. It was therefore committed to a policy of carefully adjusted *"juste milieu,"* which placed it just a little left of center. The principal threats to its continuance in office were the possibility of economic crisis, and the rise of a new group of "liberals" led by Paul Reynaud, wartime Premier and one of France's most distinguished financial experts. The "liberals" favor return to an economy of laissez-faire and oppose *dirigisme* (directed economy) of any kind, and although they declare that they would not discard the changes effected in French economy since the war, they are expected to whittle down both nationalization and social services. A victory of the "liberals" would frighten political groups of the Left, and might prove the signal for the resurgence of Gaullism and communism.

The economic crisis feared by the Queuille cabinet was precipitated in October 1949 by the devaluation of the franc in the wake of the British pound's devaluation. At that moment all labor unions—the Catholic unions, the Communist-dominated Confederation Générale de Travail (CGT), which has opposed the Marshall Plan, and the force Ouvrière, middle-of-the-road nonsectarian federation headed by Socialist Léon Jouhaux, which in 1948, after the coal strike, had split off from the CGT, demanded an increase in wages, especially for the lower-paid categories of workers, to meet price increases expected to follow devaluation. The Socialists and the MRP responded to the pressure of the Force Ouvrière and the Catholic unions, but requests for wage increases were opposed by the Radical Socialists, and Queuille offered his resignation. The subsequent failure of Socialist Jules Moch, who is regarded as one of the country's strong men, to form a cabinet, eventually formed by Bidault, was due primarily not to pressure from the two extremes—Gaullists and Communists, who have been at one in deriding the "Third Force" and demanding dissolution of the General Assembly—but to the sharp divergence on economic policy among the middle-of-the-road parties, which under favorable circumstances might constitute France's "vital center." The Socialists felt under necessity to urge satisfaction of the unions' demands, fearing that otherwise the workers would either drift back to the Communist Party or else become increasingly apathetic about democracy—and therefore left the cabinet early in 1950. Leading French Socialists believe that the most workable combination in countries predominantly or largely Catholic would be a coalition of Socialists and Catholics, who, while differing about clericalism, would have in common their desire to advance human welfare. Such coalitions, they think, might be achieved in France by the Socialists and the Popular Republicans, and in Germany by the left-wing Christian Democrats and the Social Democrats, with eventually favorable results for Franco-German co-operation in the Council of Europe.

So far, in spite of serious postwar tensions, France has succeeded in assuring political liberty for all its citizens, including the thirty per cent of voters who cast their votes for the Communists. In contrast with the immediate postwar period, when several Communists held ministerial posts, there have been no Communists in the cabinet since 1947. The Communists, however, have 165 deputies in the National Assembly out of a total of 618, and 15 in the Council of the Republic (Senate) out of a total of 938. The Queuille cabinet, through the vigilant efforts of its Socialist Minister of the Interior, Jules Moch, who is in line to succeed the ailing Léon Blum as leader of the Socialist Party, kept careful watch on Communist activities. It did not find it necessary, however, to repress Communists, to outlaw the party, or to set up machinery for inquiry into activities of Communists or Communist sympathizers that might be described as un-French. This attitude of tolerance toward sharply opposing opinions that on occasion have seemed to threaten civil strife is in marked contrast to the fear of Communists and "fellow travelers" and the accusations based on the concept of "guilt by association" which became a notable feature of political life in the United States as the "cold war" with Russia grew more intense.

Comparable tolerance was displayed in Italy, where, in contrast with France, with its long-accepted tradition of anticlericalism and separation of church and state, the Vatican retained powerful influence over public opinion. The government of Premier Alcide de Gasperi, composed of Christian Democrats, a conservative group of strongly Catholic views representing, among others, the large landowners; right-wing Socialists, led by Giuseppe Sarragat; and Republicans, led by Randolfo Pacciardi, a prominent fighter on the side of the Spanish Republicans in the 1936 civil war, has excluded Communists from its ranks, but has taken no measures to interfere with the parliamentary and other activities of the Communist Party. The Communists, headed by Palmiro Togliatti, a prominent lawyer who, paradoxical as it may seem, is an expert on ecclesiastical law and who had spent some years in Moscow, claimed a membership of nearly three million at the peak of its strength before the 1948 elections, in which the Catholic Church took an active part. Since then economic recovery, the workers' disillusionment with constant strikes, and the Vatican's vigorous drive to wean Catholics away from communism have made serious inroads into Communist ranks, with an estimated loss in 1949 of one million members.

Among the western European countries Italy is the object of particular preoccupation on the part of the Vatican. The Church is aware, on the one hand, that Italy's economic difficulties—shortage of arable land for the peasants, which land distribution may alleviate but cannot permanently cure, persistent industrial unemployment, and wide differences in economic and social status between the rich and the poor— feed the flame of Communist agitation. Today, chronic unemployment is Italy's major political problem. The usually cited figure of 2,000,000 totally unemployed out of a population of 45,000,000 should really be 4,000,000; for many are working only part time or have to lead a substandard existence. In Italy, as elsewhere, economic insecurity fosters communism. Meanwhile, the Church is determined to undermine the influence of the Italian Communists, who have hitherto contended that Catholicism is compatible with communism. In its decree of July 1949 the Vatican indicated that all members of the Communist Party, as well as "fellow travelers," would be excommunicated. Subsequently the Vatican organ *Osservatore Romano* explained that persons who supported the Communists with votes or money would not be subject to excommunication if they did not share the materialistic and anti-Christian doctrines of communism. According to the decree, however, all persons who study Communist writings are subject to excommunication. This point has been understood to mean that all Catholics must henceforth ask permission of their priests before they can study Communist doctrines. If that is true, the Vatican decree may deter the less educated elements of the Italian population, who might fear to reveal their interest in communism to their spiritual advisers, from lending an ear to Communist propaganda. Since it is the masses of poorer, less educated Italians to whom the Communists have primarily directed their appeals, the Vatican may find it possible, by threat of excommunication, which depends for enforcement not on secular punishment but on the individual Catholic's conscience, to remove a large body of actual or potential followers from the reach of the Communist Party. How long such prescription can remain effective in an era of cheap newspapers, radio, and loudspeakers unless the basic causes of Italy's economic and social maladjustments are removed remains an open question.

What the future political complexion of Germany will be is as yet difficult to determine. Until 1949 the Germans, controlled by the United States, Britain, the U.S.S.R., and France in their respective zones, had had no opportunity to give free expression to their political sentiments. As the Bonn convention, in the spring of 1949, was concluding its task of drafting the Constitution of the West German state, both the Germans and the Allies were asking themselves whether the crocuses that were springing out of earth that only the day before was powdered with snow would, like the Weimar Republic, prove a false promise, to be followed by another frost. And in blockaded Berlin, the shattered capital of would-be empire-builders, where the once arrogant statues of the Siegesallee stare disconsolately at the dreary wastes of the Tiergarten, one could not but wonder whether the Germans had really cast away the myths of nationalism.

At the Bonn constitutional convention, Germany's two

principal parties—the Christian Democrats (composed of Catholic and non-Catholic elements, of former members of the Center Party, and of parties farther to the Right) and the Social Democrats—as well as the Communists, were represented not by men newly elected in the postwar period but by leaders who had made a name for themselves before Hitler came to power and destroyed all opposition. It was therefore impossible to judge the extent to which these prewar parties and leaders accurately reflected prevailing German opinion until the elections of August 14, 1949—the first free elections in Germany since 1933—when twenty-three million Germans, or almost eighty per cent of those eligible, went to the polls to elect representatives to the Bundestag, the lower house of the new West German legislature. The two principal parties emerged almost evenly matched—the Christian Democrats with 7,357,579 votes and 139 seats, and the Social Democrats with 6,932,272 votes and 131 seats. The Communists suffered a striking defeat, even in the industrial areas of the Ruhr, winning 1,360,443 votes and 15 seats. Their defeat, due to the growing unpopularity of Russia among Germans, caused some people to wonder whether the danger of German communism had not been overrated by western spokesmen. As striking as the defeat of the Communists was the victory of Rightist parties. The Free Democrats, who draw their main strength from the upper middle class, are conservative in economic affairs, and stress freedom of the individual from state and other controls, won 2,788,653 votes and 52 seats. The Bavarian Party, segment of the Christian Democrats, intensely conservative and favorable to Bavarian separatism, won 988,606 votes and 17 seats. The German Party, which includes some former Nazi elements and favors uncontrolled economy, won 940,088 votes and 17 seats.

In the United States the German elections were hailed as a demonstration that the Germans, to quote the title of a *New York Times* editorial, are "for democracy." This was partly due to the poor showing made by the Communists, but primarily to relief felt by many here that the Social Democrats, who advocate nationalization of coal and steel, had not emerged as the leading party in Western Germany. The Christian Democrats, predominantly Catholic and conservative, had nevertheless declared in their party platform adopted at Ahlen in 1947: "The new structure of German industry must be founded on the principle that the time of the unlimited mastery of private capitalism is gone. We must, however, prevent private capitalism from being replaced by state capitalism, which is even more dangerous for the political and economic freedom of the individual." Since then the party has become closely identified with the views of Professor Ludwig Ehrard, who wants to do away with all government controls. Washington hopes that the Christian Democrats will cooperate harmoniously with the United States and not be tempted to look toward Moscow. It would be premature, however, to assume that the Christian Democrats are proponents of either democracy or free private enterprise in the American sense of these terms. The party's left wing, headed by Karl Arnold, who was unexpectedly elected president of the Bundestag, favors some degree of socialization, and after the elections urged Christian Democratic leader Dr. Konrad Adenauer to explore the possibility of forming a coalition government with the Social Democrats. But the Social Democrats, led by the fiery Dr. Kurt Schumacher, who during the election campaign vied with his Rightist opponents in violent assertions of nationalism, made it clear that they did not want to participate in a Christian Democratic government. They contend that the "no control" policies of Ehrard, already started by him when he served as Economics Minister of the Bizonal Economic Council, will lead to unemployment, chaos, and misery in western Germany. The Christian Democrats, for their part, following the elections issued a statement affirming a free-enterprise program and rejecting coalition with the Social Democrats.

Although Dr. Adenauer, who believes that coalition rule was the root of evil in the Weimar Republic, hoped to form a cabinet composed exclusively of Christian Democrats, he had to include representatives of the Rightist parties. To what extent this will force him to accept the neo-Nazi ideas of the more militant Rightists who are rapidly emerging from postwar obscurity and have begun to publish newspapers filled with nationalist and anti-Semitic declarations familiar in the days of the Nazis, and in what measure this, in turn, may cause left-wing Christian Democrats to seek affinities among the Social Democrats to form a new center, only the future can show. On one point all German parties were in solid agreement in their election propaganda. That was in their vigorous denunciation of the occupying powers, coupled with demands for restoration of Germany's prewar boundaries, including the Saar, which France wants to annex economically, and the territories of eastern Germany "assigned" to Poland at Potsdam pending conclusion of a German peace treaty.

It was to be expected that German nationalism would reassert itself the moment Allied controls began to be whittled down. Americans who had hoped to "re-educate" the Germans in a few years within the framework of a necessarily authoritarian government had not taken the strength of German traditions sufficiently into account. Dr. Carl J. Friedrich, of Harvard University, writing in the *American Political Science Review* of June 1949, made an interesting comment on this point:

Rationally speaking, it seemed so easy, once all the structures of the past had been swept away by unconditional surrender, "to build democracy from the grass roots," and eventually to arrive at one of the proven workable schemes of democratic government, whether it be the American, the Swiss, or the British. But the "grass roots" upon which the conquerors stood were, symbolically speaking, the Catholic Bavarian village and the Marxist trade union. Authoritarian faith and economic parochialism—

these were the two roots of local community which, by grafting
a synthetic nationalism upon them, the imperialism of Bismarck,
the Utopianism of Weimar, and the racism of Hitler had sought
to exploit in turn.

While Germany could not be expected to change overnight,
it is understandable that nations which only four years before
were overrun by the Germans should view this new outburst
of nationalism with little satisfaction.

Although the Christian Democrats, in their party platform,
had announced their desire to have Germany join a Western European Union, it is not a foregone conclusion that a
coalition of Christian Democrats and Rightist parties will
turn a deaf ear to approaches by Moscow. Dr. Adenauer, who
on September 7 was chosen Chancellor by the Bundestag,
stated immediately after the elections that he would not col-
laborate in any way with the Russians. Yet it was shortly
reported that Rudolf Nadolny, former Russian Ambassador
to Berlin—whose feelers for a German-Russian rapprochement in the spring of 1949 caused many Germans to recall
Rapallo—would hold conversations with leaders of Christian
Democrats and Free Democrats at Bad Godesberg. The Russians, who for the time being cannot count on a political victory of the German Communists, have two inducements to
offer to German Rightists: the hope of achieving national
unity, which remains the paramount objective of all Germans; and the prospect of markets and sources of food and
raw materials in eastern Europe, Russia, and now China.
Those who believe that conservative German industrialists
would under no circumstances do business with Stalin may do
well to remember that it was one of Germany's ablest industrialists, Walther Rathenau, who in 1921 concluded the Rapallo agreement with the Soviet regime. Meanwhile, on the
western side Winston Churchill called for inclusion of the
West German state in the Council of Europe, whose Consultative Assembly was then holding its first session at Strasbourg.

The French, who still want to be "shown" that the Germans have really changed, cautioned against undue speed in admitting the German Republic. Yet a week after the elections Dr. Adenauer suggested that Germany should be included in the North Atlantic Treaty. If the United States continues to fear Russian aggression in Europe, it may consider the possibility of making western Germany a "bastion" against Russia and communism in Europe, just as it has been considering the possibility of transforming Japan into a "bastion" against Russia and communism in Asia. Should the French oppose this course, for fear of Germany's military revival as a military power, the Germans would be in a position to play on American apprehensions about communism and to pit west against east, as Stresemann skillfully did after World War I when he balanced Russia against the Locarno powers.

Russia's principal trump card is Germany's need for markets as well as food and raw materials. As a result of postwar territorial and political developments, the West German state has over half of Germany's prewar population, less than half of its arable land, three quarters of its hard-coal production, and about one third of its brown-coal output. It must import fifty per cent of its food, as well as many essential raw materials for its industries. To pay for these imports it must increase its exports of manufactured goods above the prewar level. As long as Germany continues to obtain the bulk of its food and raw materials from the United States, it will have to sell its exports for dollars. That is, it will have to sell in the United States, which before 1939 took on the average only four per cent of Germany's exports. Its need for dollars hampers restoration of its prewar trade with non-dollar nations of western Europe, especially the Low Countries; and meanwhile American opposition to the export by recipients of Marshall Plan aid of any goods to eastern Europe that might increase Russia's "war potential" prevents restoration of its prewar trade with an area where, before the war, Germany sent from twelve to sixteen per cent of its exports and obtained a considerable portion of its food and raw materials.

These problems promise to become acute in 1950 now that the industrial production of Western Germany has reached eighty per cent of the 1936 level. Coal production in 1949 was averaging 330,000 tons a day, with 20.8 per cent of the output assigned for export under the sliding scale adopted at the Moscow Conference of Foreign Ministers in 1947. The French would like to see this export percentage raised as coal production increases—a demand resisted by the United States on the ground that recovering German industry needs more coal. Ingot steel production has risen from an annual rate of 4.7 million tons in April 1948 to a level of over 9 million tons in 1949. Assuming that Germany can solve its coal and electric power problems and obtain the necessary imports of high-grade iron ore, the ceiling production of 10.7 million tons of steel set by the Allies appeared to be within reach by 1950 or earlier. Should Western Germany then be permitted to exceed this ceiling and go up to 13 million tons, as proposed by some ECA spokesmen? Would attempts by the Western Allies to limit steel output be regarded by the German government as compatible with ideas of free private enterprise? Most important of all, from the point of view of nations that were victims of German conquest twice in the lifetime of one generation, what assurance is there that, as time goes on, Germany's industrial potential may not again be used for military purposes?

So far it has proved difficult to ascertain the views of three major groups of the population which are expected to play an important part in Germany's future political life: the youth, the women, and the eleven million "expellees" (persons of German origin expelled from neighboring countries after the war). On the whole, young people above the grammar-school age are believed, at worst, to have been strongly imbued with Nazi ideas and, at best, to be apathetic toward democracy, which for them is associated with the rule of conquering western nations. The women, who, because of the depletion of German manpower during the war, have an opportunity to exert significant influence on the country's future course, for the most part lack political experience, having been confined under Hitler to the triune objective of "church, children, and kitchen," and are still under the influence of the German tradition that "father" (or husband, or brother) "knows best." The expellees, however much they may differ on other points, are bitterly opposed to Russia and to communism, are determined to return to their homes in Sudetenland, Poland, Hungary, or Yugoslavia, and are therefore expected to become the spearhead of German irredentism. At the same time, since they find it difficult to make a living in the contracted economy of postwar Germany, they feel dissatisfied and frustrated, and their discontent predisposes them to follow any leader who might promise improvement in their lot. The existing political parties have hitherto made no attempt to absorb the expellees, and the Communists, who have sedulously cultivated the youth and the women, and under other circumstances might make a strong bid for the support of the expellees, are precluded from doing so because Russia and Russian-influenced governments of eastern Europe are blamed for the expulsions.

Germany thus contains many of the ingredients that in the interwar years went into the formation of the Nazi movement—with the added pressure of greater territorial and economic losses than it suffered after World War I. It remains to be seen whether the Allied Occupation Statute and the International Ruhr Authority, on which the West German state is to be represented, will prove a stronger dike against resurgent German nationalism than the Allied efforts at control under the Treaty of Versailles.

The principal issue in Germany, both from the point of view of internal affairs and from that of Germany's relations with the rest of the world, is whether control can continue to be divorced from political responsibility without jeopardizing the prospects for eventual democracy. Many Americans who believe that there is an intrinsic connection between democracy and free enterprise have assumed that the Germans before 1939 had free private enterprise in our sense of the term and that, once it is restored, they will have democracy. But in Germany control of the nation's production has long been highly concentrated in a few hands to a degree unknown in the United States. The Weimar Republic proved helpless to regulate the vast power held by a group of conservative industrialists who ultimately decided to throw their resources behind a demagogic leader in the hope that Hitler's form of extremism would safeguard them from the extremism of communism. Will the same process be repeated? Is it realistic to speak of "free private enterprise" in Germany, where before 1939 large-scale industries, notably the steel and coal concerns of the Ruhr, combined into powerful cartels that prevented genuine competition by controlling production and prices, and where the choice, even before Hitler, had seemed to lie between capitalistic monopolies and some form of socialism? And can the United States hope to proceed with decartelization, which so far has been decidedly sketchy, now that the West German government has been established, without antagonizing industrialists who support the Rightist parties? In Germany, the most highly industrialized country of Europe, one can see in its most naked form the fundamental political problem raised by the Industrial Revolution. For modern industrial development has created an enormous potential of national strength, which can be used for constructive or destructive purposes, depending on who controls it. Since Germany is considered to have been the aggressor in two world wars, it becomes a crucial question both for the German people and for the nations that it conquered, to determine who in the future will control the coal and steel of the Ruhr, which a peace-minded Germany operating as a workshop for the rest of Europe could use to aid its own recovery and that of its victims, but a militant Germany could marshal again to threaten the rest of the world.

The German Social Democratic Party and the trade unions that form a considerable part of its membership believe that it is necessary to nationalize coal and steel and thereby make their future utilization subject to decision by the entire German nation, not only by the industrialists. Only thus, they contend, will it be possible to use the resources of the Ruhr for the good of Germany and Europe and to assure Germany's neighbors that they have nothing more to fear from the Germans. The United States, which at home views socialism with a critical eye, has not been favorable to the socialization of Germany's basic industries, and has taken the position that return of German plants to their former managers (usually closely associated with the former owners) is necessary to assure efficient operation and prompt recovery. German trade-union leaders contend that they are asking not for sole control of industry by labor, but for a program of "codetermination" under which the development of the country's industrial system would be determined not merely by industrialists, many of whom supported Hitler even when they were not actual members of the Nazi Party, but through joint boards on which industrialists, labor, and consumers would be represented on a basis of equality—boards that in turn would be responsible to a popularly elected body.

Through this process, they believe, political democracy would be strengthened by the infusion of economic democracy, instead of keeping politics and economics in watertight compartments and pretending that one has nothing to do with the other. The time has passed, they say, when workers can be restricted to negotiations about wages, hours, and other conditions of work and barred from basic decisions about the national economy, to which they make an important contribution. Nor do German trade-union leaders agree with American spokesmen that socialization of coal and steel would spell inefficiency of operation. The Germans, they say, had discovered "the managerial revolution" long before James Burnham publicized it in the United States, and know that trained managers, not owners, are responsible for the efficient administration of factories. Under the program they propose, managers would be retained in their present posts, but would be responsible not to the owners but to the nation as a whole. In contrast with the United States, Britain, which under the Labour government has gone much farther toward nationalization than the German Social Democrats and trade-union leaders propose to do, has indicated sympathy with proposals for nationalization of Germany's basic industries. The British, however, before the establishment of the West German state, found it politic to defer to the wishes of the United States, even when in a notable instance they had to veto the constitution of one of the states in their zone, which contained a clause providing for socialization.

In eastern Europe the economic problems of recovery are greatly complicated by far-reaching political changes brought about by the rise to power of Communist parties aided by the Kremlin. But if one expects to find in eastern Europe mere carbon copies of Russia, indistinguishable from it except in name, then surprises are in store. It is just as misleading to lump Russia and the countries of eastern Europe in a single category as it would be to talk in the same breath about Argentina and Paraguay, or about Colombia and Nicaragua. A common heritage of language and some traditions does not create uniformity among the Slav countries any more than it has done in Latin America. Two nations in that area, Hungary and Rumania, in any case are not of Slav origin, and since the disruption of the Austro-Hungarian Empire have been contending, often violently, with their Slav neighbors about border problems and the treatment of respective national minorities. Nor can developments in Czechoslovakia and Poland be used to appraise the situation in the former Axis satellites—Bulgaria, Hungary, and Rumania—whose economies are bearing the charge of reparations to the U.S.S.R.

Czechoslovakia, Poland, and Yugoslavia can perhaps be taken as outstanding examples of the state of flux in eastern Europe, where nothing is definitely settled—neither boundaries, nor economic systems, nor political structure. If one goes to Czechoslovakia and Poland in the expectation of seeing downhearted people eking out a miserable existence on the verge of national economic collapse, then one has to go through a mental readjustment. Both in Prague and in Warsaw people are busy from early morning till late at night working—in Prague to keep up the productivity of an already highly developed economic system, and in Warsaw to rebuild an economy drained by war of technical skills and essential manpower.

The sharp physical contrast between Prague and Warsaw is in a sense a yardstick of the differences between Czechs and Poles. Prague, little touched by war destruction, with a population nearing one million, looks like a large, prosperous, bustling city of our Middle West, its streets swarming with workers, white-collar and manual, who are middle-class in appearance and tastes. All day solid-looking people, garbed in good-quality if not elegant clothes, pour through the main thoroughfare, bent on the many tasks of a diversified modern economy. Overlooking this incessant activity stands Prague's ancient citadel, the Hradčany, which on sunny late afternoons makes one think of Tennyson's line: "the long light falls on castle walls."

The Czechs have succeeded in preserving their capital through centuries of strife by dogged persistence in carrying on with daily life irrespective of conquest and foreign influence, always believing that, in spite of temporary adversities, the nation will live to see another day. In the process, they may have missed something—the spark of reckless heroism, the impulse to defy authority irrespective of risk that characterize the Poles—but they have gained a marked degree of steadiness in the face of recurring dangers. Their main preoccupation after the war was security in two respects: security against another attack by Germany and another Munich, which Czech government spokesmen, before the Communist coup, hoped to find in close co-operation with the U.S.S.R.; and security against another period of unemployment comparable with that of the 1930's, which they hoped to achieve through planned economy, including planned foreign trade. Today an increasing number of Czechs are preoccupied with the problem of how to get rid of domination by Russia and by the Communists, although most of them hope this objective can be achieved without another war. At the same time even the bitterest opponents of Russia and communism remain deeply affected by anxiety about the possible resurgence of Germany. The Czechs thus feel caught between two fires, one of which seems to burn more dimly only when the other rises to intense heat. The same is true of Poland, but in even greater degree, for the Poles, having acquired German territory, are fearful of a new German *Drang nach Osten,* which would leave them little choice but to rely on the U.S.S.R.

In contrast with Prague, Warsaw is but a ghost of its pre-war self. One has to see the utter desolation of the ghetto to believe what man can do to man. There is hardly a spot where the eye can rest without seeing ruins. At night, under a starry sky, this utterly shattered city looks like a lunar world where life must have been suddenly stopped by untold catastrophe. The miracle is not only that life goes on, but that these ruins pulsate with activity. Whatever one may think of Poland's political and economic system, it is impossible not to be stirred by the daily repeated act of faith of the Warsaw population—restored from close to zero at the end of the war to nearly 600,000 in 1949—who swarm over scaffoldings and trestles carrying hods of bricks on their backs, clear rubble, and keep on rebuilding their city with an incredible energy and fervor which somehow seem apart from any political ideology. All day one hears the clip-clop of horses drawing carts filled with rubble and bricks; all day one sees workers raising walls from dust heaps, building almost literally with their bare hands. Their persistent will to survive disaster, whatever its source, has been compared by an English observer in Warsaw to the will to live of the Jewish people.

In contrast to the Czechs, the inhabitants of Warsaw are poorly, although warmly clad; but their food, unrationed since Januray 1949, is plentiful and palatable in contrast with the monotonous diet, mostly composed of starches, received by the Czechs, who did not plan to end food rationing until 1950. Poland, still primarily an agricultural country, with a bumper crop in 1948, has plenty of food except for meat. The meat supply had been depleted as a result of various factors: home slaughtering of hogs in 1948 by peasants fearful of collectivization; increased meat consumption; and export of meat, notably to Britain under the Anglo-Polish barter trade agreement of 1948, providing for exchange of Polish foodstuffs and timber for British machinery and certain raw materials. Czechoslovakia, which normally balances a small wheat import with exports of beet sugar, malt, and hops, was still suffering in 1949 from the after-effects of the 1947 drought, which forced the government to divert exports assigned to pay for imported industrial equipment to the purchase, instead, of wheat and other foodstuffs. Czechoslovakia administered its rationing system with an austerity comparable to that of Britain, but following a good harvest in 1949 announced that it would deration bread and sugar.

Both Czechoslovakia and Poland are coping with political and economic problems, of which some are rooted in their long and uneasy history, while others are a direct result of war-engendered developments. As early as 1943, the Czech government-in-exile in London, headed by President Eduard Beneš, decided on expulsion of the Sudeten Germans, and after liberation in 1945–6 2,400,000 were ejected, who today, as expellees, add to the difficulties of reorganizing the political life and economy of Western Germany. These expulsions, which reduced Czechoslovakia's population from approximately 15,000,000 in 1939 to a little over 12,000,000 in 1949, have deprived the country of a considerable number of skilled workers, especially in certain export trades, such as gloves, textiles, ceramics, and glassware, that had been centered in the Sudetenland.

Government spokesmen, however, contend that the resulting economic loss is preferable to the continued presence within Czechoslovakia's borders of a population many of whom, although by no means all, proved disloyal before 1939 to the nation in which they lived. It is also argued in Prague that the Sudetenland export enterprises, such as glovemaking, were "sweated" trades, which could compete on world markets only by maintaining low wage scales. In the long run, it is said, the Czechoslovak economy will be better off if it concentrates on the export of capital goods to newly developed countries like India and the nations of the Middle East rather than on nonessential or luxury items for which, in any case, there is at present little demand by Czechoslovakia's prewar customers.

Prague also faces complex issues in establishing a workable balance between Czechs and Slovaks in what is in essence a binational state. The Czechs (over 8,000,000) are industrially advanced, and have had experience in the conduct of democratic political institutions. The Slovaks (about 3,000,000) are primarily agrarian and, in the opinion of foreign observers, decidedly susceptible to clerical-fascist ideas, as indicated by the establishment in 1939 under Nazi auspices of the puppet government headed by Monsignor Tiso. A determined effort is now being made to give the Slovaks as large a measure of participation as possible in the country's affairs under the new constitution of 1948 (some Czechs, in fact, feel that the constitution unduly favors the Slovaks) and to speed the industrialization of Slovakia through transfer to its territory of various enterprises, in some instances entire factories, from Bohemia and the Sudetenland. The predominantly rural and mountainous easternmost area of Czechoslovakia, known as Ruthenia or Carpatho-Ukraine, with a population of 824,000, was ceded by President Beneš to the U.S.S.R. in 1945. Because of its relative economic backwardness this area had been a drain on the Prague treasury during the interwar years; Moscow sought it, not for its economic, but for its strategic value.

The Poles, too, have been struggling with a population problem—the transfer of five million Poles, most of them from Eastern Poland, acquired by the U.S.S.R. in 1939, to the areas of Germany assigned to Poland at Potsdam. These areas —called by Warsaw "Recovered Lands" because the Poles held some of them in the Middle Ages—comprise two thirds of East Prussia in the north, and Silesia, Pomerania, and a small part of Brandenburg in the west. Before 1939 they were inhabited by 8,500,000 Germans and about 1,000,000 Poles. Most of the Germans either fled as the Russians approached at the end of World War II or were subsequently expelled by the Poles.

If there is one point on which most Poles, as well as the Catholic Church in Poland, would agree, it is that Polish possession of these German territories is a closed issue. Every hint on the part of the United States, notably former Secretary of State Byrnes's Stuttgart speech of 1946, that the western border remains to be fixed under the peace treaty with Germany, merely hardens Poland's determination to resist the reopening of this question. The possibility is not excluded that the U.S.S.R., too, might at some point consider the return of at least part of Poland's German lands in order to win support in Germany. The Poles, however, believe that the Kremlin would hesitate to take this step, which, in their opinion, would irretrievably break up the eastern European bloc. They are convinced, moreover, that Russia would not reconsider its own acquisition of eastern Poland in

1939. In Moscow's view, the new eastern border should end once and for all dreams of a "Greater Poland" at Russia's expense, which have been nurtured by many Polish leaders, most recently by Pilsudski in 1920. The Poles deeply regret the loss of eastern Poland, and especially of their historic city of Lwow, but they are inclined to accept the eastern border (drawn approximately along the line proposed by Lord Curzon in 1919) as final. Although many Poles look back with nostalgia to the forests and marshes of eastern Poland, the territory ceded to Russia is less desirable from the economic point of view than the Recovered Lands. Before 1939 the Poles had been a minority, although the largest one, in the population of eastern Poland, which numbered over five million Poles, over four million Ukrainians, and over one million White Russians. In 1940 the Soviet government incorporated the Ukrainians into the Ukrainian S.S.R. and the White Russians into the Byelorussian S.S.R.

As a result of postwar territorial changes, Poland today has a homogeneous population and, as one American expert has pointed out, has "become in essence a national state, which it had not been since the fourteenth century." [1] It is estimated that at present there are some forty thousand Russian troops stationed in Poland along Russia's line of communication with its zone in Germany. Poles who oppose both Russia and communism would welcome any international development that would drive the Russians back within their borders; those who regard Germany as a greater evil than Russia and agree with Communist ideology consider the presence of Russian forces in eastern Germany as a desirable safeguard against German irredentism.

In Warsaw one is acutely conscious of Poland's precarious position, poised as it is between two great and dynamic nations, the Germans and the Russians, and subject for two centuries to the intervention of both, with no natural obsta-

[1] Harrison Thomson: "The New Poland," *Foreign Policy Reports*, December 1, 1947.

cles to check invasion and dismemberment. Not that the Poles themselves have been entirely free of expansionist aspirations, as witness Pilsudski's invasion of Russia in 1920. But in the interwar years they maintained the existence of their re-united national state only by placating one or another of their powerful neighbors. Today, when Poland has cause to fear a new German irredentism spearheaded by the expellees, it sees little choice but to depend on the U.S.S.R., especially since it expects little sympathy from the United States, which, as seen from Warsaw, was not enthusiastic about Polish acquisition of German areas in the first place and is now intent on rebuilding the economy of Western Germany. Only a settlement of the German problem that would allay Poland's fear of its western neighbor, coupled with a strengthened United Nations organization capable of defending small nations against great powers, might eventually reduce Warsaw's dependence on the U.S.S.R. and make it possible for the Poles to steer a course of their own in world affairs.

In very large measure this is true also of Czechoslovakia, although the Czechs, in contrast with the Poles, have an industrial base for maintenance of a modern armed force. But when foreigners talk about the possibility of Czech military resistance to either Germany or Russia, they forget that even when Prague in 1938 had at its disposal forty divisions backed by the production of the Skoda works and other industrial enterprises, and was protected by the Carpathian Mountains, the Czechs did not put up a fight once they learned from what happened at Munich that they could not count on outside support against Hitler. It is true that when the Poles took up the Nazi challenge in 1939 and fought back, with an ultimate loss of six million out of their population of thirty million, they had been informed that Britain and France, in contrast with their stand at Munich, would fight Germany if it invaded Poland. Yet Polish leaders must have realized that, with the best will in the world, the British and French were not prepared to prevent Hitler from overrunning Poland initially.

It is a mistake to assume that either Poles or Czechs, including Communists, are uniformly pro-Russian or irrevocably committed to an exclusively pro-Russian orientation. In the past both Poland and Czechoslovakia had many ties with the West, which was not true of Russia before the Bolshevik Revolution of 1917. While the Czechs, never subjected to Russian rule, had great admiration for "the spirit of Russia," to use the title of a well-known book by Thomas Masaryk, those Poles who as a result of three eighteenth-century partitions had been ruled by the czars felt as hostile to the Russians before 1919 as their compatriots in German-administered areas felt to the Germans. Moreover, in both Czechoslovakia and Poland Communist leaders, much as they may be in agreement with the Kremlin's basic views on communism, find themselves confronted in practice with distinctive national problems; and they had hoped for greater latitude in settling those problems than, in the opinion of some, they are actually able to exercise. This seems to be true not only of Marshal Tito, the unreconstructed rebel, but also of less vigorously outspoken leaders like Wladyslaw Gomulka in Poland, Vassili Kolarov in Bulgaria, and even, if reports can be trusted, President Klement Gottwald in Czechoslovakia.

In both Czechoslovakia and Poland the Communist Party, although outwardly sharing authority with other parties of the Left in united fronts, exercises dominance through control of the government machinery, of trade unions, and of various groups and organizations. Opposition elements either have gone into exile or are under close surveillance, with no opportunity to express their views. Arrests go on, and "labor camps" exist, but foreign observers on the spot warn against generalized comparisons of conditions in Poland and Czechoslovakia with those in Russia. The power of the Communist leadership in both countries is limited by disagree-

ments in party ranks about the pace of economic development, and by the friendly interpersonal relations long in existence within groups such as the trade unions—an element
that was noticeably lacking in Russia at the time of the
Bolshevik Revolution. These factors tend to mitigate harsh
directives from the top when they have to be actually applied
to individuals.

In Poland, Communist Party disagreements were brought
to the fore at the congress held in Warsaw in December 1948
to bring about union of the Communist and Socialist parties.
At this congress the Communist leader Wladyslaw Gomulka, who had done an outstanding job as Minister for
the Recovered Lands immediately after the war, was voted
down when he opposed too rapid agricultural collectivization, and was dropped from the party's Political Bureau. A
few months later, in the spring of 1949, it was reported that
Hilary Minc, Minister of Industry and Commerce, regarded
by both Poles and foreigners as the best technician in postwar
Poland (and many say in eastern Europe), would also fall
into disfavor because of his emphasis on the need to proceed
more slowly with collectivization. For the time being, however, Minc appears to retain his strong position in the government, where he is one of the principal architects of the six-
year plan for industrialization and modernization of agriculture launched in 1950. The possibility that Gomulka,
probably the most popular figure in Poland, might become
another Tito was discounted in Warsaw in 1949, principally
because Poland's geographic position, unlike that of Yugoslavia, does not encourage comparable defiance of the
U.S.S.R.

The Communist Party in Poland, however, is faced with
two main problems, both of which involve deep-seated traditions and sentiments: how to enlist the support of the peasants, still a majority of the population, in the tasks of creating
a balanced economy combining expanded industry with mod-

ernized agriculture; and how to bring about workable relations between the state and the Catholic Church.

Peasant resistance to collectivization has proved one of the
principal stumbling-blocks to consolidation of Communist
rule in all countries of eastern Europe, including, during the
critical years of 1930–3, the U.S.S.R. In Russia peasants
emancipated from serfdom in 1861 had remained for the most
part landless, only one third of the peasants having acquired
land by 1914, either individually or as members of the village
community, the *mir*. Their principal demand, therefore, was
for individual ownership of land; and the Soviet government
had to fight a pitched battle with the villages in the 1930's
before it was able to carry through its program of collectivization at a tragic cost in human and material resources. Today
only one per cent of the Russian peasants are individual owners; the majority are now members of collective farms
(*kolkhozes*), and a relatively small number are employed as
wage laborers on large-scale state farms, which usually serve
as experimental stations for various phases of agriculture.

In eastern Europe, where individual ownership of land
was far more widespread before World War II than it had
been in Russia before the Bolshevik Revolution, Communist
governments have found it even harder than the Kremlin to
force through a program of collectivization; they have been
faced with passive resistance that has threatened to cut off
supplies of food for the towns and raw materials for the
factories. Moreover, in contrast with Russia, peasant parties
had come to play a significant part in eastern European countries before 1939, and thus the peasants, to a far greater extent
than in the Soviet Union, could have proved the backbone of
resistance to communism. After World War II popular peasant leaders like Stanyslaw Mikolajczyk of Poland, Juliu
Maniu of Rumania, and Nikola Petkov of Yugoslavia clashed
directly with the Communists, who did not believe they could
achieve the desired degree of national economic integration

and planning if so important a sector of the nation's economy
as agriculture remained in the hands of small individual producers under no responsibility to gear their production to the
needs of government programs.

This dilemma, one of the principal factors that caused
Marshal Tito to defy the Kremlin, was revealed again and
again in discussion of Poland's six-year plan. The announced
aim of this plan, successor to the three-year reconstruction
plan inaugurated in 1946, is not to create socialism but to
build its foundations. The pace of socialization, especially
with respect to agriculture, was vigorously debated at the
Warsaw congress of 1948. In spite of the fact that Gomulka
was demoted at that time for urging a policy of gradualism,
it was made clear during the congress that undue haste in
attempting to achieve agricultural collectivization should be
avoided for fear of antagonizing the peasants. The Polish
peasants, like other peasants of eastern Europe and the Balkans, and to a far greater extent than Russian peasants before 1917, have had experience with the concept and practice
of private property and resist any hint that their land and
other possessions might be pooled in collective farms.

Yet Hilary Minc has stressed, notably at the plenary session of the Central Committee of the Polish Workers' Party in
July 1948, that the party's program must be based on Marxist-
Leninist theory. Warning "that the party's program . . .
will not be accepted and understood at once by all social
groups and strata, nor even by all of the working population,"
he added: "without a program there is no winning over the
people for the party." The task of the government, he said, is
"to persuade the working population of the soundness of our
program." Instead of urging agricultural collectivization,
Minc proposed the voluntary formation of "production co-
operatives"; but even this proposal was interpreted as a step
toward collectivization by the peasants, who proceeded to
slaughter hogs for home consumption.

Owing to peasant resistance, the Polish government for the

time being exercises great caution in formulating its plans for agricultural co-operatives. Thus it faces the problem of an economy divided into a nationalized sector of industrial production and a privately controlled sector of agricultural production, which cannot be closely meshed into a national economic program. In 1949 government spokesmen estimated that the nationalized sector, including industrial co-operatives, employed 75 per cent of all workers engaged in industry and handicrafts and produced 85 per cent of the output. By contrast, state farms, comparable to the Russian *sovhozes*, and usually run, as in Russia, as model farms, comprise about 10 per cent of the total acreage and yield about 7.5 per cent of the grain output. The government is aware that even if collectivization were not resisted by the peasants, it would be limited for the time being by lack of modern agricultural equipment. Stations similar to those in Russia, where agricultural equipment can be rented by the peasants, have been established at one thousand points in the country, and tractors and other machinery are being imported from Czechoslovakia, Britain, and the U.S.S.R., but the shortage remains acute.

It is the opinion of economic experts that Poland has made considerable progress toward industrial recovery, especially in the textile industry, which ranks first in employment, and in coal mining; and it is generally acknowledged to have the highest coal productivity per man in Europe. In 1948 coal and coke constituted fifty per cent of the total value of Poland's exports. Poland's rapidly expanding merchant fleet operates through the ports of Gdynia, Gdansk (Danzig), and Szczecin (Stettin), and orders have been placed abroad for modern ships, including two oil tankers in Britain. In spite of these achievements, Poland is handicapped by lack of technicians and skilled workers owing to wartime loss of manpower. It also needs all kinds of machinery both to rehabilitate existing enterprises—notably the coal mines it took over from Germany in Silesia—and to equip factories blueprinted in its six-year plan. Efforts are being made to increase productivity by "labor competitions" similar to the Stakhanovist movement in Russia, with money incentives offered to record-breaking workers; since real wages have not increased, workers have shown considerable aversion to such competitions. Poland is also seeking to overcome some of the problems of industrial backwardness by collaboration with the more advanced economy of Czechoslovakia. A number of Polish-Czechoslovak commissions have been established to eliminate overlapping in production and to study the possibility of integrating the industrial output of the two countries, but so far apparently have achieved no concrete results.

Czechoslovakia itself, however, is faced with the need to import new machinery and spare parts for machines already in operation before it can measurably increase its exports to neighboring countries of the west, where it hopes to purchase necessary equipment. The Prague government, too, places increasing emphasis on labor productivity, and strenuous attempts are being made to cut down absenteeism, which according to some foreign observers, is due not so much to sabotage, as has frequently been reported, as to lack of material incentives. Nationalized factories, which include all enterprises employing more than fifty workers, are administered not by workers' councils but by managers—in many instances former managers or owners—who are responsible to the government. Far from holding out the promise of an easy life, government and trade-union leaders point out that the country's standard of living cannot be maintained, nor can the social services Czechoslovakia has developed since its emergence as a national state in 1919 be kept up, unless all groups of the population increase their output. Czechoslovakia, like Poland, lags in capital formation, and Czech Premier Anton Zapotocky in 1949 emphasized that wages must not "eat up the results of increased production," and that nationalized industries must provide funds for capital investment. "For," he added, "if they do not improve and expand, we shall not be able to compete with foreign countries and buy the necessary raw materials." In spite of these problems of production and distribution, non-Communist foreign observers—for example, Joseph Harseh of the *Christian Science Monitor*—believe that the enhancement of prestige and larger opportunities for education and leisure activities that the Communist governments have given industrial workers, especially in Czechoslovakia, provide a form of nonmaterial compensation that has strengthened the position of the Communist Party among workers' groups. By contrast, growing restrictions on political liberty, loss of prestige, and economic deterioration have alienated the middle class, which, however, played an important part only in Czechoslovakia; while fear of collectivization has aroused resistance among peasants.

In the countries of eastern Europe whose populations are predominantly Roman Catholic, the Communist parties face not only stubborn opposition from the peasants but also opposition from the Catholic Church. This has proved true in Yugoslavia, where Archbishop Stepinaz was sentenced to prison; in Hungary, where Cardinal Mindszenty was brought to trial in 1949 for alleged treason and condemned to life imprisonment; in Czechoslovakia, where the struggle between the Prague government and Archbishop Joseph Beran, outwardly over religious issues, was complicated by the political conflict between the advanced Czechs, many of whom are Protestants, and the more backward Slovaks, who are Catholics. The situation in Poland, where ninety per cent of the population are Catholics, is perhaps the most clear-cut example of the conflict waged between church and state in eastern Europe.

The Catholic Church had historically been one of the bulwarks of the Polish nation in its resistance to foreign oppression, had once taken an active part in political life, and remains a vital force that cannot be disregarded or defied with impunity. Instead of attempting a frontal attack comparable to the attack of the Russian Communists in 1917 on the far weaker Orthodox hierarchy, the Polish government is seeking to limit the scope of the Church's activities in three main sectors. First, it has proposed that religious instruction, compulsory in all schools and given by priests who receive their salaries from the state, should be made voluntary, at the discretion of parents. At the same time, pleading a variety of reasons, it has shut down the relatively few schools directly administered by the Church. Second, it has suppressed most Catholic newspapers and restricted those still published to discussion of nonpolitical subjects. And, third, it has curtailed the activities of Catholic organizations. At the Warsaw congress of December 1948 Communist Party spokesmen declared the party would insist that the Church withdraw completely from political life and cease its extrareligious educational activities, especially among the youth. The clergy, they contended, must give proof of loyalty to the regime—a contention that has caused some observers to assume that the Polish government, while preserving the Church, wants to terminate its international ties with the Vatican and transform it into a distinctly national institution.

In spite of governmental restrictions, churches in Poland are full to overflowing, and the large number of young people among the worshippers is notable, as is also the number of soldiers, who are expected by the Army to attend church services. In Warsaw demolished churches, including the Cathedral, are being rebuilt at state expense, with as meticulous care to reproduce them in their original form, no matter how ancient, as in the case of other edifices.

The Catholic hierarchy in Poland, for its part, has been pondering the course it should follow. Should it fight the government openly, as Cardinal Mindszenty did in Hungary, at the risk of martyrdom, which might rally the people to its side? Should it reach some kind of *modus vivendi* with the government at the risk of diminishing its spiritual influence? Or should it take a firm stand on such issues as religious education, but avoid a showdown with the government and concentrate on preserving the concept of the dignity of the individual until such time as this concept can flourish in Poland? No decision had yet been reached in 1949, but the new Primate, Archbishop Stefan Wyszynski, who that year succeeded the late Cardinal Hlond, in a pastoral letter signed by all bishops and read in all churches, condemned the government for its attacks on priests. Some members of the hierarchy attributed these government attacks not to Poles, nor even to Polish Communists, but to Russia and "the Jews" —this despite the fact that the Nazis reduced the Jewish population of Poland, once estimated at over three million, to a mere handful, The Catholic Church has been so identified with the Polish nation throughout its history, and has had such deep-rooted international ties, that the Polish Communists have a far different problem in their attempt to work out new church-state relations than was faced by the Russian Communists in 1917.

While the political situation in the countries of eastern Europe and the Balkans, usually referred to as Russia's"satellites," remains in a state of flux, with the possibility that nationalism may deeply affect the practices of communism within individual nations as well as their relations with the U.S.S.R., the Russians, too, have been facing difficult political problems stemming from the disorganization and material destruction wrought by war. In spite of the outward appearance of a "monolithic" state where neither political "deviations" nor departures from rigidly planned economy can occur, the U.S.S.R. has undergone many internal changes during the more than thirty years of Communist Party rule. The leadership of the inner party group, the Politbureau, which to the outside world looks like a close-knit dictatorship, as unshakable as the rock of Gibraltar, has in actuality been rent again and again by dissension. Party policies have been attacked first from the Left, represented by Trotsky, advocate of "permanent revolution" as opposed to Stalin's policy of consolidation through "building socialism in one country"; and then from the Right, represented by Rykov, Bukharin, and Tomsky, who reflected the discontent of such diverse groups as peasants, intellectuals, and trade unions. Military leaders like Tukhachevsky and prominent figures in administration, industry, arts, and sciences have been executed or sent to "labor camps" for "re-education," on the accusation that they had been hatching treasonable plots against Stalin or seeking the aid of foreign countries—notably in 1936 of Germany and Japan—in alleged plans to overthrow the Kremlin dictatorship. Russian engineers, as well as foreign technicians brought to Russia by the Soviet government to assist in its program of industrialization, were charged in the 1930's with "sabotage" of industrial enterprises. Nationalist movements, particularly in the Ukraine, a hotbed of irredentism since its subjugation by Czarist Russia in the seventeenth century, have been suppressed, most recently since World War II; Ukrainian nationalist leaders, some of whom had counted on German support (as had also happened during World War I before the Bolsheviks seized power), have been "liquidated"; and in contrast to prewar years, anti-Semitism has emerged, largely because the Jews are suspected of being "cosmopolitan" and pro-Western.

After 1945, too, Politbureau chiefs appear to have had serious divergences of views about Russia's future course in foreign policy. These divergences in certain respects recalled the controversy between Trotsky and Stalin after Lenin's death in 1923 concerning their estimates of the "world conjuncture" and the effect it might have on Russia and on world communism. Some of the Politbureau members, particularly Andrei Zhdanov, able "trouble-shooter" who among many important tasks headed the defense of Leningrad during the war and had then served as Russian commissioner in Finland, were reported to believe that the end of capitalism was in sight; that the United States would suffer a severe depression, which would open the way to the triumph throughout the world of communism, anticipated but not realized in 1919; and that Moscow, without resort to war, could hasten this process through active propaganda and non-co-operation with the Western World. Others, among whom are thought to be Stalin himself and Gregori Malenkov, who now occupies a key role in the Communist Party comparable to that held by Stalin twenty years ago and who is said to be the marshal's choice as his successor, either were inclined to let "permanent revolution" take its course, but without making a break with the West; or else favored a policy of international reconstruction, accompanied by active economic relations with advanced Western countries from which Russia could obtain tools, machinery, and raw materials. This latter policy was comparable to Stalin's earlier program of "building socialism in one country," which was based on the assumption that the U.S.S.R., while not expending its own resources and avoiding collision with other powers, would by its example encourage the development of communism in other countries.

So far as can be determined, Zhdanov exercised strong influence on the Kremlin's policy in the immediate postwar period, supported and justified by the calculations of the economist Vozhnesensky, who predicted the early collapse of capitalism. The views of Vozhnesensky, however, were challenged by Eugene Varga, who predicted that Western capitalism, modified by a growing measure of state control even in the United States, would continue in existence much longer than had been foreseen by some of the Marxist prophets in Russia and elsewhere. Although Varga was vigorously criticized and temporarily discredited, his influence began to be felt again after the death of Zhdanov, in 1948, and the subsequent emergence of Malenkov as the real power behind the Kremlin. Unless a great depression in the United States materially alters the world situation in the immediate future, it may be expected that the U.S.S.R. while continuing to avoid close contacts with the West, which, in the opinion of its leaders, might endanger the Soviet state by contaminating the Russian people with "cosmopolitanism" and "bourgeois" ideas, will endeavor to achieve at least temporarily the "peaceful coexistence" previously urged by Stalin through the development of trade relations between East and West.

Such a course probably offers Moscow the best promise of stabilizing Russia's internal situation, of reconstructing devastated areas, and of achieving a level of production that would assure the country's security by the establishment of heavy industries, yet at the same time leave a margin for the output of consumer goods, a demand for which has been rising in the postwar period. The Russian people, who have been struggling for thirty years with "blood, sweat, and tears" to create a modern industrial economy in what was for the most part a backward agrarian country, only to suffer a disheartening setback during World War II, are eager to have their hopes for a better life realized as soon as possible. Moreover, at least two million Russians, soldiers and officers in the armies of occupation who had a glimpse of life in eastern Europe, and especially in the eastern zone of Germany, have brought back new ideas about standards of living. Although "reoriented" in special training camps on their return, they have urged economic and social improvements in the communities where they resumed civilian tasks. This does not mean that the Russians are discontented to the point of revolt against the existing system—although there are many individuals among the new middle class of engineers, administrators, and intellectuals who are deeply irked by restrictions on freedom of expression, particularly in science and the arts. First-hand reports from Russia indicate that the young generation, who are free both from the fanatical hatreds of the "old Bolsheviks" and from the nostalgia for the pre-1914 past that swayed many of the opponents of communism, believe that Soviet institutions are good, and even better than those of other countries; but they want to improve these institutions, and particularly to rid them of bureaucratic red tape and the more crude and irksome forms of "thought-control."

In spite of internal tensions, the Russians have made considerable progress in recovering from the havoc wrought by the Germans in the industry, transportation, and agriculture of the occupied areas in the Ukraine and the Donbas, one of the principal production regions of the U.S.S.R. According to official Soviet statistics, over-all industrial production in 1949 was well above the level of 1940, the last prewar year, and agricultural output for 1948 was close to prewar figures. While Western observers discount some of the Russian claims, it is probable that reconstruction of both heavy industry and agriculture has been rapidly advancing since VE-day. In the immediate postwar period Russia had serious bottlenecks in the output of coal and steel, and consequently in the restoration of transportation and the production of agricultural machinery, especially tractors. The Soviet government reports that some of these bottlenecks have now been broken; that in 1948 the output of coal, steel, and related metals exceeded prewar marks; and that tractors and farm machines are being supplied to collective farms in larger quantities than in 1940. If these reports prove to be accurate, the current fourth Five-Year Plan may be completed in its main features in four years, and the fifth Five-Year Plan will be launched in 1950. The goals set for Soviet economy by Stalin in his pre-election speech of February 9, 1946, inaugurating the fourth Five-Year Plan, were an annual production of 500 million metric tons of coal, 60 million tons of steel (the United States produced 100 million tons in 1949), 60 million tons of oil, and 50 million tons of pig iron—with approximately half of these figures to be reached by 1950. At that time Stalin told the Russian people that "special attention will be devoted to extending the production of consumer goods, to raising the living-standards of the working people."

The U.S.S.R. is still faced with serious economic problems,

some of which are similar to the problems of western European nations devastated by war; others are attributable to the character of Soviet economy. Russia, like many nations in Europe, is suffering from acute housing shortages, especially in Stalingrad and other devastated cities, and has found it difficult to replace wartime losses of livestock. The output of consumer goods, although improving, remains very low compared with the needs of the population of two hundred million. The intensive development of heavy industry, and the relative neglect of light industries producing consumer goods, have been a notable feature of Soviet economy since 1917. The objective of Lenin, furthered by Stalin, was to create as rapidly as possible a base for future large-scale modern economy through electrification and the creation of heavy industries. But, since Soviet leaders took the view that without heavy industries a modern nation is vulnerable to foreign attack, an important although statistically undetermined proportion of the industrial output of the U.S.S.R. was systematically set aside for armaments, and many factories were so planned as to be readily converted from peacetime to wartime purposes—for example, tractor factories were used to build tanks during World War II.

There is nothing in the economic theories of the Russians, or of Communists in general, to indicate that they intend, as a matter of principle, to concentrate all production in perpetuity on heavy industry. On the contrary, Soviet leaders have constantly held out to the Russians the promise that, once the initial stages of industrialization had been passed, "life would be better and gayer." The discrepancy between the output of heavy and light industry is due not to Communist theories as such, but to the fact that Russia in 1917 was still in the early phases of the Industrial Revolution and, under the Soviet program, had "to catch up with and outdistance" the advanced capitalist nations. Before World War II many Westerners regarded the elaborate Soviet heavy-industry program as either an aberration of theoretical economists or a dictatorially imposed and ruthlessly administered policy designed to keep the Russians forevermore in a condition of poverty, and hence of enslavement. Since then, however, many of the advanced nations of Europe, with Britain in the lead, have discovered that, because of their wartime economic losses, they have had to devote their efforts primarily to the reconstruction and modernization of heavy industry before they could begin to satisfy consumer needs; have introduced "austerity" programs of varying severity; and have frankly told their people that postponement of all but "essential" needs was required for national survival. It is entirely possible that, once the U.S.S.R. has laid a firm basis of heavy industry and, at the same time, has come to feel that it is not in constant danger of foreign attack—as it did during the period 1917–41—more and more attention will be given by the Soviet government to production of consumer goods and improvement in the standard of living. It is significant that the Russians since the war have been drawing on the eastern zone of Germany and on their neighbors of eastern Europe, not only for "essential" products needed for heavy industry, but also for consumer goods that Russia does not yet produce in sufficient quantities—for example, shoes, hats, and crockery from Czechoslovakia, textile goods from Poland, and tobacco from Bulgaria.

The attention of the Western World, and especially of the United States, has been fixed so steadily on Russia and on communism since 1945 that it has sometimes seemed as if the future of Europe depended solely on Moscow's decisions and Washington's counter-decisions. This view overestimates the power and influence of the U.S.S.R. and underestimates the staying qualities of the United States and of European countries outside Russia. The U.S.S.R. has loomed important in the period since World War II partly because the West had forgotten that Russia, in the days of the czars, had been one of Europe's great powers, and had come to discount it in that role, regarding Moscow primarily as the center of world communism; and partly because the West, including the United States, had lost its sense of direction and its faith in the original concepts of democracy. Both western Europe and the United States had long been accustomed to thinking of the West as the focus of the universe, with less advanced peoples, including Russia and the nations of Asia, eking out a rather obscure existence along the periphery. They found it difficult to adjust themselves to a new world balance in which backward peoples inspired by Western democratic traditions at least as much as by communism, if not actually more so, also sought to reach the center of the world stage, thus reducing Europe to the lesser proportions of one of the five continents—historically the most advanced, but clearly not predestined to remain for all time master of Asia or Africa.

This reversal in Europe's position, which had been coming about gradually for at least two centuries with the develment of other continents, encouraged by European explorers, settlers, and traders, had passed relatively unnoticed until World War II brutally revealed the change in the world balance of power. With the defeat of Germany and Italy and the weakening of France and Britain and their overseas empires, the U.S.S.R. emerged as the principal power on the continent—not because it was itself so strong, but because its possible contestants had grown relatively so feeble. Had the other European nations maintained their strength and influence, it is difficult to believe that the Soviet government, no matter how far-reaching its ambitions to enhance the territorial, strategic, and economic position of the Russian nation or how fervent its desire to advance the cause of communism, could have exerted as much influence as it did in the immediate postwar period. But even at the peak of this period the U.S.S.R. did not reach much farther in Europe than it had done under the czars, when Russia was deeply involved in the affairs of countries along its western border from the Baltic to the Black Sea, sought to unite all Slavs under its leadership, sent its armies as far west as Paris during the Napoleonic wars, and took an active part in all conferences on the continent's affairs, including such decisive nineteenth-century conclaves as the Congress of Vienna in 1815, the Congress of Paris following the Crimean War in 1856, and the Congress of Berlin in 1878.

It is true that in communism the Soviet leaders found a weapon for extending Russian influence throughout Europe that had not been available to the czars. By 1949, however, it looked as if this weapon might be transformed into a dangerous boomerang by the nationalism of countries that had come under Communist rule. Moreover, in its bid for international communism, appealing to all workers across national frontiers, the Kremlin had come into head-on collision with the Vatican's international Catholicism, which claims the allegiance of all Catholics, irrespective of national affiliations. And it had also discovered that, contrary to the assumption of Marx and Lenin, "workers of the world," far from uniting, were as deeply divided along national, political, and ideological lines as any other group—with the trade unions of western Europe breaking off in 1949 from the World Federation of Unions (WFTU), dominated by Communists, to form in London a new international organization on democratic lines.

Meanwhile the United States, which until 1917 had been eager to trade with Europe and to share in the cultural heritage of the Western nations, but had consistently refrained from long-term political and military commitments on the continent, in the course of two world wars had become deeply involved in the affairs of Europe. Had this country maintained on the continent the military strength it had brought into play during World War II, it may be doubted that the U.S.S.R. would have been able to assert its influence as it did between 1945 and 1949. For the United States, by its presence on the continent and by demonstration of its intention to participate in Europe's affairs in time of peace as well as war, would then have balanced the U.S.S.R., thus offsetting the weakness of the nations of western Europe. As events turned out, however, the United States abruptly withdrew both military strength and political attention, leaving on the continent a vacuum that the western European nations were then too prostrated to fill. The U.S.S.R., itself gravely shaken by the war, had sufficient momentum and confidence to seize this moment of interregnum and renew the bid for power and influence that it failed to carry through in 1917.

Alarmed by this unanticipated challenge—for most Americans had assumed that once the war was over, the Russians would go back to their own territory, mind their own affairs, and even co-operate with this country—the United States retraced its steps. Beginning with Byrnes's Stuttgart speech of 1946, it endeavored to rebuild the military, political, and economic position it commanded on the continent at the end of the war, but voluntarily abandoned after VJ-day in response to vigorous domestic demands to "bring the boys home" and return as soon as possible to "normal" life. With the threefold development of the European Recovery Program, various projects for Western Union, and the North Atlantic Treaty, the United States in 1949 reached a point where it could hope to weight the other end of the European scales against the U.S.S.R. Thus in the middle of the twentieth century we see the balance of power in Europe, traditionally fostered by Britain, re-created again—but this time on one side by a non-European power, the United States, and on the other by the U.S.S.R., which is only partly situated in Europe.

The future of Europe, in whose determination the United States and the U.S.S.R. since 1945 have come to play a decisive part, depends on the answers events may give to six big ifs. *If* this country succeeds in avoiding a major depression that would precipitate an economic crisis in the rest of the world; *if* we recognize our responsibility to take the lead in effecting transfer of relations from the national plane to the plane of the United Nations; *if* western Europe not only restores its productive facilities, but also finds it possible to sell its goods abroad, and thereby regains some measure of independence from the United States; *if* both the United States and the countries of western Europe reorganize their political, economic, and social life in such a way as to avoid the rise, or recrudescence, of fascism allied with reactionary religious groups; *if* the Kremlin decides that the "world conjuncture" is not favorable to the spread of communism in Europe and returns to "building socialism in one country," thereby conceivably raising the standard of living of the Russian people, with the possibility that this might eventually encourage greater political flexibility; and *if* the nations of eastern Europe and the Balkans which now have Communist governments insist on adapting communism to their particular national conditions, irrespective of Russia's wishes and practices and came to abandon the subversive techniques Communists developed in the years when their party was defeated as illegal—then Europe, as well as the United States, may be on the threshold of a new and invigorating era that would see larger fulfillment of the promises of democracy and industrialization than has proved possible in the past. But this will not depend, as many Americans believe, solely or chiefly on what the U.S.S.R. may do in Europe. It will depend even more on the use we make in Europe of the vastly increased material power we now command as a result of our own tremendous economic growth and the coincident decline of other Western nations.

PART III

The United States in Europe

Chapter VII

SHAPING THE GRAND DESIGN

World War II marked the great divide in our relations with the rest of the world, but particularly with Europe, which for us has a priority of sentiment as well as of strategic and economic interests. Until then we had been so absorbed with the manifold tasks of creating here a democratic society, and building a vast and varied industrial economy, that relations with other nations had remained on the periphery of our preoccupations. Not that isolationism is peculiar to Americans. Other nations, less favored by geography, have also sought to withdraw into themselves, witness the "Little Englanders" in Britain. And as a matter of fact few Americans have ever advocated one-hundred-per-cent isolationism. From the earliest days of the Republic we have wanted to trade with other lands, to travel, and to share the heritage of world civilization. There is little here of the apprehensive isolationism that the Kremlin has imposed on the Russian people since World War II, prohibiting the most trivial contacts with foreigners and foreign ideas. Our isolationism, in the past, has consisted largely of hesitation to undertake political and military commitments embodied in formal alliances that would automatically "involve" us in the political quarrels of other continents and in wars precipitated by such quarrels.

It was not until World War II that we began to be aware that noninvolvement in world affairs, far from being an insurance against war, might actually endanger our security by permitting, without intervention on our part, the rise on other continents of nations that could challenge or even physically attack us. Moral considerations, among them our well-nigh automatic reflexes of wanting to help other peoples to win or regain freedom and to relieve human suffering, played an important part in altering our attitude toward the rest of the world. But so did political and strategic considerations, as we came to realize that this country, fronting on two oceans hitherto patrolled by Britain's Navy, was no longer invulnerable in an age of far-reaching weapons—among them our own wartime invention, the atomic bomb, which can be delivered by long-range planes to any point on the globe.

Since 1945, slowly, with many waverings and setbacks, but on the whole with a growing sense of direction and an increasing measure of public support, we have been developing a new policy of co-operation with other nations. Our co-operation fans out in concentric circles from our still relatively loose connection with the global framework of the United Nations and the Specialized Agencies, which is constantly threatened by regression to unilateral national action, to the closer bonds we have forged with the North Atlantic region, and the still tighter inner group we have tended to form with Britain and Canada. This policy of co-operation represents a veritable revolution. For it is based on recognition that we must work with other nations, but especially with western Europe, not only temporarily in an emergency as we did in 1917 and again in 1941–5, but permanently, in time of peace also. Under the San Francisco Charter the United States accepted the concept of peacetime co-operation with members of the United Nations—although we have departed from this course again and again when national interests appeared to demand unilateral action, as in the case of the Truman Doctrine, the Marshall Plan and the North Atlantic treaty. At times our commitments to western Europe have seemed to cut across our broader commitments to the UN; on other occasions we have tried to carry out national policies through international agencies, as in the case of Point Four. We are still in the process of shaping the grand design of our foreign policy. The over-all pattern still looks confused, many lines run counter to others, and much erasing and redrafting remain to be done.

In formulating our policy in Europe we have labored under the handicap of having to start practically from scratch as compared with older European nations, which, living side by side, had for centuries found it necessary, if not always agreeable, to develop workable relations with one another. Not that older nations have always acted wisely or have shown invariable foresight in foreign policy. The British have acquiesced in the prevailing impression that they "muddle through." While this apparent muddling is often a screen for shrewd and hardboiled bargaining, the British have barely missed catastrophe often enough to make one wonder whether they are as certain about ends and means as they appear to be in the eyes of less experienced Americans. The Russians wrap themselves in the apparently impenetrable mantle of Marxist infallibility. Yet this mantle, when rent from time to time, reveals a stubborn predisposition on the part of Soviet leaders, in spite of their often uncomfortably penetrating appraisal of the forces at work in the contemporary world, to miscalculate the attitudes even of close neighbors like Finland and Yugoslavia.

Nor are other peoples more free of contradictions than we are, or better prepared to march foward to their destiny without the bother of having to reconcile seemingly irreconcilable impulses. The British have for centuries been torn between "Little Englandism" and the drive for empire, between a deep-seated desire for insularity and an equally deep-seated interest in the universe, between their ties to overseas dominions and possessions and their concern to hold the balance of power on the European continent. The Germans have oscillated between conflicting orientations toward east and west, between peaceful technological development, at which they are peculiarly adept, and recurring thirst for militarism and expansion. The Russians have been in the ambiv-

alent position of living astride two continents, never entirely
committed to either Europe or Asia, eager to acquire the
techniques of the West, yet inwardly in revolt against Western materialism. While we make many mistakes in foreign
policy through lack of knowledge and experience, we have
one great advantage over the older nations of Europe. The
very fact that we have had to start in modern times practically
with a *tabula rasa* liberates us from the dead hand of tradition, from the frustrating attitude that "we can't do this because we have never done it before," from the weary cynicism
of many European statesmen who have been forced to look at
the same issues so long that they have become astigmatic. To
Europeans we often seem naïve and immature, or tiresomely
inclined to be "eager beavers"—and there is truth in these
strictures. Yet our inexperience has a constructive aspect: for
it gives us courage—perhaps the right term is "nerve"—to try
new, and seemingly impossible, approaches to ancient problems, just as we are more ready than Europeans to experiment
with untried techniques of production.

Our policy in Europe is still so much in the formative stage
that it would be premature to sum it up in a cut-and-dried
formula. But with the announcement in September 1949 that
an "atomic explosion" had occurred in the U.S.S.R. we
reached a milestone in our postwar foreign policy. From this
new vantage point we can look back with greater clarity on
what we have endeavored to achieve, as well as forward to the
objectives we must now seek.

The main outlines of our grand design in Europe have
been fairly clear. After Germany's "unconditional surrender"
many here thought that the danger of war and of political extremism on the continent was over, and that postwar problems of security and recovery could be peaceably settled either
in the recently organized United Nations or through negotiations between the wartime Allies. The desire to return to
peacetime tasks at home as soon as possible was uppermost in
the thoughts of the American people. Immediately after VJ-

day we drastically curtailed our political, economic, and military commitments on the continent, except for the responsibilities we had assumed during the war for joint Allied occupation of Germany and Austria. Only after we had come to the conclusion that Russia and communism directly threatened the security and economic recovery of Europe, and thus indirectly our own, did we actively reappear on the European stage in 1947. When we did so, our two main objectives, which became closely intertwined, were to "contain" Russia and communism, and to restore the economy and security of Europe. Danger seemed imminent, especially from the guerrilla war in Greece and, later from the Communist attacks on the Marshall Plan in France and Italy. We did not take time to make a thorough analysis of Europe's postwar problems, to discover whether fears of German resurgence in France and eastern Europe were justified, whether those who opposed communism on the continent were genuine supporters of our democracy or reactionaries who were taking advantage of our apprehensions.

It would not be fair to say that at the outset we held Russia and communism solely responsible for Europe's ills. Secretary of State Marshall made it clear in his Harvard speech that these ills had deep roots in Europe's past. But we operated on the oversimplified formula that if people would have enough to eat they would become immune to Communist propaganda; and we concentrated our efforts on restoration of European economy—only to discover two years later, in 1949, that Europe needed, not restoration, but far-reaching changes that its old-guard political and business leaders viewed as tantamount to revolution. By that time, however, we had established ourselves as defenders of the existing order against all attempts at change. We were thus placed in the mentally distracting position—described by some of our transatlantic critics as schizophrenia—of wanting Europe to alter its economic structure from top to bottom so that it could produce and export more, yet of feeling at the same time that proponents of change were somehow tainted by communism. Lacking an initial frame of reference, we were further confused by the circumstances under which we had returned to Europe. For at a time when we urgently needed to define our own objectives, we found it necessary to take over, at short notice, responsibilities and commitments Britain had assumed at the peak of its nineteenth-century strength—in the Mediterranean, in Greece, in Turkey, along Europe's Atlantic seaboard. In many instances we have discovered that our new world interests coincide with those of Britain, and this has caused us to take a more charitable view of the growth and practices of the British Empire than we had held in the past.

To a far greater extent than was true in the days of the Monroe Doctrine, the New World has been called in to redress the balance of the Old. With the decline of the leading nations of Europe, the United States, aided and advised by Britain, has sought, not always consciously, to establish a new balance of power. In so doing we have at many points retraced the pattern of Britain's traditional policy, one of whose major objectives in Europe was to "contain" Russia by preventing its emergence from the Baltic and the Black Sea into the Mediterranean and the Atlantic. Today American naval power, joined to that of Britain, which it now surpasses, and enhanced since Hiroshima by common possession of the atomic bomb, confronts the land power of Russia, backed by a modern air force, at some of the same strategic points where in earlier centuries Britain, either alone or aided by France and Turkey, strove to check Russia's drive to the open seas—in the North Sea, the Scandinavian region, the Mediterranean, and the Dardanelles. For its part the U.S.S.R., having emerged from World War II as a leading nation on the continent and one of the world's two superpowers, has transferred to the United States the apprehensions, suspicion, and hostility with which the Russians had traditionally viewed the British. On Russia's centuries-old attitude toward any nation that attempted to check its seaward drive has been superimposed in our time the determination of Soviet leaders to propagate communism throughout the world and bring about the collapse of capitalism, now symbolized for Moscow by the United States. This country in turn, alarmed by the Kremlin's support of Communist groups outside the U.S.S.R., has deployed great efforts to rout communism throughout the world and to foster the development of political democracy and free private enterprise on the American pattern. Thus in Europe, and more recently in Asia, the struggle for strategic bases, spheres of influence, allies, and resources, waged before 1914 between Britain and Russia, has been transformed into a struggle between the United States and the U.S.S.R.—at the same time becoming almost indistinguishably fused with a new conflict between political ideologies and economic systems in which this country is cast in the role of protagonist of the West and Russia in the role of protagonist of the East.

In this twofold wrestling of giants, in which all other nations have in some measure become involved, our actions in Europe have been inevitably affected by our attitudes toward the principal nations of the continent. In theory the United States might be expected to get along with Britain far better than with any other country. The two nations have ties of fundamental importance—not only a common language, but also a common heritage of ideas in law, in politics, in literature, and in concepts of morality. Most Americans, moreover, have been convinced by the experience of World War II that the British Isles are absolutely necessary to the security of the United States. Every strategic plan made in Washington starts out by assuming that Britain will be our loyal ally in any future war, and will again serve as a giant aircraft-carrier for American planes and as a base for either defense against attack launched from continental points or a new invasion to liberate a conquered Europe. One of the first precautions taken by this country in 1948 against possible Russian aggression was to station sixty B-29's on British soil. Yet in

1949 many Americans were not yet ready to share with Britain the secrets of atomic-bomb manufacturing processes developed since the MacMahon security law of 1947, in spite of the fact that British scientists had shared in the wartime research work that resulted in the invention of the bomb. By one of the most interesting transformations in history, the descendants of the American colonists who nearly two hundred years ago challenged Britain's domination have now fallen heir to many of its world undertakings, and through the harsh experience of two world wars have discovered the extent to which the destinies of the two peoples are intimately intertwined. Today relations between Americans and British come close to the "fraternal association" advocated by Winston Churchill at Fulton, Missouri, in 1946.

Yet there remain a number of elements in Anglo-American relations which are apt to create friction in seemingly unexpected ways, recurrently causing surprise in both the United States and Britain.

Both we and the British tend to forget, until some issue like the partition of Palestine or the disposal of Italy's African colonies brings it back to our minds, how subtle but far-reaching is the influence still exercised here by anti-British sentiment that can be traced to the revolt of the American colonies. Moreover, the Irish, who play an important role in the political life of some of our large cities, particularly Boston and New York, nurture here their old grudges against Britain for maintaining the partition of Ireland. And many Zionists continue to resent Britain's opposition to partition of Palestine and its arms aid to the Arabs.

In one sense, the American Revolution was the revolt of a group that in current terminology could be described as *petit bourgeois*—the Puritans and other middle-class immigrants—against what they regarded as the yoke of the British monarchy and aristocracy. This aspect of social revolt can still be seen in the revulsion of American opinion against monarchy—for example, in present-day Greece—although most

Americans see no inconsistency in displaying at the same time an avid and friendly interest in the private life of the British royal family.

The American rebellion against Britain's colonial rule has deeply affected our attitude toward colonialism in general. In the grimmest moments of World War II, when Britain's very existence was at stake, Americans were apt to ask: "And after the war what will happen to India? What will Britain do about Palestine? Must we help Britain if, when the war is over, it simply reverts to its traditional colonial policy?" The decision of the British Labour government in 1947 to grant independence to India and Pakistan was warmly applauded in the United States, even after we had begun to realize that the freeing of these Asian nations would probably raise as many problems as it had seemed to solve.

Our ingrained anticolonialism has proved difficult for many Britishers—especially Tories—to understand. The British, deeply convinced that their colonial administration in Asia and Africa can be credited with genuine accomplishments, are amazed to find that most of us brush aside these accomplishments, fastening instead on faults and failures. The British regard this attitude of ours as either naïve ignorance or willful blindness to the issues at stake, with tragic consequences in either case for the white man, who is no longer encouraged to carry the burden of developing backward areas. By contrast, those Britishers—particularly among Labourites—who have shared the American desire to see colonialism brought to an end as soon as possible through the grant of independence to dependent peoples have viewed with some concern the proclamation of President Truman's Point Four about technical assistance to underdeveloped countries, fearing that it might prove to be old-fashioned imperialism in newfangled garb.

In essence the American Revolution held the seeds of future dissolution of all colonial rule, and was so interpreted by some contemporary observers, among them the French philosopher Turgot, who wrote at the time: "I firmly believe that all the metropolitan countries will be compelled to abandon all command of their colonies, to allow them a complete freedom of commerce with all nations, to be content to share this freedom with the others and to preserve with their colonies only the bonds of friendship and fraternity"—a description that admirably fits Britain's present relationship with India. Since World War II the United States has given concrete proof of its own reluctance to perpetuate colonial domination by granting independence to the Phillippines, as promised, in 1946. Applauding Britain's conduct in India, this country has more recently addressed its anticolonial strictures to other Western nations that sought to prolong the colonial system—France in Indo-China, and the Netherlands in Indonesia.

Many of us understand more clearly today than in the past that the European colonial powers need the economic resources of their colonies, if only to fulfill the Marshall Plan; and we see better now than in 1939 that some colonial peoples, for example the Burmese, are probably not fully prepared to assume the responsibilities of independence. Yet by and large the American public is convinced that the events of the postwar period have incontrovertibly demonstrated the urgent necessity of liberating colonial peoples as rapidly as possible, not only so that they may gain the political experience they lack and might otherwise seek by force, but also in order to prevent the U.S.S.R. from winning an easy propaganda victory against the West. Particularly repugnant to Americans is the prospect, occasionally suggested by the colonial powers, that the United States might send troops to suppress colonial unrest in Malaya, Indo-China, or Indonesia, or furnish weapons to the armed forces of the Western nations for this purpose, perhaps under the North Atlantic Treaty. European requests for arms to be used in the colonies have been refused by Washington—except in Indo-China.

American anticolonial sentiment does not lack economic

undertones. There has been a strong conviction here that political independence will bring in colonial areas a release of productive energies comparable to that of the nineteenth century in the United States, although usually little thought is given to the vast differences that exist between the resources and skills, say, of southeast Asia and those of the American continent. Some of our European critics are apt to think that the United States is interested in termination of colonial monopolies solely because it hopes to find new markets for American products. It would be a mistake, however, to underestimate the fundamentally philanthropic, if oversimplified and overoptimistic, desire of many Americans to see backward peoples attain a higher standard of living.

European observers, on occasion, wryly point out what they regard as similarities between the outlook of the United States on colonial problems and that of the U.S.S.R. Actually the Soviet government, which in 1917 denounced Czarist unequal treaties with China and Iran and aligned Russia on the side of colonial peoples against "imperialist exploitation," has since World War II resorted in neighboring countries to many "imperialist" practices for which we once criticized the Western colonial powers—even to the extent of modeling its 51–49 per cent of shares accords with Hungary and Rumania on the oil-development agreement of the Anglo-Iranian Oil Company with Iran. Yet it is one of the paradoxes of American-Russian relations that in the colonial sphere Washington, in theory, is far more in accord with Moscow than with Paris or The Hague.

Here, however, the United States finds itself in a dilemma. Either it must remain faithful to its anticolonial tradition, in the hope of winning a moral and propagandist victory over Russia, but at the risk of losing the friendship of the Western colonial nations, whose economic and military assistance is essential for us in case of war with Moscow; or it must align itself with the colonial powers, in the hope of gaining their loyal assistance against Russia in Europe, but at the risk of losing the game to communism in Asia. This dilemma is not limited to Americans. All Western nations possessing colonies are faced by a profound division of opinion between those who for economic and strategic reasons, or from a desire to salvage vested interests, want at least to prolong, if not indefinitely maintain, the colonial system, and those who for humanitarian, political, and ideological reasons insist on termination of this system, or at least its modification by such measures as the transfer of some backward areas unprepared for independence to the Trusteeship Council of the United Nations.

People unfamiliar with American thought might jump to the conclusion that opposition here to British monarchy and colonialism would create genuine enthusiasm for the British Labour Party. This, as we know, did not prove to be so. On the contrary, the program of nationalization and social services introduced by the Labour government was widely criticized in the United States. Most of us are still little aware of the degree of socialization that exists here—for example, our system of public schools and universities, and more recent developments like the Tennessee Valley Authority. Moreover, American critics of the Labour government usually overlook the historical development of British democracy, the decline of competition among British industries, with the growth of cartels, the consolidation of the trade unions, the insignificant part played by Communists, and the extent to which the younger Conservatives have accepted the basic premises of the Labour government's program. Events in both Britain and the United States during 1949, however, have moderated some of the harsh judgments earlier pronounced here on the Labour government. Once the American public has become accustomed to viewing British socialism in the context of Britain's special conditions, which are vastly different from our own, we may be able to throw off the fear still prevailing in some circles that the British example may lead us down the primrose path toward totalitarianism. We shall then be able to benefit by the adjustments of democracy to industrializa-

tion that the British have effected with their customary sense
of proportion and respect for individual liberties, just as
Britain, in the reorganization of its production, may benefit
by our technological achievements. When that stage of mutual accommodation has been reached, the United States and
Britain may enter on an era of exceptionally harmonious relations, for one of the cardinal differences between us—the
difference about colonialism—would have meanwhile been
relegated to the archives.

But, admitting that the interests of the United States parallel those of Britain at many points, is it accurate to say that
they are identical, and should we act as if they were? On this
issue there is among us a considerable division of opinion.
Some Americans who for the first time are reading the memoirs of Lord Palmerston think that Washington must start its
role as a world power at the exact point where the British
Empire laid down the "white man's burden." Others contend that this country risks dissipating the goodwill it had
previously gained among colonial peoples if it plays too rigidly the exact role of the British Empire and, without careful
study of American objectives, becomes involved in the traditional conflict for power between Britain and Russia.

The first group would be inclined to follow Churchill and
accept integrally his Fulton, Missouri, concept of "fraternal
association." They would like to see a close "union now" between the United States and Britain—a union that might then
serve as the nucleus of a world organization from which Russia would be excluded or would exclude itself. The second
group insists that the American government should examine
each problem *de novo,* not in the light of the experience, good
or bad, of the British, even if through this process of examin-
ation it would arrive at the same conclusions as Britain. They
point to the divergences that have already appeared between
the United States and Britain in some of Europe's trouble
spots—in Italy and in Greece, not to speak of the Middle East.

Our preoccupation with Russia has caused us to work more

closely and more uncritically with Britain in the Mediterranean, in eastern Europe, and in the Middle East than we
might have done under different circumstances. This co-
operation has confronted us with a new set of problems. For
the Labour government, progressive as it is at home, has not
yet shed the traditional faintly contemptuous attitude of the
Foreign Office toward "backward" peoples in Europe, not to
speak of other continents. Unless we can gracefully dissociate
ourselves from this heritage by positive demonstrations of our
concern for the welfare of areas outside western Europe, then
the resentment aroused over the years by the British may
prove a heavy liability to us when we undertake to improve
our relations with Russia or to bolster our influence in Asia.
Moreover, by linking our course to that of the British in an
approximation of "union now with Britain" we have risked
losing the confidence and support of the continental nations,
particularly France, which strongly doubt Britain's willingness to participate in any form of European union. Paradoxical as it may seem, these doubts have been reinforced by the
attitude of the Labour Party, which has proved more
provincial-minded than the Conservatives and has concentrated on a national program of socialism instead of fostering
international, or at least regional European, action. We shall
have to steer a firm course between Britain and the continent
if we are not to alienate the continental nations, especially
in the economic sphere, where, some of them feel, we have
repeatedly given the advantage to the British.

The transfer of world responsibility in politics and strategy
from Britain to the United States has been complicated, and
in 1949 was overshadowed, by problems of international trade
and finance. Britain is gravely but by no means fatally weakened by the material losses of two world wars and the obsolescence of its production facilities. Yet it remains our principal
competitor in world markets, at least during the temporary
eclipse of Germany and Japan. We thus find ourselves in the
schizophrenic condition of insisting that Britain increase its

production and exports so as to become less dependent on us, and at the same time worrying about the competition of British products. The fundamental economic readjustments both Britain and the United States must undertake have already been discussed in Chapter 4. Our joint success in effecting the change-over in our respective roles—with the British accepting the role of debtor and we the role of creditor nation—and the atmosphere of mutual understanding that can be developed in the course of this delicate operation, which is bound to affect many vested interests on both sides of the Atlantic, will more than any other developments determine the future course of Anglo-American relations.

The attitude of most Americans toward France is at the other pole from their attitude toward Britain. In contrast with the hostility aroused here by the revolt against English colonial rule, we take pleasure in recalling France's friendship in the critical days of 1776. The name of Lafayette, invoked at all ceremonies commemorating Franco-American friendship, symbolizes the singularly favorable auspices under which relations were established between one of the most ancient nations of Europe, then seemingly a stronghold of feudal monarchy, and the new American Republic, born of revolution. The French Revolution frightened many Americans, but the antimonarchism of France, corresponding to the antimonarchism of the young Republic, the historical coincidence of the two revolutions, and their interpretation across the Atlantic by such eloquent spokesmen as Thomas Jefferson and Benjamin Franklin created a remarkable rapprochement between two revolutionary nations in a world that remained conservative. It is interesting to recall today that when Tom Paine visited France he proclaimed himself a standard-bearer of "world revolution." This ideological rapprochement, if one may use a modern term, has remained at the basis of Franco-American relations even in periods of serious divergences such as we have experienced during and since World War II.

The affinity of ideas between the United States and France has been further strengthened by the profound and sincere admiration of Americans for French culture and French *esprit*. Several generations of Americans—and not merely expatriates who found themselves more at home on the Left Bank than in what they regarded as the raw life of "uncultured" American cities—have felt intoxicated by the potent distillation of French thought and arts. In France Americans have discovered nonmaterial values that until recently had been lacking in a young nation preoccupied to the exclusion of practically all other interests by the concrete problems of opening up, industrializing, and peopling a continent.

Yet while admiring France's beauty and spiritual qualities, many Americans deplore its material backwardness. They point to the lack of hygiene, of concern for social welfare, of large-scale industrial equipment, of up-to-date technological training. In these respects France seems to Americans sadly inefficient as compared with Germany. Can France, it is asked, even with the aid of the ERP and the fulfillment of the Monnet plan, hope to compete effectively with Germany? Will France modify its way of life, based on the craftsmanship of individual artisans and the output of small farms, and accept the advantages, as well as the vicissitudes, of mass production? Or must the United States indefinitely keep German industrial output at a level sufficiently low to prevent it from threatening the economy, if not the security, of France? American critics fail to note that the very fact that France, unlike some of the other nations of western Europe, had not hitherto become heavily industrialized now redounds to its benefit; for today it has the good fortune of possessing an economy well balanced between industry and agriculture and, unlike Britain and the West German state, is at least capable of feeding its population. Moreover, Americans seldom realize that France has a substantial modern industry, especially in steel and automobiles, or that the French, according to ECA labor experts, are actually more ready to adopt new techniques and use modern equipment, on farms as well as in factories, than the seemingly more advanced British and Germans. And, paradoxically, even those Americans who would like to see France increase its industrialization would be the first to deplore any deflowering of French culture, which has drawn much of its strength and savor from a diversified economy and a democratic social system.

Just as Americans have found it difficult to understand the character of the French, so they have felt at a loss to estimate the role France might play in the contemporary world. There is always a time-lag in the judgments nations make about one another. We have continued to think of France as the nation of Louis XIV, of Napoleon, or at least of 1914 and the "miracle of Verdun." The great contribution the French made to the Allied victory in World War I encouraged the illusion here that France had retained the international position it commanded in its periods of military glory, without considering the terrible cost it had paid for victory; and its rapid defeat in 1940 shocked the United States. American opinion, always mercurial, reversed itself overnight. Having expected, for no concrete reason, that France would vigorously resist the Germans (although we ourselves were then neither ready nor willing to help the French), on the morrow of France's defeat we jumped to the other extreme and decided that France was finished and should be written off as a decisive factor in world affairs. In a period when the power of a nation is measured by its industrial resources, France, it seemed in the United States, had been reduced to a secondary position in which it would no longer be able to defend itself unaided against any enemy nation possessing industrial equipment—whether Germany or Russia—and would henceforth depend on this country for its defense.

This contemptuous attitude, not unlike the attitude of Stalin, who at Yalta in 1945 refused to have France admitted to the negotiations of the great powers because of its lack of military strength and the paucity of its contribution to Germany's defeat, was at least as responsible for the disregard shown toward General de Gaulle as the fear, expressed by President Roosevelt and others, that the general was a potential dictator. At the same time France's demonstrated weakness made it less vulnerable to our anticolonial criticism, and leading American colonial experts like the late Raymond L. Buell have contended that French administration in Africa (although not in Indo-China) is in some respects superior to that of the other colonial powers. Another favorable result of France's relatively modest degree of industrialization is that French manufactures do not seriously compete with American exports. Franco-American relations, therefore, are not threatened, for the time being at least, by economic friction. On the contrary, the luxury products of French craftsmen have found a ready market in the United States, the only important market for "nonessentials" left in the world.

The paradox of relations between the United States and France is that Washington, while convinced that France is industrially too weak to resist aggression without our assistance, has found it difficult to understand the preoccupation of the French with the problem of security in Europe. During the interwar years, when Americans imagined that Germany had been defeated once and for all and felt great pity for "the poor Germans," this French preoccupation, voiced by Clemenceau and Poincaré, was regarded by many of us as an unhealthy obsession unjustified by reality. Even after the grueling experience of World War II the United States, to the amazement of the French, returned to the idea that this time, beyond the shadow of a doubt, German war potential had been shattered and Germany's capacity for destroying others had been neutralized. Whenever French spokesmen voiced doubts on this score, Washington pointed to German factories shattered or damaged by precision bombing.

What many Americans fail to grasp is that even after two smashing military defeats and vast material destruction the Germans have retained two important advantages over

France and other countries of Europe with the single exception of the U.S.S.R.: Germany still has the largest population
on the continent, a population containing an exceptionally
high number of young men and women capable of raising
large families; and the Germans possess technical *know-how*
to a degree unmatched in France and in other continental
countries except Belgium and Sweden. And when we speak
of *know-how,* it should be noted that in this respect Germany
is probably fifty years ahead of its only conceivable competitor
on the continent, the U.S.S.R. This means that even if France
could, in the future, renew the alliance it made with Russia
after the consolidation of the German Empire under Bismarck and Wilhelm II to check the possible military resurgence of Germany, such an alliance would not relieve France
of its anxiety about German industrial might. The French
would still face the problem of reorganizing their economy
so as to attain a level of technical development comparable to
that of Germany. Biology and technology thus combine to
perpetuate French fear of German nationalism and militarism—a fear that French Foreign Minister Robert Schuman
has tried to alleviate by close co-operation with the United
States and Britain, but which is constantly fanned at one extreme by General de Gaulle, who urges the French not to depend on outside military aid and to build up their own armed
forces, and at the other by the Communists, who contend that
only a Germany friendly to Russia can be safe for France.

The French have been disturbed since the war by what
they regard as a troubling ambiguity in American policy toward Germany. They have watched, with mounting anxiety,
the rebuilding of western German economy under American
direction and with strong transfusions of American funds.
When we tell the French that this reconstruction is necessary
to improve the economic situation of the rest of Europe, their
answer is that they have no more desire than we do to starve
the Germans or to deprive them of employment. On the contrary, the French realize just as well as we that an impover-

ished and discontented German nation would be a cancer constantly threatening Europe's body politic. They insist, however, on knowing what the Germans will do with their industrial machine once it has been reconstructed. Will they operate it peacefully, for their own benefit and that of Europe, as hoped by the United States, or will they turn it against their neighbors, as happened three times in the memory of one French generation? Being thrifty themselves, the French listen with genuine sympathy to our plea that the German economy must be rebuilt so as to ease the burdens of the American taxpayer. But, like the Chinese and the Filipinos when confronted with a similar argument about the need to rehabilitate the economy of Japan, the French ask whether, in the long run, it would cost the American taxpayer less to keep paying for food and raw materials imported by Germany than to foot the bill for another war.

It often surprises Americans to discover that the French, who have had to endure three German invasions, are still more fearful of Germany than of Russia, which invaded France only once, in 1814, when Russian soldiers reached Paris as part of the coalition that defeated Napoleon, and Czar Alexander I became a prime mover in the making of the Peace of Vienna. In French opinion, the real danger presented by Russia is not that of war, but of internal unrest and upheaval stirred up by native Communists; and against that danger military weapons, including the atomic bomb, will prove powerless. Only improved economic and social conditions assuring a measure of political stability will eventually check the influence of communism, say the French. In their view, preparation for war, involving diversion of manpower and material resources to the creation and supply of armed forces, would jeopardize democracy instead of assuring its salvation.

Through this process of reasoning the French have arrived at the conclusion that they cannot hope to attain security by military preparedness. This conclusion is sharpened by their unwillingness to participate in any future war. The French contend that they have had enough of being bled white every thirty years or so, and no longer want their country to serve as a battlefield. Again and again one hears Frenchmen who will have no truck with communism say: "You will not see us rushing again to defend our frontiers," and "We are tired of being liberated." This, in a sense, is an admission of France's industrial and military inability to sustain another major conflict. But it is also more deeply the expression of the prevailing sentiment in Europe that wars settle nothing and that therefore other exits must be found out of current crises.

As a result, the North Atlantic Pact did not arouse the enthusiasm among the French that we might have expected. Had this pact been consummated in 1919, when France desperately desired a guarantee from Britain and the United States against German resurgence, its reception would have been very different; and the mere existence of such a guarantee might have changed the course of history in Europe. But much water has flowed under many bridges since 1919. In 1949 the French welcomed the assurance that the United States considers it has a permanent stake in the security of western Europe and will aid any country that becomes the victim of aggression. Like other Europeans, however, the French have grown wary of pledges unless they can see them implemented. They want the United States to cross its "t's" and dot its "i's" before they rejoice. They know, better than we do, the weakness and lack of equipment of their own armed forces and the extent to which their economy is already being drained by the maintenance of 150,000 troops in Indo-China to fight the guerrilla forces of the Viet-Minh leader Ho Chi-minh. Nor were the French reassured by reports that some of our military leaders had counseled the inclusion in the North Atlantic Pact of Spain, and of armed forces recruited in Germany.

But if preparation for military defense against aggression

by Germany or Russia is not viewed with hope in France, what other method might be tried to relieve the tension in Europe? With little fanfare, the French have done more thinking than they are given credit for in the United States about the possibility of organizing a federation of Europe, in which the West German state would be integrated. Aristide Briand's vision of a United States of Europe lives again in the thoughts of many Frenchmen, who see in it both a genuine safeguard of France's security and an opportunity for France to resume a role of greatness as the nucleus and animating spirit of such a federation. Foreign Minister Robert Schuman has discreetly explored at unpublicized gatherings of representatives of the two recently warring nations the possibilities of rapprochement between French and Germans within the framework of a European federation. What many Frenchmen would like best of all would be to see the entrance into the proposed federation of separate German states, for the hope lingers on in France, as it did after World War I, that some of the German states, particularly Bavaria, would, if left to their own devices, work much more closely with France than a centralized unified German Reich. This hope, however, seems as obsolete as the desire of French supporters of the *ancien régime* for restoration of the monarchy.

On what general bases could a European federation such as that envisaged by France be founded? The French are convinced that Britain will never be truly interested in a European union because of its ties with the Commonwealth, yet will be reluctant to see a union formed without its participation, for fear that it might some day become a coalition inimical to Britain's traditional concept of a continental balance of power. Therefore, the French predict, the British will continue to stall on projects for European union, without, however, rejecting them outright. Hence many Frenchmen believe that France, the standard-bearer of European culture, is destined to take the leadership in a federation, with the close co-operation of Italy.

But is it possible for disparate political and economic systems such as those of France and Germany to join in a European federation? Can there be an agreement as to ends and means between France, with its coalition government left of center and its partly nationalized economy, and the West German state, whose economy remains in the hands of industrial magnates and whose government may turn out, at best, to be conservative or at worst, neo-Nazi? The French Socialists and Popular Republicans are eager to have the Bonn republic join the Council of Europe, believing that after a year of contacts with the west the Germans would throw Dr. Adenauer out of office and form a coalition, comparable to that of France, consisting of the left-wing Christian Democrats headed by Karl Arnold (corresponding to the French Popular Republicans) and the Social Democrats. Yet should co-operation between left-of-center coalitions be achieved across the Rhine, would the United States oppose it on the ground that even a modest degree of socialization might slow down Germany's recovery?

Among both French and Germans there is much talk that only some form of socialization of the resources of the Ruhr would create a sound base for European federation. German trade-union leaders contend that, once the key enterprises of coal and steel, which are also the sinews of war, have been nationalized, the French need no longer fear the use of these resources for war purposes. In France the Socialist André Philip has long urged the establishment of a Ruhr Valley Authority on which France, Germany, and other interested nations would be represented—an authority that, combining German coal and steel and French iron, could undertake a large-scale industrial development of western Europe which would constitute a new and fructifying element for the continent's economy as a whole. Such a development, in the opinion of French and Germans who have given it thought, would go far to reduce the effectiveness of Russian propaganda, which has accused the United States of simply transferring control of the Ruhr from the hands of German to

those of American capitalists. It would also give the West a
bargaining-point in future negotiations with the U.S.S.R. and
countries of eastern Europe concerning similar utilization of
the coal and other resources of the Silesian basin, now controlled by Poland, for the benefit of the entire surrounding
region. The evolution of such plans, however, depends on
the policy of the United States toward Germany.

The French, as well as many other Europeans, have been at
a loss to understand our attitude toward Germany. This is
partly due to the indelible impressions left by the Germans
on the peoples they conquered—impressions the United
States had only a limited opportunity to share in two world
wars; but more fundamentally because Europeans are baffled
by American estimates of the German nation.

It is difficult to explain to Europeans that many Americans
—often quite unconsciously—admire in the Germans the very
characteristics they find lacking in otherwise more sympathetic nations like France and Italy. We admire the German
capacity for organization and great aptitude for industrial
techniques, while recognizing that the Germans, in contrast
with the British and the French, have hitherto proved to be
singularly deficient in the talents requisite for political democracy. Many Americans who have had business dealings
with Europe also contend that the Germans have a higher
level of commercial honesty than some of their neighbors.
These two aspects—technical know-how and reputation for
honesty—cause Americans to think that Germany, speaking
strictly from the business point of view, is a better risk for
loans and private investments than, for example, France,
which, it is argued, is plagued by unstable governments and
a financial system in chronic disequilibrium.

Americans also find the Germans' cleanliness and preoccupation with hygiene wholly admirable, and feel materially
more comfortable in Germany than in France, where the
plumbing often leaves much to be desired and elevators are
inclined to be temperamental. By contrast, the French are

inclined to think that cleanliness and hygiene are not essential aspects of culture, and that the great epochs of the flowering of the human spirit, like the golden age of Greece and the Italian Renaissance, did not suffer from absence of modern conveniences. Nor is it easy for Europeans to forget that in the charnel-houses of Dachau the Germans had posted their accustomed notices proclaiming cleanliness to be a virtue. From the American point of view, however, the central fact is that, of all the countries of Europe, Germany has developed a material way of life that most closely resembles ours. True, German anti-Semitism profoundly shocked the American public; yet Americans quartered in Germany who had either open or latent anti-Semitic tendencies did not feel out of harmony with the Germans. In many respects American victors in Germany, like the Romans among the Parthians, have taken on some of the less attractive characteristics of the conquered. Perhaps the greatest shock for all thoughtful Americans familiar with American Military Government has been the discovery that the Germans are not alone in calmly assuming the omniscience of military decisions or in accepting without question the concepts and practices of authoritarianism.

Not only have Americans admired the technical achievements of the Germans, but before 1939 we had no such fear of German competition in world markets as we did of the British. On the contrary, we have found certain German products, notably dyestuffs, chemicals, and various precision instruments, very useful in our industries. In those instances where fear of competition had begun to be felt, or where American enterprises wanted to share the secret of German inventions, the mechanism of prewar cartels providing for reduction in output, maintenance of fixed prices, and opportunities for American industrialists to benefit by the special experience of German technicians, had in general served to alleviate tensions between the highly developed economies of the two great industrial nations. Since World War II the American government has brought here an unrevealed number of German scientists who have continued their work on the atomic bomb and other German secret weapons—as the U.S.S.R. had done before us—thus making it possible for American laboratories to draw on scientific advances achieved by the Germans under the Nazis.

While the war was still raging, American opinion on the future of Germany became sharply divided. One group insisted that Europe would always remain in mortal peril if Germany was allowed to retain its industrial plant and equipment. The main thesis of this group—which supported the Morgenthau plan for German deindustrialization—was that peace could be assured only if Germany was transformed from an advanced industrial nation capable of again creating a vast military potential into a pastoral nation, through the outright destruction of industries designed primarily for war purposes and the dismantling and transfer of others as reparations to countries conquered and looted by the Germans.

Others contended that the Morgenthau plan was neither fair nor susceptible of realization. Their main thesis was that the Germans, who in Hitler's day had already been too numerous for the Reich's resources and had therefore been captivated by Hitler's promise of greater *Lebensraum,* would be unable to subsist even at a very low standard of living within the postwar territorial confines of Germany unless they not merely maintained, but greatly expanded their industrial system. According to this group, the imposition by force of a pastoral way of life not only would fail to supply the minimum needs of sixty-five million Germans, but would have the effect of a time-bomb, encouraging the eventual explosion of fanatical nationalism which would prove even more violent than Nazism.

The conflict between these two American approaches toward Germany brought about a prolonged and at times bitter discussion concerning the "level of production" that should be fixed for the Germans in a peace treaty not as yet concluded. Should it be the so-called pastoral level, leaving to the Germans only a few industries necessary for the processing of agricultural products and the output of consumers' goods? Should it be the level of 1932, when Hitler was coming to power—a level that had been in considerable part subsidized by private American and British loans during the interwar years, and proved adequate for the creation by Hitler within a few years of armaments destined to conquer Europe? Or was it necessary to reorganize the German economy in such a way that production (except for the output of war weapons) would remain more or less the same as in the past, but control of production and distribution would be transferred from the German industrialists who had been Hitler's allies to the German people as a whole through nationalization of strategic raw materials like coal, and of key industries like steel? If socialization was deemed possible, was it reasonable to believe that the industrial workers and the lower middle class would prove more democratic, less militaristic, and less nationalistic than the military and industrial leaders of prewar Germany?

The controversy between the two groups was in part resolved—even before Russia had aroused our fears—early in the postwar period with the abandonment of the Morgenthau plan, which had never stirred much enthusiasm or won much support in European countries conquered by the Germans. By 1949 the main issue in the United States lay, on the one hand, between American military leaders and ECA officials who for reasons of either security or economy or both were convinced it was necessary to reconstruct German industry as rapidly as possible and, on the other hand, those Europeans and Americans who feared that German industry rebuilt without adequate safeguards might again become the instrument of a new German military clique. One of the principal tasks of American policy in Germany thus became the discovery of a formula that would make it possible for the German economy to develop to the limits of its capacities, for the benefit not only of the Germans but of Europe as a whole, and at the same time would assure Germany's neighbors that they need no longer fear an armed attack by the Reich. This country believed it had evolved the necessary formula following the breakdown in 1947 of four-power negotiations on Germany in the Council of Foreign Ministers. At that time the United States, Britain, and France agreed on a series of measures, including the organization of a West German state with its own constitution, adopted by the German Council at Bonn in May 1949; the economic unification of the three western zones; the adoption of an Allied statute governing the relations of the three Western powers with the new state; and the creation of an International Ruhr Authority, composed of American, British, French, and German representatives, whose function was to supervise and control distribution of the products of the Ruhr area, sinews of Germany's peacetime as well as wartime industry.

On the question of Germany's industrial reconstruction the difference between the United States and the U.S.S.R. has been a difference of degree and of method rather than of principle. It has sometimes been asserted here that the Kremlin was seeking to destroy the German economy, and when the U.S.S.R. began to oppose the Marshall Plan in 1947, it was commonly said that the Kremlin opposed the reconstruction of Europe in general. The discussions of the Council of Foreign Ministers do not reveal opposition by Russia to the continued existence of Germany as an industrial state. Even during the war, when the Germans deliberately destroyed the industry and agriculture of the areas they occupied in the U.S.S.R. the Kremlin refrained from urging a policy of revenge, and proposed nothing resembling a Morgenthau plan for Germany. On the contrary, the Soviet government has been intensely interested in obtaining from the Germans, as reparations, goods valued at the Big Four conference of Moscow in 1947 at ten billion dollars—not merely products of light industries, such as were available in the Russian zone of Germany, but principally capital goods from the Ruhr.

To fulfill these demands German industry would have to be reconstructed, and probably even expanded, if at the same time it were to export goods for dollars, as desired by the United States, and supply some of the needs of western European nations. If other factors did not enter into the picture, it is quite conceivable that, for different reasons, the United States and the U.S.S.R. would be in agreement on the necessity of developing German industry to its full capacity—an agreement noted with some alarm by the French. Here, however, emerged a fundamental divergence between the two countries. Until now the United States, differing on this point from Britain, has opposed socialization of the raw materials and industries of Germany, and in his famous Law No. 75 of November 11, 1948 on the Ruhr, General Clay, former American Military Governor, proposed to return these enterprises eventually to German owners, some of whom had been appointed to act as trustees for their properties. The U.S.S.R., by contrast, has insisted that the German industrialists should be deprived of their economic authority and that mines and industries in the Ruhr should be placed under workers' administration.

The problem of Germany's economic future has been inextricably linked from the outset with the problem of its future political organization. As the war drew to an end, Americans hoped that in Germany, as well as in Japan, it would prove possible in a relatively short period of time to achieve "re-education" of the population and to transform the Germans into a democratic nation. It has been difficult for us to imagine how a people so advanced in scientific knowledge and methods could have remained at so low a level of political experience and mere humanity. Refusing to accept this ambivalence in the attitude of Germans, many Americans believed that a distinction should be made between the government of Hitler on the one hand and the German people on the other, and that when the Nazis had disappeared it would become fairly easy to remake the German mentality. It was therefore a shock for us to discover after four years of occupation characterized by vigorous efforts at denazification and re-education, and before the Germans had acquired freedom to dispose of themselves, that nationalism, anti-Semitism, and revived belief in Nazi doctrines had emerged into the open. There is no doubt that Russia's 1948–9 blockade of Berlin, the activities of German Communists in the Russian zone of Germany, and the Soviet government's policy of draining the zone of economic resources in the form of reparations to the U.S.S.R. have aroused German hostility both to Russia and to communism. But it was far from clear in 1949 whether the Germans, if left to their own devices, would adopt demo-cratic practices patterned on those of the United States, Brit-ain, and France, or would hearken again to the blandishments of new demagogic leaders like Hitler, promising the ultimate triumph of the German master race through fresh resort to force.

On the issue of Germany's political structure, as on that of its economic recovery, the two great protagonists, the United States and the U.S.S.R., differ less on the ultimate objective than on the method of achieving it. On occasion it has been contended in this country that the Kremlin opposed German unification. It would be more accurate to say that both Wash-ington and Moscow have wanted the unification of Germany, provided it could be achieved on terms each would regard as acceptable. Moscow has wanted a Germany unified by a po-litical group that would be in sympathy with Russian ideas—that is, Communists or groups willing to work with the Com-munists. Washington has wanted a Germany unified by po-litical groups that would be in sympathy with American, or at least Western, ideas. As in the economic sphere, so in the sphere of politics the United States felt it was making consid-erable progress toward German unification on Western terms after it had reached agreement with Britain and France in 1948 on the creation of a West German state. The Bonn Constitution, drafted by German representatives in consultation with the military governments of the three Western powers, represented a compromise between strict centralization and a loose federation. It also conformed with Western democratic principles by providing for freedom of the person, including freedom of movement, freedom from arbitrary arrest and detention, freedom of association and assembly, freedom of speech, press, and radio, freedom of all democratic political parties and freedom of elections, and independence of the judiciary. The constitution, moreover, envisaged increasing scope for Germany to associate peacefully in economic and political but not military fields with Europe and with international agencies. The Paris conference of the Council of Foreign Ministers in May 1949 reached no decision on German unification, and a West German state was established following the elections of August 14, 1949.

What kind of leaders will free Germans bring to power in the West German state? This key question cannot be answered adequately today any more than after 1919. Is it true that the Western Allies of World War I, because of their fear of Bolshevism, nipped in the bud the revolution that seemed in the making following the Kaiser's downfall, and thus left the Germans in a state of arrested political development that made them peculiarly susceptible to Nazi doctrines? What assurance is there that the Bonn Constitution will prove more of a safeguard against extremism than that of Weimar? Is democracy a matter of constitutions, or does it grow out of a conscious struggle for liberty such as characterized the English Revolution of 1688, the French Revolution of 1789, and the American Revolution—the kind of struggle that has been notably absent from the history of the German people? Which of the existing political groups in Germany is genuinely in sympathy with Western ideas? The Christian Democrats? The Social Democrats? Can there be political democracy in Germany if economic control remains in the hands of a small group of industrialists who are under no obligation to give any accounting of their activities to the representatives of the German people?

The answers to these questions will determine, in the long run, the role the United States can effectively play in Germany. For the time being, this country holds strong cards, for the Germans urgently need American financial aid under the Marshall Plan to reconstruct their industries. Once reconstruction has been achieved, however, and the Marshall Plan comes to an end, West German industries will have to find markets for their products if Germany is to be able to purchase abroad the food and raw materials it needs. Can Germany find adequate markets in the United States? Or will it have to turn again, as it did after World War I, to eastern Europe and the Balkans, where during the inter-war years it sold between 12 and 16 per cent of its exports, importing in return food, raw materials, and timber? Will German industrialists then follow the example of Walther Rathenau and arrange another Rapallo deal with Russia? Will they, like the German military leaders who in 1939 persuaded Hitler much against his will to conclude the German-Russian nonaggression pact find it possible to strike a new bargain safeguarding Germany in the east and return to their dreams of establishing a German industrial empire on the continent? Whatever may be the answers to these questions, it has become increasingly clear that dissensions among the Allies have strengthened the bargaining position of the Germans, who are now again able to play west and east against each other. It should be no cause for surprise if Germany, like the legendary phœnix, should emerge once more from the ashes of war as the only real victor in Europe.

During the postwar period, however, Russia, not Germany, has loomed most important, and relations between the United States and the U.S.S.R. have become the focal point not only of Washington's foreign policy, but also of all international discussions. The axis United States-U.S.S.R. acts as a magnet drawing to it all the forces, the anxieties, and the hopes of the world.

Since the United States had few contacts with the Russian Empire, American-Russian relations from the birth of the American Republic to the Bolshevik Revolution of 1917 were relatively colorless. When the new American government sent its first Ambassador, John Francis Dana, to the court of Catherine the Great in St. Petersburg, the position of the two countries was exactly the reverse of what it has become in our times. Then it was America that had emerged from revolution, while Russia was a bulwark of the *status quo*. While Catherine had been interested in the iconoclastic ideas of Voltaire, republicanism in practice represented a threat to Russian totalitarianism of that period; and the American Ambassador was forced to return home empty-handed, without being received by the Empress.

Even after the young Republic had been recognized and diplomatic relations had been established, difficult moments arose between the two countries, separated though they were in terms of geography. It is often forgotten that the Monroe Doctrine was proclaimed in 1823 partly at least to warn Czar Alexander I that the Holy Alliance, of which he was the principal architect, could not intervene in the affairs of the republics of the Western Hemisphere, then closely linked to Spain, without meeting determined opposition on our part. Historians of the future may see in the Monroe Doctrine a precursor of the Truman Doctrine, inaugurating a policy of "containment" of Russia within the geographic limits then accessible to the United States, but subsequently reaching farther and farther out with the spread of American interests, influence, and power.

Approximately at the same time Americans became alarmed over the voyages of Russian explorers and fur-hunters who visited our west coast, some of them settling there, as one can still see today in some communities of the San Francisco area inhabited by descendants of Russian settlers. Russia, however, was then so little interested in the possibility of territorial expansion in the New World that in 1867 it sold Alaska for five million dollars to the United States, which, for its part, was so indifferent to the potentialities of this now highly strategic area that the purchase, transacted by Secretary of State Seward, became known as "Seward's Folly".

By contrast to these uneasy moments, Americans felt grateful to Russia during the Civil War when, at a critical moment in 1861, Russian naval vessels appeared at the port of New York. Unpleasant as it is to destroy a legend, it must be noted that this gesture was inspired not by Russia's desire to help the North against Britain, but by its fear that the British, who had expressed great sympathy for the Poles then in revolt against Russian rule, might attempt to seize these vessels if they remained on the high seas.

Toward the end of the century clouds again appeared on the horizon when the United States, in the 1890's, strongly protested against the Jewish pogroms staged by the Czarist government—protests comparable to those Washington has made in our time against acts of repression committed by Moscow and by Communist regimes in the countries of eastern Europe. And, just as the Monroe Doctrine had been inspired by Russian actions, so another famous doctrine, the policy of the Open Door in China, proclaimed by Secretary of State Hay in 1899, was directed primarily against Russia, whose infiltration into Manchuria, to use a modern term, was believed to be threatening American trade interests.

In fact, the United States was becoming increasingly perturbed over the expansion in Asia of Czarist Russia, which at the end of the Sino-Japanese War of 1896, disastrous for China, had intervened on China's side and, in return had obtained concessions in Manchuria and at the ports of Port Arthur and Dairen—again developments that have had parallels in our time. The United States was therefore not displeased when Japan, in 1904, delivered a sneak attack on

Russia at Port Arthur—as the Russians no doubt recall today, now that we are in control of Japan. President Theodore Roosevelt encouraged the Japanese until it appeared that Japan was winning its war against Russia with alarming ease, and then offered his good offices to arrange the Treaty of Portsmouth of 1905, by which Russia lost most of the advantages it had acquired after 1896, among them its leaseholds at Port Arthur and Dairen. In Russia the crushing defeat inflicted by Japan crystallized popular dissatisfaction with the Czarist government, precipitating the revolution of 1905, which forced the Czar to grant a limited form of parliamentary government. It also set the stage for the more profound convulsions of March and November 1917, brought about by Russia's military rout at the hands of Imperial Germany. One of the first acts of the Soviet government that issued from the Bolshevik Revolution was to repudiate all unequal treaties concluded by the Czars, notably with China. But twenty-eight years later, at Yalta, Stalin, who had combined Russian nationalism with the doctrine of international communism, returned to the course set by the Czars and demanded, as the price of aiding China in the war against Japan, support by Britain and the United States for Russia's claims to special rights in Manchuria, Dairen, and Port Arthur.

It is from the Revolutionary period of 1917 that one must date the beginning of fundamental controversies between the United States and Russia which have cast an ever darkening shadow on all areas of the globe where the two nations claim interests; and, since they emerged out of World War II as the two remaining great powers, this means over the entire globe. The United States rejoiced at the fall of Czarism, believing that it would bring about in Russia a democratic system comparable to that of advanced nations of the West. Few Americans were then aware not only that Russia in 1917 was an economically underdeveloped country, still in the early stages of industrialization, exporting grain and raw materials like oil in exchange for manufactured goods it had no facilities to produce, but also that the Russians had remained outside the main stream of western Europe's historical development. Unfamiliar with Russia's history, and intent on comparing Russia with the West instead of trying to evaluate it in terms of its particular experience, Americans felt deeply disillusioned by the weakness of Russia's handful of politically inexperienced liberals, the Soviet "dictatorship of the proletariat," the ruthlessness of the agrarian collectivization, and the political purges of the 1930's. This disillusionment, which more adequate information might have averted or at least placed in perspective, has continued to color the attitude of the American people with respect to the U.S.S.R. Moscow, for its part, has done little to alleviate American fears and suspicions, persisting in its own conviction that the United States, as the last bastion of capitalism and imperialism, will sooner or later seek to destroy the "socialist fatherland" of workers and peasants. This mutual distrust, which on both sides has at times threatened to assume the proportions of hysteria, has been aggravated by several factors.

In the early days of the Bolshevik Revolution, and for a decade after—until the inhumanities of the Soviet collectivization campaign shocked American opinion—a number of Americans were greatly impressed by events in Russia, communicating their enthusiasm to the American public. John Reed wrote lyrically about "Ten Days That Shook the World." William C. Bullitt, now a vigorous denouncer of the Soviet system, saw hope and promise in it when, as a young man, he visited Russia in 1919 to report to President Wilson and the Paris Peace Conference. A long list of experienced observers and literary figures, from Walter Duranty and Louis Fischer to Vincent Sheean and André Gide, sought in still primitive Russia answers to all the problems of modern industrial civilization, hoping that the U.S.S.R. would prove synonymous with Utopia. In the retrospect of history this search may appear due far less to false promises held out by the Russians than to a form of escapism on the part of Western intellectuals disheartened by the less attractive features of industrial society—an escapism that has reasserted itself in the period after World War II when some of those who felt let down by Russia turned for inspiration and consolation to India, counterposing the non-violence and passive resistance of Gandhi to the violence and assertiveness of Stalin.

When it turned out that Russia was not Utopia and could offer few answers to the problems of the industrial West— although it may well have some answers for the problems of still more backward countries in Asia—these journalists, most of whom knew little or nothing of Russia's pre-Revolutionary conditions, its history or its language, became disillusioned, and communicated their deception to the same readers in the United States whom they had previously assured that all was for the best in the best of Russian worlds. Other Americans, who had become admirers of Trotsky as the apostle of permanent world revolution and the true exponent of Leninism, bitterly denounced Stalin for what they described as his betrayal of the Bolshevik Revolution; and today it is among American Trotskyists that one finds the most implacable enemies of the U.S.S.R.

The Bolshevik Revolution, with its accent on liquidation of private property, dealt a blow to the concept of the sanctity of private enterprise, which for most Americans is intimately linked with political democracy. Few Americans in the early days of the Soviet system took the trouble to study the economic conditions of pre-Revolutionary Russia, where capitalism such as we know it in the West had been still in its infancy. The extraction of raw materials and the development of railways, electricity, and other public utilities were financed, as in Latin America and in colonial areas, not by Russian but by foreign capital—Belgian, French, German, British, and some American, Russian private financial resources being either tied up in land or invested in a few light industries, such as sugar and textiles. The Communist attack on capitalism in Russia was in essence an attack on "exploitation" of native resources by foreign capital—the kind of attack that has also been made by non-Communist nationalist leaders—for example, Perón in Argentina, as well as by non-Communist critics of foreign activities in China. It would be interesting to know whether the Soviet leaders, for their part, might not have taken a different view of the character and survival prospects of modern capitalism if they had studied the American economy, which in a number of fundamental respects differs from the capitalism of western European nations, especially as practiced before 1917 in colonial areas. The Russian Communists had derived their initial impression of capitalism from Marx's mid-nineteenth-century analysis of Britain and from Russia's early twentieth-century sweat-shop factory conditions. Without examining the situation in the United States at first hand, they lumped all forms of capitalism in one category uniformly denounced as "exploiting," "imperialist," and "war-mongering"; and these denunciations were then echoed uncritically by Communists of other countries.

So deep was the hostility aroused in the United States by the anticapitalism of the Soviet government that it has proved extremely difficult for Americans to look with any degree of objectivity at the more constructive aspects of economic programs not only in the U.S.S.R. but also in countries governed since World War II by Communist regimes—Poland, Czechoslovakia, Hungary, and Yugoslavia (until Tito defied Stalin). While Soviet spokesmen have persisted in believing that American capitalism is set in an unalterable mold and is bound to crack under the impact of another great depression, Americans have become almost as rigid in assuming that the Soviet system is monolithic and inflexible and can never succeed in improving the standard of living. (What most American critics usually mean is that the Soviet system cannot offer a standard of living comparable to that of the United States, which is quite different from saying that it may not provide a rising standard of living in terms of Russia's past conditions.) If both nations continue to wear blinders when looking at each other, it is quite possible that each has a surprise in store when it discovers that the other not only has survived, but may be entirely capable of further growth, adaptation to changed conditions, and improvement in years to come.

Americans were also shocked by the antireligious policy of the Soviet government, especially by its brutal mockery of religion in antireligious museums. It is not so much that we are all profoundly religious, but we feel that the state should respect all organized religions, and assure the freedom of its citizens to believe what they want, or not to believe at all. This aspect of the Soviet system has particularly disturbed the Catholic Church (although there are few Roman Catholics in the U.S.S.R.) because of the effect the Russian antireligious campaign might have, and in fact has had since World War II, in predominantly Catholic countries subjected to Communist rule.

So strong has been the feeling aroused by the Soviet government's attitude toward religion that it has proved difficult for Americans to evaluate the pre-1917 problems arising from the special position of the Russian Orthodox Church. In keeping with the Byzantine concept of close relations between religious and lay authorities, that Church had been an instrument of Czarism, not an independent body, and had supported the Czars in their opposition to expansion of education, fearing with good reason that education unaccompanied by reforms would encourage political rebellion. The Church, like the monarchy, was one of the great owners of land at a time when Russian peasants, emancipated in 1861 but in considerable part still land-hungry, were susceptible to Communist promises of "land, bread, and peace." And in contrast with the organized churches of advanced Western nations, the Orthodox Church had displayed little interest or concern for the social conditions of the masses.

The establishment of diplomatic relations between the United States and the U.S.S.R. in 1933 after a lapse of sixteen years did not materially affect the conflict of ideas between the two countries. Recognition was due primarily to a desire on the part of American business men to trade with Russia, as Britain and Germany had been doing since the 1920's, and determination on the part of Washington to counterbalance Japan's rising power on the Asiatic mainland. Recognition, however, left unaltered the various currents of anti-Soviet sentiment here; and the Kremlin, on its side, by continuing its propaganda for world revolution and the downfall of capitalism, did little to encourage the friendship of the United States. The conclusion of the Russo-German pact in 1939 proved another great shock for the American public—although there is no evidence that the United States would have been either willing or able to defend the U.S.S.R. against Germany had Hitler, as Soviet leaders firmly believed, decided to invade Russia at that time, when the Russians felt ill-prepared to resist. Without analyzing possible motives for the Kremlin's actions, most Americans had expected that Russia would oppose Hitler in eastern Europe, even at the cost of German invasion and even if the western nations of Europe were interested in a military arrangement with Russia only for their own protection and merely hoped to divert Hitler to the east. Moreover, the attitude of Communists in all countries, who in the early stages of the war opposed British and French resistance to Germany and denounced the "imperialism" of the Western powers, created in the United States, as in Europe, deep suspicions about the motives of the Kremlin.

All this, however, changed from one day to the next with the German invasion of the U.S.S.R on June 22, 1941. The United States was not yet formally engaged in the world conflict, but already considered Russia as an ally—at least an ally of Britain, to whom American aid was being given in increasing measure. The heroic resistance of the Russians, especially at Stalingrad, and the very fact that so backward a country as

Russia could defend itself successfully against an advanced industrial nation like Germany, made a powerful impression in the United States, where some experts had predicted that "the Germans would go through Russia like a knife through butter." Jumping from one extreme to another, we tried to convince ourselves that the very fact of fighting together against a common enemy would change Russia from top to bottom and that the war would create a durable basis of cooperation between the United States and the U.S.S.R. This was the great dream of President Roosevelt—a dream he hoped to realize by organizing the United Nations with the aid of Russia before the end of hostilities. At the conferences of Teheran and Yalta Roosevelt labored to lay the groundwork for what he hoped would be a fundamental and lasting accord.

Since then some critics have accused Roosevelt of trying to "appease" Stalin and of having, by this method, encouraged Russian expansionism. It is extremely difficult for a contemporary historian to judge with any degree of objectivity the epoch in which he lives. This, however, may be said: that during a bloody war there is usually between members of a coalition no question of "appeasement" in the sense of attempts that were made at Munich and elsewhere to achieve "peace in our time" with Hitler. The main, and most often only, objective in time of war is to keep the coalition together, at any price, for a fight to the finish against a common enemy. And in the case of the United States at Yalta, there were two enemies—Germany and Japan—both of which were also enemies of Russia. At Yalta one could hope for the defeat of Germany, although the Battle of the Bulge was still a recent and poignant memory. But President Roosevelt had to project his strategic plans beyond victory in Europe. He had to prepare for what was then foreseen as a conflict to the death with Japan. At that time, as many hindsight interpreters have since tended to forget, it was not yet known that the invention of the atomic bomb would soon be successfully completed. (Stalin was officially told about it for the first time at the Potsdam conference of July 1945 by President Truman, a month before Japan's surrender.) Although we subsequently learned that Japan was on the point of collapse before Hiroshima, when the Yalta conference met, our military chiefs, as Secretary of War Henry L. Stimson has told in his memoirs,[1] anticipated a nightmare struggle in which American soldiers would have to conquer the Japanese islands inch by inch against determined and ruthless resistance. The United States therefore sought to obtain assurances in advance that Russia would remain at our side after victory in Europe and would enter the war against Japan at the earliest possible moment. Stalin, heartened by Russia's impressive record of victories over the Germans, but aware of the drain of four years of constant warfare on Russian resources of manpower and materials, was ready to give this assurance—at a price. This price consisted of substantial concessions by China, which was not represented at Yalta and was not consulted at that time. It is entirely justifiable to argue that this price was too high, and that neither Roosevelt nor Churchill had the right to pay it at China's expense. And now that we know how close we then were to discovering the secret of atomic-bomb manufacture, it is possible to assert that the United States would not have needed Russia's aid for victory in Asia. More, Russia's intervention, which took place exactly as promised, three months after VE-day, not only was superfluous, but proved actually embarrassing to this country, and dangerous for Chiang Kai-shek, when the Russians subsequently turned over to the Chinese Communists stocks of Japanese arms they had seized in Manchuria. But whatever legitimate criticisms may be made of the Yalta decisions, these decisions must be judged in the light of the situation as it seemed at that time, not as it turned out to be.

Among the factors that had to be weighed at Yalta were the

---

[1] Henry L. Stimson and McGeorge Bundy: *On Active Service in Peace and War* (New York, Harper & Brothers; 1947).

magnitude of Russia's military achievement, which had materially altered the balance of power in Europe and Asia; the ambiguity of relations between Britain and Russia; and the strain under which President Roosevelt labored at the conference, two months before his death. It has often been contended here since the war that the Russians won only, or primarily, because of the military equipment, valued at eleven billion dollars, which they received from us under lend-lease. Some military experts, however, believe that Russia's victory was due principally to its military organization and the armaments furnished by its own factories in Siberia, many of which had been transferred there as the Germans advanced into the industrial area of the Don Basin,[1] and that while the United States furnished mobility through trucks and other motorized equipment, the Russians had to depend largely on their own airplanes, tanks, and guns. The knowledge of this accomplishment, as well as of the high cost in human lives paid for it—higher than that of any other nation arrayed against Germany, except Poland—unquestionably influenced Stalin's calculations at Yalta.

So did his doubts about the readiness of Britain to concede a special position to Russia in eastern Europe and the Balkans once the war was over. Many witnesses have testified to the mutual distrust that, in spite of official expressions of goodwill, persisted between Churchill, who in the 1920's had described the Russian Bolsheviks as a horde issuing from the ghettos of eastern Europe, and Stalin. The British, while preparing for the invasion of France, were still intent on their traditional policy of preventing Russia's emergence out of the Black Sea, and at the Teheran conference Churchill had proposed an Allied invasion of the Balkans. This proposal, in Stalin's opinion, not only was a poor substitute for an attack on Germany in the west but seemed to represent one more

---

[1] General Augustin Guillaume: *Soviet Arms and Soviet Power: the Secrets of Russia's Might,* with a foreword by Lt. Gen. Walter Bedell Smith (Washington: Infantry Journal Press; 1949).

effort by Britain to checkmate Russia in a long-disputed area —an area, too, where after prolonged discussions the Kremlin, on the eve of World War II, had succeeded in breaking up the establishment of a German sphere of influence. When Roosevelt, at Teheran, came out against a Balkan campaign, Britain began to consider the possibility of dividing the area into spheres of influence with Russia for the duration of the war. According to former Secretary of State Cordell Hull, Britain in June 1944 proposed to Russia the division, for military purposes, of eastern Europe and the Balkans into spheres of influence, Russia to control 80 per cent of Hungary and Rumania against 20 per cent for Britain, Yugoslavia being divided 50–50, and Greece assigned entirely to Britain.[1] Britain apparently had not intended to consult the United States about this mathematical apportionment of influence, but Russia insisted that Washington should be informed. Against the advice of Hull, who told British Ambassador Lord Halifax that the United States objected in principle to spheres of influence (Churchill countered this argument in a subsequent telephone conversation with President Roosevelt by contending that the United States had a sphere of influence in Latin America), Roosevelt acquiesced in Britain's proposal for a three-month period, provided that it was only a military measure; and the division was carried into effect six months before Yalta.

It would be interesting to know what Stalin thought when, during that conference, Churchill and Roosevelt insisted that Russia should undertake to hold "free unfettered elections" in countries that Britain and the United States had just acknowledged, at least for wartime purposes, to be within its sphere of influence. Whether or not Stalin at Yalta had an elaborate master-plan for the installation of Communist regimes in eastern Europe remains a matter of dispute. His policy, however, clearly reflected the interests of Russia as a

[1] Cordell Hull: *The Memoirs of Cordell Hull* (New York: The Macmillan Company; 1948), 2 volumes.

national state, interests that had been pursued a quarter of a
century before by the Czar. It is all the more surprising to
find that American negotiators, although probably not the
British, were surprised when Stalin, among other claims,
asked for the Dardanelles. It should be noted that, until the
Western powers began actively to intervene in the affairs of
eastern Europe, the Kremlin abstained from action in Greece,
and even in Italy, where Stalin, to the surprise of many Western observers, recognized the government of Marshal
Badoglio.

Whether President Roosevelt, had he been well, might
have held the balance between Churchill and Stalin at Yalta
and after as he had done previously, must remain a matter for
speculation. What we do know is that the President was then
mortally ill, and in a hurry to reach an accord with Stalin
about the war against Japan—perhaps without giving
sufficient thought to the consequences of the concessions demanded by the Russians, or possibly hoping that in time a
more favorable agreement might be worked out within the
United Nations. It is also known that before his death, in fact
almost immediately on his return from Yalta, Roosevelt began to have doubts about the possibility of co-operation with
the U.S.S.R. It is entirely conceivable that, had he lived, he
might have decided to change his tactics and inaugurated a
stiffer policy toward the Kremlin. To ask now what Roosevelt
would have done "if" this or that had happened is to raise
what he liked to call "iffy" questions. We do know that,
shortly after Harry S. Truman had succeeded to the Pres-
idency, he was persuaded by some of his military and State
Department advisers that it was necessary to adopt a "firm"
tone toward Russia and even to impress on them the strength
of American military power. And this the President did in
his first talk with Molotov, in April 1945, on the eve of the
San Francisco conference summoned, in accordance with
previous plans suggested by Roosevelt, to draft the Charter
of the United Nations.

At that conference, which got off to an inauspicious start when the United States used its influence to bring about the admission of Argentina, whose dictatorial government had been criticized by the Roosevelt administration—as Molotov was quick to remind the delegates—it immediately became clear that the halcyon period of American-Russian relations, if it had ever been more than a war-induced mirage, had come to an end. Even before VE-day it was evident to close observers that the United States and the U.S.S.R. had begun again to distrust each other's motives and ultimate objectives. It also was obvious that Britain, represented by its suave Foreign Secretary, Anthony Eden, who offered a striking contrast to Foreign Minister Molotov, blunt to the point of uncouthness, had assumed the role of "honest broker" and was attempting to strike a new balance of power, this time between the two worlds of America and Russia—or, as some less charitable observers claimed, to drive a wedge between its two great partners in the anti-Hitler coalition. Less than a year later, at Fulton, Missouri, Churchill denounced Russia and called for a "fraternal association" of Britain and the United States.

That the U.S.S.R., after 1945, began to assert its influence in eastern Europe and the Balkans at a rapidly accelerating tempo is now a matter of record. It would be interesting to know whether American policy based on a more extensive knowledge of the historic objectives of the Russian nation apart from those of communism might have achieved better results and avoided some of the postwar clashes between the United States and the U.S.S.R., but this is a point to be settled by future historians. Whatever may have been the initial reasons for these clashes, today the main problems of American-Russian relations fall into four main categories: political, economic, security, and ideological.

In the political sphere the United States finds it impossible to accept the Soviet dictatorship, with its apparatus of a one-party totalitarian government, suppression of all opposition, secret police, "labor camps," and restrictions on liberty of religion, press, science, art, education, and so on. Even if the American government were to admit that the Russians can do what they want in their own country, it cannot accept the imposition of similar totalitarian regimes on Russia's neighbors in Europe and Asia through propaganda, infiltration, or outright use of force. On this point it is difficult to discover a basis for agreement so long as the Soviet government remains unchanged. But what if it should turn out, as seems to be the case in Yugoslavia, that Russia's neighbors want communism—without pressure from Russia, and even in actual defiance of communism as interpreted by Stalin? Do we oppose all dictatorships, whatever their political outlook—in Spain as well as in Russia, in Portugal and Peru as well as in Poland—or only Communist dictatorships? Do we in fact oppose all Communist dictatorships, or only dictatorships that are associated with the U.S.S.R.? In Latin America, where this country, by use of its influence, is in a better position to foster democratic institutions than in eastern Europe, dictatorial governments dominated by military or fascist elements, notably in Bolivia, Peru, and Venezuela, have been accepted in the United States with little criticism, and the Perón dictatorship in Argentina, although criticized here, has on the whole enjoyed support from Washington, notably when it sought admission to the United Nations. When Marshal Tito defied the Kremlin, he too began to be treated in a more friendly way by Washington, although he claimed to be a purer Communist than Stalin and did not abandon the totalitarian features of his administration. The United States has also on occasion given the impression that it might get along with the Chinese Communists provided they took no hostile measures against American business interests. Is the United States, then, concerned primarily with the Russian form of government—or with Russia's ambitions as a great power? If the latter, is there any assurance that a change in Russia's government would bring about a change in its foreign policy, which under the Soviet government has at many points paralleled the policy of the Czars?

In the economic sphere direct controversy between the United States and the U.S.S.R is less acute today than during the interwar years, when the "Red trade menace" and "Russian dumping" of the products of "slave labor" were featured in our newspaper headlines. Since then Americans have become accustomed to see the emergence of other systems of controlled and planned economy, and the Russian system, although still regarded with repugnance, no longer appears as startling as it seemed in 1917. Nor does the United States feel threatened by the economic competition of the U.S.S.R., whose products, to the extent that they are at all available for export, are still of a quality too low to challenge American goods in Europe, although they might eventually be sought in the less advanced countries of Asia and the Near East. On the contrary, the United States stands to benefit by the import of some of Russia's strategic raw materials, especially manganese, chrome, and platinum, which are in short supply here.

Actually, the shoe is on the other foot. It is the U.S.S.R. that needs goods produced in the United States, particularly capital equipment and tools for the rehabilitation of its war-devastated industries and mines. At the end of World War II the Soviet government had hoped to obtain here a six-billion-dollar credit for such purchases. But as American-Russian relations deteriorated, and especially after Moscow in June 1947 had refused to join in the Marshall Plan, extending its injunction to neighboring countries of eastern Europe, prospects for an American credit grew dim. The United States adopted a policy of licensing only such exports to Russia and its neighbors as would not increase their "war potential," and since in modern warfare almost anything can contribute to war potential this meant, in effect, that exports to Russia and eastern Europe came practically to a standstill. In addition, the United States indicated to Marshall Plan countries that it would not be desirable for them to ship to the east goods that American manufacturers were not permitted to sell, and in April 1949 Britain issued a list of prohibited items. This list, however, was short and precise and included only items used solely for war purposes. With the United States in control of exports from western Germany, where a licensing policy comparable to that of Washington has hitherto been followed, Russia and eastern Europe were effectively shut out of sources of industrial equipment except for what could be furnished by Russia's industries, already strained by the needs of its own reconstruction, and by Czechoslovakia, which, with a population of twelve million, can hardly fill the needs of all eastern Europe and the Balkans. This economic dilemma was probably one of the principal reasons why the Kremlin decided to lift the Berlin blockade in May 1949, in the hope, apparently, of reaching an economic settlement with the West that would permit access to the industrial output of the Ruhr.

There is another side to this picture, however. If Russia and eastern Europe need machinery and tools from the west, so do some of the western countries—particularly Britain—need to find sources of food, timber, and raw materials for which they will not have to pay dollars, as well as markets for their industrial exports. The real economic issue, then, is not directly between the United States and the U.S.S.R., but between the United States as spark-plug of western Europe's recovery and the U.S.S.R. as self-appointed controller of eastern European sources of supply. This economic discussion centers on Germany, both because Russia and its neighbors hope to obtain from the Ruhr equipment they have no dollars to purchase in the United States, and because West German industry, as it revives, will probably seek to recover its traditional markets in the east.

Underlying American-Russian discussions of political and economic problems is concern on both sides about the respective security of the two countries. The United States has been seeking to protect countries along Russia's European periphery both against Communist infiltration and against military and economic pressure by the U.S.S.R., notably in Greece and Turkey. It has worked on the creation of a North Atlantic security zone, stretching from Norway to Italy, which might serve as a rampart against westward expansion by Russia. It has favored the revival of Germany and Japan as "workshops" of Europe and Asia, and as potential bastions for defense of the two continents—or, if worst came to worst, as possible bases from which American military power could roll back the Russian tide.

The U.S.S.R., for its part, has indicated that it fears the military resurgence of both Germany and Japan. Opinion differs as to whether Russia's postwar moves have been designed to provide it with springboards for further expansion or with a safety belt to prevent attack by others. The second theory appears to be supported by the Kremlin's efforts to create and consolidate in neighboring countries governments that could be counted on to be "friendly" to Russia and not susceptible of being taken over by potential enemies, as was the case with the fascist or semi-fascist regimes of the interwar years. While the United States has insisted on guarding the secret of manufacturing the atomic bomb, regarded by Churchill and others as the chief postwar deterrent to Russian aggression, until such time as the Kremlin is ready to permit international inspection of industrial installations, the U.S.S.R., which has discovered the secret, has been demanding that the United States destroy its bomb stockpile before it would consider any form of international control.

In debates about military security against the U.S.S.R. some Americans are beginning to ask themselves whether military and economic warfare would prove adequate in case the conflict should turn out to be a conflict of ideas rather than of arms. Here is probably the most difficult aspect of American policy toward Russia. For it becomes increasingly clear that communism gains adherents particularly in nations that are a prey to economic or social maladjustments and are suffering from moral disequilibrium or internal disintegration. The Marshall Plan recognized that communism thrives on misery and chaos, and that what is needed is not to fight the outward symptoms but to eliminate the basic conditions that breed communism. This, however, is not an easy task. In order to combat communism effectively, the United States may have to propose and help to carry out some of the economic and social reforms urged by the Communists—in China, in southeast Asia, in Africa, in Latin America, not to speak of eastern Europe and the Balkans. Should this happen, the ideological issue between the United States and the U.S.S.R. may boil down to divergence not so much about ends as about means.

Both superpowers face dilemmas. The dilemma of Russia is how a still backward country, where nationalism was strongly fostered during the war as a prerequisite of victory over a traditional enemy, can continue to propagate the idea of a world revolution, which according to Lenin was supposed to cut across all nationalisms, and at the same time furnish out of its as yet meager resources the industrial equipment necessary to create in other underdeveloped areas an industrialized economy and a higher standard of living. The dilemma of the United States is how to reconcile the principles of political liberty, which are an essential part of the heritage of Western civilization, with the primitive conditions of backward countries, and to furnish these countries not only the equipment needed to modernize their agriculture and establish some industries, but also the ingredients of genuinely independent political life—even if their governmental practices should turn out to differ markedly from those of our democracy. The two dilemmas are illustrated by the situation the United States and the U.S.S.R. face in two key areas of the continent: in eastern Europe and the Balkans, and in the countries bordering on the Mediterranean.

In both areas, from the Baltic to the Dardanelles, Russia

has repeatedly asserted its interests for several centuries against Teutons, Swedes, Poles, Tatars, Turks, Britain, and modern Germany. It is the United States, not the U.S.S.R., that is the newcomer. To the extent that this country, consciously or unconsciously, takes over the role played by Russia's previous opponents, of containing Russia or menacing its security by building alliances and acquiring bases along its periphery, to that extent we must be prepared for an eventual military showdown with the U.S.S.R. If our purpose is to put an end both to Russia's military power and to the Soviet system, then war probably offers the only effective course, and the risk envisaged by some of our advocates of atomic warfare, although a desperate gamble that might plunge the whole world into chaos, could be regarded as a well-calculated risk. This course, however, could be justifiably adopted only if there is reason to assume that, once Russia has been defeated and its system destroyed, the countries of eastern Europe and the Balkans will immediately repudiate communism and by an overwhelming majority choose to restore the governments that ruled them before 1939. It is on this assumption that Washington has apparently based its policy since 1945, denouncing not only Russia's "imperialism" in neighboring nations, but also communism as practiced by these nations. At the same time we have not been prepared to go to the lengths of intervening by force on behalf of the individuals and groups whose fate we have deplored—Mikolajczyk and his Peasant Party in Poland, Cardinal Mindszenty in Hungary, Beneš and Archbishop Beran in Czechoslovakia, Juliu Maniu in Rumania, Petkov in Bulgaria. By this policy of now blowing hot, now blowing cold, we have antagonized the new regimes of eastern Europe and the Balkans, whose initial suspicions of the West have been confirmed by our sympathy for opposition leaders; yet we have bitterly disappointed the men who had thought they could count on our support for their plans to overthrow communism. The net result, by 1949, was that while Russia's dictatorial attitude toward its neighbors had begun to undermine its influence in eastern Europe and the Balkans, traditionally a twilight zone between east and west, we had made no significant gains at Russia's expense.

If we are to avoid confusion and achieve concrete results, we shall have to draw a clearly discernible line between what we think of the conduct of the U.S.S.R. as a great power and what we think of communism as a way of life. When the Kremlin resorts to political ruthlessness, military pressures, and economic exploitation with respect to its weaker neighbors, we should be just as critical of its actions as we would be in the case of other great powers, ourselves included. "Imperialism" is no better when practiced by the East than by the West. If we take this stand, we shall find support among Russia's neighbors, including Communists, as we can already see in Yugoslavia, where Marshal Tito has denounced Russian "imperialism" with a greater wealth of concrete details than the Western powers, but at the same time has made it clear that he does not intend to whitewash the conduct of the West. Yugoslavia's defiance of Stalin and its unvarnished attacks on the Cominform, however, do not mean that it intends to give up either communism or the methods of the police state. This creates a problem for us. For if we are able to do business with the Yugoslav Communists, may we not find it possible to follow the same course with the Communists of other countries once they have dissociated themselves from Russia? And if we deal with Communism at all, to what extent shall we be forced to abandon our postwar demands for "democracy" and "free, unfettered elections" in eastern Europe and the Balkans?

What we shall have to recognize, over the long run, is that we were misled, or misled ourselves, in 1945 when we thought that once Russia had been "contained," democratic conditions would naturally come about in an area that, with the exception of Czechoslovakia, had had practically no experience with the institutions and methods of Western democracy. If the Russians, once the war was over, had promptly withdrawn into their borders, the likelihood is that fascist or semi-fascist regimes would have come to power from the Baltic to the Black Sea, except in Czechoslovakia. The persistence of fascist influence can be readily noted even in a Westernized nation like Austria, where, with the four Allies still in control, a neo-Nazi party succeeded in winning twelve per cent of the votes in the 1949 national elections. Nor does the experience of the interwar years give any evidence that anti-Communist regimes in eastern Europe and the Balkans would have introduced democratic practices. What the Communists have been doing to anti-Communists would have been done to them. Our choice there has been not, as often asserted, between communism and democracy, but between communism and some form of fascism. Our decision about working with communism must thus depend on our estimate as to the potential capacity of Communist regimes to create conditions of literacy and improved living-standards which might eventually facilitate the growth of political liberties. The most likely prospect, if we can take Yugoslavia's experience as a guide, is that neither the United States nor the U.S.S.R. can hope to win a clear-cut victory in eastern Europe and the Balkans; and that the mingled influences of East and West will gradually be fused into systems that will not be patterned exclusively either on American capitalism or on Russian communism.

The Mediterranean, once claimed by Italy as its own private sea—*Mare Nostrum*—and in more recent times regarded by Britain as the "life-line" of its Empire, linking the British Isles through Gibraltar and Suez with India and the Pacific, has since World War II become an arena of controversy between the United States and the U.S.S.R. Here, in the three strategic instances of Spain, Italy, and Greece, may be seen in microcosm the clashing interests that are not always so clearly evident in larger theaters of action such as Germany and China.

Until 1939 the United States had little interest in the Mediterranean region. At most a few American concerns, particularly oil companies, had then begun to get acquainted with internal developments in countries of the Near East, where oil resources were being explored or developed; American schools and colleges at Beirut and Cairo had laid a basis for cultural ties with the Arabs; and American Zionists were hoping to establish a Jewish state in Palestine. These various interests, however, were not closely related to American policy in Europe. It is true that some links had been forged through immigrants from Italy and Greece who, after settling in the United States, where they contributed to the physical development of the American continent, remained in touch with their homelands, writing about the wonders of the New World, revisiting their families from time to time, and, most important of all, sending home remittances that became an important invisible item in the balance of payments of the two Mediterranean countries. More recently the civil war of 1936 in Spain had precipitated a conflict here between Americans who were sympathetic to the cause of the Spanish Republicans and those—particularly in the Catholic hierarchy—who wanted the United States to aid General Franco, considered as a pillar of Christendom and a bulwark against communism.

It is only since World War II, however, that the United States has become thoroughly involved in this historic region of world strategy. The very fact that American forces started their European campaign in North Africa fixed American attention on the Mediterranean. The long and arduous conquest of Italy plunged the United States into the complex problems of the Italian people, demoralized by twenty years of Fascism. Britain's postwar weakness threw new responsibilities on the United States, especially when it began to appear in 1947 that the decline in British military and economic strength would tempt or encourage the U.S.S.R. to make a bid for strategic positions in Greece and Turkey, gateways to the Near East, where by that time American interests had passed from a passive to an active phase. Farther east, Moscow's desire to maintain its wartime influence in Iran, the necessity of developing Near Eastern oil resources to fill both Marshall Plan requirements in Europe and the expanded needs of the American Navy, and since 1947, conflicts between Jews and Arabs in Palestine, all contributed to enlarge the political, economic, and strategic stake of the United States in the Mediterranean.

Not only has this country inherited many of Britain's former problems and obligations, but it has been confronted with many others that either had not arisen in prewar years or else had not then preoccupied the British. Like Britain at the apogee of its power in the nineteenth century, the United States had discovered that possession of a large navy leads to the acquisition of bases. In addition to bases already held by the British at Gibraltar and Malta, which withstood the impact of air warfare in 1939–45, the United States has obtained from Portugal, Britain's ally since the thirteenth century, the right to make use of bases in the Azores. Like Britain, too, this country has become interested in the possibility of obtaining bases on the African coast of the Mediterranean, which during World War II proved vulnerable to attack and invasion by the Germans; and since 1945 has been concerned with the disposal of Italy's former colonies in Africa. Greece and Turkey, traditionally involved in great-power maneuvers for control of the Balkans and the eastern Mediterranean, have again emerged into the limelight, their strategic significance enhanced by the possibility that, if held in the Western orbit, they could serve not only as naval bases but also as bases for the launching of air attacks on the U.S.S.R.; and, if brought into the orbit of Moscow, they might become Russian outposts for further extension of Soviet influence into Africa and the Near East. Meanwhile General Franco, having survived the vicissitudes of war, which brought disaster to Hitler and Mussolini, has sought to convince the United States that Spain could serve as a valuable base for defense against Russia or, alternatively, as a springboard for reconquest of the continent—reviving memories of Wellington's Peninsular campaign against Napoleon. If, however, the Western powers should decide against the inclusion of Spain in their military calculations, and in their list of recipients of American aid, Franco indicated that Spain, in Russian hands, would become a great danger to the Atlantic community. Thus Spain and the Arab countries joined hands in offering to underpin American defense measures against the U.S.S.R.

The policy of the United States in the Mediterranean has been determined primarily by considerations of security, with the emphasis on containment of Russia and of communism. Setting ideological considerations aside for a moment, the policy of containment is not a novel development in the Mediterranean area. As already pointed out, Britain for two centuries sought by all means at its disposal to confine the Russians in the Black Sea and enlisted for this purpose the aid of Turkey, guardian of the Dardanelles, which itself had fought eleven wars with Russia for control of this strategic gateway. In 1856 Britain and Turkey were assisted by France and Sardinia in the Crimean War, which proved costly for Russia and like other Russian military defeats hastened social unrest that resulted in the emancipation of the serfs by Alexander II in 1861. When the Russians, in 1878, inflicted a serious blow on the Ottoman Empire—the "Sick Man of Europe"—by helping their Slav "brothers," Serbs and Bulgarians, to overthrow the Turkish yoke, Britain and France, with the aid of Bismarck at the Berlin peace conference forced the Czarist government to abandon the advantages it had gained in the course of the Russo-Turkish War. After promising Russia in 1915 that it would receive control of the Dardanelles as the spoils of a common victory, Britain and France in 1919 decided they were under no obligation to fulfill this undertaking because the Czarist government had meanwhile been overthrown. The Lausanne Treaty of 1923, giving Turkey special advantages at the Straits, aroused resentment in Moscow, which insisted on its revision at the Montreux conference of 1936, when terms more favorable to Russian claims were agreed to by the other powers.

Throughout this long history of struggle, with the goal again and again almost within grasp but always eluding it, Russia, both under the Czars and under the Soviet government has been more concerned to exclude all possible enemies from the Black Sea than to assure itself an exit into the Mediterranean. Recognizing its weakness as a naval power, as well as the vulnerability of its important industrial and agrarian areas of the Ukraine and the Don Basin to naval and land attack, and now to air plus atomic-bomb warfare, the Soviet government has sought to prevent other nations from obtaining a foothold within striking-distance of Russian soil. In view of this policy, consistently and stubbornly followed by Czars and commissars, one can but wonder at the assumptions made by former Secretary of State James F. Byrnes, who in describing the Yalta conference said: "How unrealistic of Stalin to ask for the Dardanelles at a time when atomic warfare has made all bases obsolete." [1] Not only was Stalin at Yalta hewing to a line set by Russia for two centuries, but other great powers had at that time given no hint that they were prepared to abandon bases they possessed; nor have they done so since the revelation of the atomic bomb, which, it should be recalled, was still in the experimental stage in February 1945.

If considerations of strategy alone are taken into account, it is possible to find, as some American military leaders have done, that Spain could play a role, although not necessarily an important role, in case of war with Russia and that for this reason it may become necessary for the United States to "do business" with Franco. In general Washington has been little affected by the popular sympathy for Spanish Republicans that exists in Britain, in France, and in some other countries

[1] James F. Byrnes: *Speaking Frankly,* cited.

of Europe, where the Republicans were regarded as the vanguard of the world's struggle against fascism. One of the principal reasons for this difference has been the great influence exercised in this country by the Catholic Church, representing 26 out of 150 million citizens—an influence that no American government would want openly to defy. In addition, some American business men, like the business men of England and France, have seen nothing wrong in trading with Franco, provided that Spain would give trustworthy guarantees of financial stability—as the Spanish government did in 1949 by offering gold deposits in London as guarantee on a loan granted by the Chase National Bank.

American public opinion, so far as it is expressed in the press and in public discussion, has been opposed to rapprochement with Franco, on the ground that this would constitute repudiation of our support of democracy and would play directly into the hands of Russia and of Communists everywhere. But as fear of Russia and communism grew here in 1948–9, more and more people in Washington began to think that Spain might be useful to the United States. It was admitted that Spanish military forces would be neither large nor very reliable. The principal motive affecting those who favored reconciliation with Franco was fear that Spain, as a result of economic collapse, might succumb to communism and thus become a Russian base for operations in the Atlantic—a fear sedulously fanned by Franco. The essential goal, then, became the avoidance of disorder in Spain that might bring about any change in the government that could prove favorable to Russia. Consequently, efforts were made to maintain the *status quo,* even at the price of leaving the Spanish people at their present low level of economic development and standard of living, which, over the long run, might foster the very extremism feared by the United States. At the same time it must be recognized that economic measures against Franco would certainly not improve the lot of the Spanish people. Conflicts in American attitudes resulted in a vacillating policy toward Spain, with the United States at one time acquiescing in the recommendation of the United Nations General Assembly that member nations should withdraw ambassadors from Madrid in token of disapproval, and later urging the rescinding of this resolution and giving the impression that it would not oppose Spain's admission to international agencies like the International Civil Aviation Organization, although not to the UN itself. Doubts as to the course advocated by this country were at least temporarily set at rest in April 1949 and January 1950 when Secretary of state Dean Acheson declared that the United States would not seek rapprochement with the Franco government as long as the Spanish nation did not enjoy certain basic liberties.

The strategic problem is even more complicated in the case of Italy, for there the question is not to establish or maintain in power a dictatorial government, but to reorganize the economy of the country to the point where the Italian people will become less and less susceptible, because of poverty and hopelessness, to the promises and influence of communism. This is a far-reaching task, for Italy has long suffered from a surplus of population. What can be done with the nearly two million totally unemployed Italy had at the peak of Marshall Plan aid in 1949—two million who might sooner or later fall prey to Communist propaganda? In an earlier and happier period emigration offered a remedy, especially emigration to the United States and to a lesser extent to Latin America. Today, however, most countries, the United States especially, no longer want to open their doors wide to new settlers; and even displaced victims of Nazi conquest, who had a particular call on the generosity of the World War II victors and who numbered fewer than a million, experienced great difficulties in finding new homes. Emigration, moreover, is only a palliative, since the place of those who leave is quickly filled by newborn children in a country like Italy, where religious beliefs and social conventions have combined to defeat measures of planned parenthood.

Colonies overseas might conceivably offer a population outlet. But Italy, arriving late in the colonial struggle, after the formation of the Italian state in the 1860's, succeeded in acquiring in Africa only meagerly endowed territories that had been passed over by the great European powers. And in any case it lacks the financial resources necessary to develop colonies to the stage where they could offer a fruitful new homeland for Italian colonists—as Mussolini, in spite of his grandiloquent invocations of the glories of the Roman Empire, discovered when he set out on colonial adventures. Moreover, in Italy's former African colonies—Libya, Eritrea, Italian Somaliland—Britain, seeking to maintain its influence in the Arab world, has not felt free to back Italy too openly. Meanwhile both Britain and the United States, concerned with problems of naval and air power, have themselves become interested in these colonies and are determined not to let them fall into the hands of the U.S.S.R., recalling with misgivings Moscow's demand for Tripoli in 1945.

Italian workers might find employment in some of the European countries suffering from labor shortages, notably France. But Italy has never liked to lose citizens to other countries, and at the present time is not eager to part with skilled workers it needs for its own economy; and it is the skilled workers who are most in demand abroad. Nor is land reform a long-term solution, for redistribution of land, even accompanied by modernization of agricultural methods and by mechanization, would add to the unemployment problems of urban centers. The remedy for surplus population that offers the most hope is a radical solution: birth-control, accompanied by more thorough education and training of Italy's children and youth in various skills. It is difficult, however, for the United States to advocate birth-control, which is opposed by the Vatican and resisted by American Catholic leaders. How far can the United States go in helping Italy to maintain a standard of living that would preclude resort to extremist movements—either communism or reviving Fascism—without being forced, in self-defense, to recommend certain fundamental social reforms that, in the eyes of Italian conservatives, might appear not to differ very markedly from reforms advocated by the Communists? The alternative to such reforms might have to be a decision on our part to subsidize Italy for an indefinite period of time, with no assurance that this drain on American economy could be stopped.

Similar problems, in an even more acute form, present themselves in Greece. This little country lacks the natural resources that have made it possible for Italy to establish viable industries at least in the north, and since the war has been the scene of battles between Greeks which at the same time are battles, reminiscent of the Balkan wars before 1914, between Greece and other nations of that area and, in a larger sense, between the great powers. Compared with the financial assistance we have given in other parts of Europe, American aid to Greece has been comparatively modest; and our aid has accomplished some constructive purposes, such as restoration of ports, building of roads, and so on, in addition to the achievement of our military objective—the containment of Greek rebel forces and of Russian influence in Greek territory. But as long as guerrilla warfare continued, it was impossible for the Greeks to reconstruct their economy, poor as it is even in times of peace; and American subsidies, earmarked in the first instance for the rehabilitation of Greece, had to be diverted primarily to military expenditures, thus postponing for the time being the thoroughgoing reforms that would be necessary to inflict permanent defeat on extremist elements and to stabilize the political and economic situation. Like Italy, Greece has a surplus population in terms of the country's resources and employment facilities, and would like to send at least two million out of its seven million people to settle in other lands. The United States thus finds itself in a dilemma. Americans, by and large, do not approve of the conservative Greek government, which has shown little or no concern for the welfare of poorer groups of the population; but Washington has been reluctant to let that government fall, for fear of encouraging the spread of communism. Meanwhile some American officials realize that Greece's present leaders hope to retain power indefinitely by continuing their intermittent struggle with the guerrilla troops. As long as this struggle persists, it may be expected to enlist American sympathy and, with it, American financial aid.

These three brief case histories of Mediterranean countries where the United States and the U.S.S.R. are in conflict raise four principal questions concerning American foreign policy.

First, is it possible to confront countries like Spain, Italy, and Greece—and this becomes even more problematic when one turns to Asia, Africa, and some of the Latin-American nations—with a "we or they" choice between the democracy of the West and the totalitarian system of the East? Is it feasible to develop institutions of political liberty in countries that for one reason or another are still relatively retarded? Or would it be wiser to accept things as they are, not to view them in terms of black and white, and to exercise some patience while these countries raise their very low standard of living, and subsequently their level of education and political experience? Are there individuals or groups in these countries capable of effecting a minimum of reform? Is it the task of the United States to discover such individuals or groups and then to give them all possible support until they have grown in strength and confidence? Or will it prove impossible to find a middle ground there at the present time—as George C. Marshall found it impossible to discover a middle ground between the "extremists" around Chiang Kai-shek and the Communist extremists?

Second, is it practicable to offer these countries a clear-cut choice between the free-private-enterprise system, considerably qualified in practice, of the United States, and the Russian system of strictly controlled economy? Or can mixed systems be developed that might be better adapted to local circumstances? Is it possible to have economic and social reforms in these countries without a certain measure of governmental intervention—whether that of their own rulers or of the United States? Is it possible that in some respects Russia's experience might be useful to these countries, for example in establishing machine and tractor stations that can serve numbers of farms, and thereby reducing the need for agricultural machinery that is in short supply—an arrangement used during the war by the Middle East Supply Center, organized under the guidance of Britain and the United States, and since the war by French landowners in Algeria? Should the United States, because of hostility to communism, reject *in toto* all that the Russians have done in industry and agriculture? Or is it possible to find a practical mixture of American know-how and Russian production methods evolved for a still backward, predominantly peasant population?

Third, to what extent should military considerations determine the foreign policy of the United States in these countries? The United States is at present the greatest naval power, as well as the greatest air power in the world, with the hydrogen bomb potentially superseding the atomic bomb as a winning card in its hands. An armament race between the two superpowers can have only one foreseeable result—a more destructive war than any yet known in history. And meanwhile the efforts and resources that could be expended by us on the development of backward areas, and by Russia on its own development, are being drained off into military preparations. Have we exhausted all possibilities on both sides of finding a basis for peaceful "coexistence"?

Fourth, by what methods will it be possible to avoid a military showdown and lay the bases for peaceful reconstruction of the world? What are the alternatives? Must the superpowers establish new spheres of influence, of which eastern Europe, the Balkans, and the Mediterranean would be examples in Europe? Is it possible in our time to undertake a new division of spoils, such as Britain and France made in Africa after Fashoda in 1899 or Britain and Russia in Iran, Afghanistan, and Tibet in 1907? Or has the world become too small for such deals between great powers, and public opinion more sensitive than it used to be about the disposal of territories without the agreement of their inhabitants?

Must we then endeavor to strike a new balance of power, not only in Europe or Asia, but all over the globe? If so, how will it prove possible to avert conflicts that in the past have eventually arisen between the two sides of every balance? Or can we find a new form of balance, this time within the framework of the United Nations, where the small and middle nations can serve as shock-absorbers cushioning controversies between the great? Must one or the other of the two superpowers inevitably seek to impose its own world domination—*Pax Americana or Pax Sovietica*—or can they become reconciled to the idea that other nations will not want to become mere carbon copies of either America or Russia? It is in the context of these larger ultimate issues that the accomplishments of the European Recovery Program, of efforts to create a European union and a North Atlantic community, and even of the United Nations must be appraised.

Chapter VIII

AFTER ERP WHAT?

In Europe our postwar policy of peacetime co-operation with other nations, like a triptych, consists of three panels: economic—the European Recovery Program; political—proposals for a Western European Union; and military—the North Atlantic Treaty and the accompanying military aid program. This policy, new for the United States, represents a novel development also for the rest of the world. For it is based on the concept that national states (in this case western European) must voluntarily accept economic, political, and military limitations on their sovereignty, and must achieve ever greater integration between their economies, their governmental systems, and their armed forces to the point where a new form of federation—federation not only of contiguous territories in western Europe but also, across the Atlantic, of Europe with the United States and Canada—might be accomplished. This new policy, initially formulated with the object of rehabilitating western Europe and safeguarding it from Russia and communism—and, more remotely, from a resurgent Germany—is already having far-reaching effects on the United States itself and on our relations with other areas of the world. As time goes on, especially if fear of Russia and communism should abate, it is conceivable that a recession of American interest in international co-operation might set in, and energies and funds now concentrated on such undertakings as ECA might be diverted to projects for further development of this country, especially in the South. It is doubtful, however, that, having meshed our thinking, our preoccupations, and our hopes so closely with those of Europe and the rest of the world, we could revert to isolationism.

The first panel in the triptych of American policy toward Europe—the European Recovery program—had been presented in bold outline by Secretary of State Marshall in his address of June 5, 1947 at Harvard University, but, before that, had already been sketched out by his Assistant Secretary Dean Acheson in a less publicized speech at Cleveland, Mississippi.

The objectives of the Marshall Plan cannot be defined in terms of black and white. The motives of all human beings, and this means of all nations, are mixed. The point of departure of the plan was the realization, two years after the end of World War II, that the rehabilitation of Europe would take much longer than had first been expected in the United States, and that in the meantime economic dislocation threatened to undermine the morale and the political stability of the continent, opening the door to all types of extremism, but particularly to communism. This realization caused a profound shock in the United States; for the majority of Americans were still unaware either of the scope of the destruction and demoralization caused in Europe by two world wars, or of the resulting economic, social, and political deterioration. Washington then decided that it was necessary to help Europe maintain the momentum of its own recovery efforts by providing it with food, raw materials, and essential industrial equipment—not in the form of loans which the Europeans would have to repay, thus indefinitely prolonging their postwar crisis, but for the most part in the form either of gifts or of direct subsidies for American exports to Europe.

As originally outlined, the Marshall Plan was neither anti-Russian nor anti-Communist. "Our policy," said Marshall at Harvard, "is not directed against any country or doctrine, but against hunger, desperation and chaos." Its objective was "the revival of a working economy in the world, so as to permit the emergence of political and social conditions in which free institutions could exist." It is important to stress this concept of the Marshall Plan because it was subsequently obscured by two developments: the previous proclamation in March 1947 of the Truman Doctrine, which pledged American aid to all "free" nations menaced by Russia and communism through a policy of "containment" that emphasized military rather than economic measures; and the refusal of the U.S.S.R., on its own behalf and on behalf of its eastern European neighbors, to participate in the plan, followed by Communist attempts to prevent its realization in the recipient nations. Two years later, in 1949, the United States undertook to supplement the economic assistance given to western Europe under the ERP by military measures under the North Atlantic Treaty, which carried forward on a broader geographic scale the objectives of the Truman Doctrine that had originally appeared to be designed to cover only nations along the immediate periphery of the U.S.S.R.

Thus the Marshall Plan had as its first objective the economic, and consequently social and moral, reconstruction of Europe. This reconstruction, it was hoped, would eventually result in political stabilization of the continent, and the consequent weakening, or even some day eclipse, of communism. Even today the Economic Cooperation Administration recognizes that the root of the trouble in Europe is not communism, but the accumulated heritage of war. The problem of Europe's balance of payments, said the ECA in its third, 1948, report to Congress, "is an outgrowth of World War II, which not only destroyed or disorganized a large part of Europe's productive capacity, but also consumed much of the foreign investments and service facilities that formerly provided a major source of income." [1] By contrast, the Truman Doctrine, improvised in short order to meet what seemed to

---

[1] *Third Report to Congress of the Economic Cooperation Administration* for the Quarter ending December 31, 1948 (Washington: Government Printing Office; 1949), p. 2.

be a catastrophic emergency provoked by Britain's decision to withdraw its small force from Greece (this force was actually not withdrawn until the autumn of 1949), attacked the symptoms rather than the causes of the disease, which sprang from political and economic disorganization within various nations, as well as disequilibrium of forces between the great powers directly resulting from the war.

It would be hypocritical to assert that the Marshall Plan was inspired solely by generosity. Unadulterated generosity on the part of any nation would be more than human, and attempts by American commentators to interpret it in that sense have not sounded convincing to skeptical Europeans. The American people and their representatives in Congress were certainly inspired in part by genuine sympathy for the plight of Europeans, but in part also by the national interests of the United States. They recognized—and this was a great step forward in the direction of developing an intelligent and constructive foreign policy—that if Europe's crisis were to continue, the United States would suffer from it sooner or later. It was becoming increasingly clear that isolationism and neutrality, no matter how desirable, were no longer practicable, and that the United States was closely tied to the misery or prosperity of other nations.

An important aspect of American self-interest was the realization that this country's industry, vastly expanded during the war to meet the needs of our own armed forces and of our allies all over the globe, might undergo sudden and dangerous shrinkage unless outlets could be found abroad for its increased output. Fear of the unemployment that might ensue, and bitter memories of the 1929 depression—not merely the need for European rehabilitation—were in the minds of those who drafted the European Recovery Program. The American public was growing aware that if this country was to maintain exports to Europe at a rate sufficient to keep up production in our industries, we would have either to increase our imports from Europe, or to send our goods to the continent at our own expense, underwritten by the government, which means by the taxpayers. Even had we wanted in 1947 to increase our imports of European products on a vast scale, this would have proved impossible in practice, for the shattered industries of the continent were then unable to produce adequately for export.

It was a revolutionary change in American thinking, however, to recognize that we cannot hope to export without importing; and this change has gradually shaped the main lines of our foreign economic policy. But pending the recovery of Europe's export industries, the Marshall Plan served to meet both the needs of Europe for goods from this country which they themselves could not purchase because of shortage of dollars, and the need of our own economy to continue industrial and agricultural production at approximately the wartime level. Under the Marshall Plan, Europe was promised for four years approximately twenty billion dollars' worth of food, fuel, certain raw materials, and industrial equipment, while American producers were assured of a market for their goods during the same period.

Many Americans have asked what the United States could hope to receive in return for its assistance to Europe. One answer is that this country would be amply rewarded if our own stability and security were strengthened by the reconstruction of Europe on a firm basis. This is a sound argument, but somewhat too abstract for the general public of any nation. Very naturally some Americans have pointed out that, important and necessary as aid to Europe was, it would create difficult problems here by curtailing goods available for home consumption and keeping up the level of domestic prices, thus merely postponing the hard moment of readjustment from war to peace conditions that our American economy was bound to undergo. For it must be recalled that, contrary to Communist assertions, the Marshall Plan was proposed and adopted not during a period of depression and lack of employment here, but during a period of great economic activity when American industry and agriculture were striving to fill the needs of our own people, postponed by war —a period of full employment for industrial and agricultural workers and of full utilization of raw materials and essential industrial materials like steel. Thus the United States at that time was sending goods to Europe not out of a surplus that would have caused an immediate slump unless exported, but out of many shortages, with consequent strains on the domestic standard of living and danger of further inflation. It was therefore essential at that time to convince our people that the real sacrifices we were asked to make for the Marshall Plan not only were necessary, but would bring about genuine returns, if not in material terms, at least in other substantial forms. It was only two years later, when the postponed demands at home had been more or less satisfied, that the ERP began to be regarded here as a valuable, in fact essential, safety-valve for our own economy—especially our surplus of agricultural products.

To repeated questions concerning the advantages of the Marshall Plan for the American people, two main answers were offered here. The first, and the one that received the widest publicity, was that the program of aid to Europe constituted the strongest weapon at our command against communism. At times—especially during Congressional hearings on the ERP appropriations—this aspect was presented in a sensational manner, designed to make the public feel that an armed attack by Russia or a series of Communist upheavals in European countries were imminent, and that American aid should therefore be continued or stepped up. Since this kind of appeal was likely to bring public support more readily than less dramatic interpretations, the Marshall Plan was increasingly pictured as a method for checking Russia and communism—in far greater measure than had been originally conceived by its proponents—and in the minds of many people both here and in Europe it became increasingly identified with the "contain Russia" objectives of the Truman Doctrine. Meanwhile the actions of the Soviet government, first in refusing to participate in the Marshall Plan, then in seeking to defeat it by Communist propaganda and acts of sabotage, and the extension of Communist rule in eastern Europe and the Balkans, climaxed by the 1948 coup in Czechoslovakia, provided justification in Washington for transforming the ERP from a measure to alleviate misery and economic chaos into a weapon for fighting the "cold war" against Russia and communism.

The second answer to American questions about the advantages this country can hope to derive from the Marshall Plan—and the one that carries most weight over the long run—is that the countries receiving American aid must, in return, demonstrate a genuine intention to help themselves and each other as much as possible, through mutual aid in a western European union, accompanied by measures of closer political and military co-operation. It is entirely natural, and wholly in the American tradition, to expect and hope the Europeans will resort to mutual aid. The concept of self-help—the effort of each individual to make his own way without undue dependence on his family or his community—is deeply ingrained in our memories of American pioneer life; and so is the concept of co-operation between individuals, of teamwork in the twentieth-century community, but without dependence on the state, regarded here as inimical to individual liberty. Americans are very generous—more generous perhaps than other peoples have been in comparable periods of national wealth and power—but they do not like to have others take advantage of their generosity, and they want to see the recipients of their assistance do something to rehabilitate themselves. Many feel that some of the European nations do not help themselves sufficiently, or count too much on the prospect that this country will continue to help them after 1952. This was one of the reasons for fixing the time limit of four years for the Marshall Plan. The United States has tried to leave to each country receiving ERP aid the decision as to how hard it thinks its people can work and what sacrifices it can demand from them. But on the issue of mutual aid among the beneficiaries of ERP aid the United States has felt that it had the right to make its views known, since the problem of mutual aid goes beyond the frame of national economy and becomes an international problem.

To put it bluntly, many Americans by the end of 1949 had come to the conclusion that the countries of western Europe had not made enough of an effort to co-ordinate their economic plans and thus demonstrate to the United States that after 1952 they would be able to maintain by their own efforts a viable standard of living without continuing to receive what in effect are subsidies from this country. When in January 1949 Robert Marjolin of France, secretary-general of the Organization for European Economic Cooperation, said that if western Europe did not reorganize its economic relationships it would face an economic catastrophe in 1952, when it would have a deficit of three billion dollars in its trade with the United States, this warning did not reassure the American public—nor did it visibly needle the ERP countries into action.

Some Americans, notably Thomas E. Dewey during the 1948 Presidential election campaign, have contended that the United States should use the ERP as a goad to force the western European nations into forming an economic union before the 1952 deadline. Others, without pressing for such a showdown, had hoped that western Europe would voluntarily achieve "integration" as the only feasible alternative to increasing autarchy. The case for integration was put most forcefully by ECA Administrator Paul G. Hoffman before the OEEC in Paris on October 31, 1949, when he urged "the building of an expanding economy in Western Europe through integration." He declared:

The substance of such integration would be the formation of a single large market within which quantitative restrictions on the movements of goods, monetary barriers to the flow of payments and, eventually, all tariffs are permanently swept away. The fact that we have in the United States a single market of 150,000,000 consumers has been indispensable to the strength and efficacy of our economy. The creation of a permanent, freely trading area, comprising 270,000,000 consumers in Western Europe, would have a multitude of consequences. It would accelerate the development of large-scale, low-cost production industries. It would make the effective use of all resources easier, the stifling of healthy competition more difficult.

He also expressed the conviction that integration would "set in motion a rapid growth in productivity." [1]

When Europeans, in answer to American appeals for integration, point out the many obstacles erected by tradition, vested interests, nationalism, and so on, Americans think these objections are exaggerated and unrealistic. Europeans retort by asking whether we, for our part, have not overestimated the ease with which old nations that for centuries fought to delimit their small territorial areas and defend them against encroachments can from one day to the next jettison their sovereignty and their deep-rooted economic interests and merge their separate economies into a viable union. They find comparisons between Europe in the twentieth century and the thirteen American colonies two centuries ago not only unduly facile, but actually inaccurate. Perhaps we could appreciate their problems better by imagining how we would feel if we were asked by the ERP nations to join them in a still larger transatlantic union, scrap our tariffs, and eliminate those of our industries that might prove unable to compete with industries of western Europe— for example, watchmaking or shipping.

This discussion about integration, however, has proved useful for both sides. The Europeans have come to realize that the United States is deadly in earnest in urging reorganization of the continent's economies and have given in-

_____
[1] *New York Times*, November 1, 1949.

creasingly serious attention to the creation of at least a limited economic union, possibly composed of the Benelux and Franco-Italian customs union, familiarly labeled Fritalux, with the eventual inclusion of the West German state. They continue to fear, however, that without Britain such a union would prove unworkable, in view of the dependence of many European nations on the sterling area, and would eventually come to be dominated by Germany. Americans, meanwhile, have become aware that integration cannot be achieved overnight and, most important, cannot be crammed down the throats of the Europeans by us. We have also begun to understand that Britain, for the time being, prefers to hold aloof from a continental economic union; and that it will take time and tactful handling to iron out differences in policies between countries committed to planning, like Britain and the Scandinavian nations, and those like France, Belgium, and Italy which allow greater play for free private enterprise.

We now realize, too, in a more sober mood, that the United States, no matter how generously inclined, cannot under the most favorable political circumstances re-establish the economy of the continent on the foundations of 1914 or even of 1939. Some of these foundations, as already noted, have vanished beyond salvaging; others are perhaps not a total loss, such as the resources of colonies in southeast Asia, but their intrinsic value has greatly diminished, and their future contribution to the continent's economy remains in doubt. No power on earth can remedy Europe's impoverishment as a result of two world wars. The only remedy one can recommend for the future would be the avoidance of conflicts so costly in terms of human values and material wealth. Whatever we do, Europe will sooner or later have to adjust itself to a radically altered world economic situation and face the fact that the singularly favorable position it enjoyed during the five centuries following the discovery of the Indies and of the New World and the conquest of colonies in Asia and Africa is now drawing to a close. While Russia and the Communists have capitalized on the predicament of western Europe, they did not bring it about. It would therefore be dangerously short-sighted to deal with Europe's economic problems in the future as if they were entirely the handiwork of the Cominform.

In seeking answers to these problems the United States finds itself involved in contradictory attitudes. The majority of Americans would probably want to see in Europe restoration where it once existed, or inauguration where it was non-existent, of the system of free private enterprise. Yet officially we urge the western European nations to integrate their economies, to limit or abandon some of their existing branches of production and institute others—a program that would require in many instances far more extensive government controls than have so far been practiced in western Europe, would unfavorably affect the interests of some private producers in industry and agriculture, and would call for planning and directed economy on a regional scale. Thus we, who regard ourselves and are regarded by others as champions of free enterprise and freer world trade, often appear in Europe as advocates of closely regulated national economies and some form of industrial combinations—even if these become known by some name other than cartels, a term we hold in ill repute. Paradoxical as it may seem to us, the one country in Europe that has remained dedicated to free enterprise—Switzerland—declined to accept Marshall Plan aid precisely on the ground that this measure would require planning and controls on the part of recipient nations; and alone of the nations of western Europe it has continued to trade freely not only with the United States, but also with Russia and eastern Europe. For our part, we urge Europeans to reduce their prices and export more to us, yet fear their competition in a buyers' market both at home and abroad. We tell them to remove their tariff barriers and accept the International Trade Organization charter—yet have not ratified the ITO ourselves, and blanch at the thought of cutting our own tariffs on the principal items sold here by our European friends.

What can we do to keep the economy of Europe on an even keel and prevent further crises that might encourage extremism of Right or Left? The most urgent thing is to recognize that the recovery phase in Europe is over, and that the purpose for which the Marshall Plan was originally devised has been achieved. The Marshall Plan was admittedly a short-term emergency operation. As such, it has been described as "a brilliant success" by Paul G. Hoffman—who then had to add that it would leave Europe by 1952 "in only precarious balance." Some European economists, notably in Britain, have urged that the United States promptly cut the umbilical cord, wind up the Marshall Plan in 1950, and start fresh with a long-term program of far-reaching reconstruction, not only in Europe, but in other continents closely linked to Europe's economy. Only such a program, in their opinion, can really succeed in readjusting world economy to the major development of the past quarter of a century—and that is the emergence of the United States as the principal producing and creditor nation of the world.

Unless major changes now unforeseen occur in 1950, we shall be faced with four alternatives in our economic relations with Europe, all bristling with difficulties:

1. We might have to increase imports from western Europe to the tune of some two billion dollars—the estimated amount of the trade deficit between Europe and the United States upon termination of the Marshall Plan. The chief difficulty is that, as the United Nations 1948 survey pointed out, Europe's exports to the United States were traditionally restricted to a few specialized items, and in 1937, the last normal prewar year, the share of European manufactures in total American consumption amounted to only about 0.6 per cent. Not only will the European countries have to diversify their exports to us, and improve their quality while

keeping prices down, but we, for our part, will have to organize here an import drive in their favor, ease our customs procedures, consider tariff reductions on the principal items of European exports—for example, British woolens, and provide reconversion subsidies for American enterprises injured by imports.

2. We might undertake to do what many Europeans heartily wish we would do—and that is voluntarily curtail our exports to other markets where we compete with leading industrial nations, notably Latin America. This would not only require a spirit of self-sacrifice rarely displayed by any nation, but also probably make it necessary for us to introduce planning and control in foreign trade—a procedure that would be unpalatable to those of us who support free enterprise. The UN Economic Commission for Europe candidly emphasized a point that official presentation of the Marshall Plan here had generally avoided. It is that by 1953 the United States would face the "anomalous" prospect of having surpluses and excesses of production capacity in commodities for which, through the ERP, it has helped to develop substitute sources of supply in western Europe.[1] Since the Marshall Plan has in effect achieved its purpose by the end of 1949, this problem has already emerged. American observers, for example, noted that world oil markets that had been in the hands chiefly of United States concerns since the inception of the industry were definitely passing to British interests, which processed oil from the Middle East in refineries built in Europe with Marshall Plan funds, and then sold it in the sterling area to countries that did not have dollars to purchase American oil.

3. We might continue to give aid to Europe for an indefinite period after 1952 by subsidizing our exports to that area, as we are in effect doing under the ERP, but perhaps with a smaller expenditure of funds—for example, by reducing the annual sum of five billion dollars now spent on the

[1] United Nations: *Economic Survey of Europe for 1948,* cited.

program to the three-million-dollar estimated trade deficit. In the near future this alternative may appear the least distasteful of the four to Congress and to the American people. Europeans, however, would not regard prolongation of the ERP as entirely satisfactory, because, as the UN survey points out, the emergency character of American aid tends to perpetuate various emergency measures taken by other countries and defeats our own long-term plan for revival of multilateral trade through the International Trade Organization by obstructing progress toward freer and less discriminatory trading conditions. It is the considered opinion of United Nations economic experts that international governmental loans and grants afford only a temporary solution of international commercial and financial problems.

4. The fourth alternative, favored both by the recipients of ERP aid and by the United Nations Department of Economic Affairs in a report published in December 1949, is a large-scale program of capital investment abroad by the United States for specific development projects over a period of time, the funds not to be explicitly tied to expenditures on American goods. The UN report pointed out that during the period from 1874 to 1914, when many areas of the world, including the United States, were being developed and industrialized with the aid of foreign capital, the foreign long-term investments of Britain, France, and Germany grew from 6 to 33 billion dollars, yielding an average annual income of about five per cent. If the United States is to take the place in the world's economy of Britain and other western European nations, a program envisaging long-term investments of 20 to 30 billion dollars, it is contended, would not be unduly large. It must be admitted, however, that conditions under which investments can be made abroad today differ in many respects from those which prevailed before World War I. A century ago investors felt free, as they would not be now, to disregard the welfare and desires of native populations in backward areas, and even then fre-

quently had to take heavy losses on their investments. Nor did many of their restrictions on trade and currency convertibility which developed during the interwar years and were further accentuated after 1945, hamper world trade at every turn. If the contemplated American investments abroad are to be undertaken primarily by the government, this would mean added governmental planning and control of commerce and finance. If they are left for the most part in the hands of private investors, as President Truman has recommended under Point Four, then private investors will, quite understandably, want both from Washington and from the investment-seeking countries guarantees against foreign risks over and above those incidental to business operations at home, such as currency inconvertibility, confiscatory or discriminatory taxes, confiscation, seizure, or expropriation.[1] Such guarantees, however, and especially their enforcement, could all too easily provoke charges of "imperialism" against the United States and of "capitalist exploitation" against private American investors if large-scale investments are made by this country unilaterally. It was therefore wise for the United States to submit its Point Four program to the Economic and Social Council of the United Nations; and all future attempts to fulfill this program will prove most effective and least open to criticism if undertaken through the machinery of the UN.

The problem of accepting repayment of our investments by the European nations, however, would remain. For sooner or later they would have to pay us back, and this they could do only in the form of additional exports or services, which would bring us right back to our first alternative—of increasing imports sufficiently to close the existing trade gap between the two continents, a problem that import-hungry Britain did not face in the nineteenth century. This problem will become more acute as the world enters a period of

[1] See International Chamber of Commerce: *Draft International Code of Fair Treatment for Foreign Investments* (Paris, 1949).

buyers' markets, when the United States may become involved in intensified competition with the industrial nations of western Europe. And competition will be particularly lively now that devaluation has made it easier for
western Europe to trade with the non-dollar area than with the
dollar area.

Nor is there much prospect of achieving genuine currency convertibility and of reviving world trade as long as
Britain continues to owe sterling debts of approximately
one billion dollars to India, Pakistan, Iraq, Egypt, Argentina, Brazil, Uruguay, Israel, and Ceylon, for payment of
which it must set aside unrequited exports that might otherwise be sold in the United States. In view of this situation,
some ECA experts have urged that it would be a good
investment for Washington to use remaining Marshall Plan
appropriations to liquidate Britain's sterling indebtedness.
This discussion has revealed that plans for integration of
western Europe alone, or for continuance of bilateral trade
between western Europe and the United States, however
financed, will not remove the main obstacles to freer world
trade. Above all, they have clearly shown that a regional solution may represent a setback at a time when what is
needed is trade revival all over the globe.

The complex issues raised by the new relationship of our
economy to that of Europe, however, cannot be discussed
apart from the political and military issues with which they
are closely linked, and the attitude of this country toward
projects for western European political union, the North
Atlantic Treaty, and co-operation between the Western
Hemisphere and Europe within the framework of the
United Nations.

Chapter IX

WESTERN EUROPE: ILLUSION OR REALITY?

In the course of Congressional discussions of the Marshall Plan several members of Congress expressed the point of view that Europe would be unable to rehabilitate its economy if fear of aggression persisted, beclouding the economic outlook and jeopardizing political stability. They contended that the program of economic aid to Europe would therefore have to be accompanied by a program of political union between the countries benefiting by ERP, and by a program of mutual military assistance. During the first year of operation of the ERP, 1948–9, this larger concept of relations within the Marshall Plan group of nations, as well as between this group and the United States, gained more and more adherents both in official circles and among the American public.

It is difficult for us to understand the division of the European continent into a large number of small compartmentalized nations, each with its full panoply of frontier and tariff restrictions, which, as seen from here, only serve to block trade and communications between people who for their own good should be co-operating with each other as much as possible. Since Americans are convinced that the great economic upsurge and prosperity of the United States can be explained in large part by the fact that this country, continental in expanse, is free of tariff barriers, they believe that for the permanent rehabilitation of Europe it is absolutely necessary to abandon its ancient system of small national states and to create some form of tariff-free economic union. There is a strong belief here that it will prove impossible to establish such a union unless there is a political federation on the continent, at least of western Europe if not of Europe as a whole. Senator Fulbright of Arkansas expressed this sentiment when, in 1949, he introduced in the Senate a resolution favoring immediate formation of a European union.

Europeans who have given thought to federation possibilities find the American program too schematic, not sufficiently aware of the special conditions created in Europe by a long and tumultuous history of clashes between peoples and repeated efforts to assert and preserve national characteristics, traditions, and aspirations within given territorial confines. Even those European spokesmen who are themselves genuinely eager to see the development of a union on the continent and the disappearance of barriers between nations feel that we expect too much in too short a time. They urge patience, and contend that a union hastily contrived to meet the deadline of the ERP's termination in 1952 might cause more harm than good by disrupting efforts now being made by each nation to achieve recovery and political stabilization. The most optimistic European supporters of union believe that it will take at least twenty or twenty-five years to lay the groundwork for a practicable system and resolve such problems as Britain's reluctance to become too closely linked with the continent, the role of Germany in a European federation, and the relationship of this federation to the U.S.S.R.—central problems that, according to our friends across the Atlantic, have received insufficient consideration in the United States.

Practical experience with European problems gained by many Americans through the operations of various government agencies, particularly the European Cooperation Administration, has served to moderate the impatience earlier displayed here toward what had been considered undue slowness on the part of Europeans in framing plans for con-

tinental or western European union. We have begun to
realize that if the movement for federation is to play a vital
role, it must come from Europe itself and not be imposed
by the United States. Nevertheless, many thoughtful Americans—and this is not always adequately understood in Europe—believe that the beneficial effects of the ERP will be
dissipated in the long run unless the European countries
make use of the respite thereby gained to reorganize fundamentally both the economy and the political structure of
Europe. ECA Director Paul Hoffman said in February 1950
that Europe must accomplish in the remaining twenty-five
months of the ERP what would normally take twenty-five
years. The only steps taken so far toward economic integration are the Franco-Italian customs union of 1949, as yet
not implemented, and the Benelux customs union of 1947,
which eliminated all duties among the three countries, but
left untouched trade restrictions such as quotas, import and
export licensing, and currency control. The final stage is
to be full economic union, which is to go into operation on
July 1, 1950.

Discussions of economic integration in the OEEC and the
ECA indicate that perhaps the most practicable immediate
approach to economic problems will not be through rapid
and grandiose attempts to break down all lines of division
between Marshall Plan nations, but rather through patient
efforts to weave across these lines an ever growing network
of co-operation in many different fields that would gradually
convince the inhabitants of each of the compartmentalized
nations that greater freedom for movement of goods and for
communications of all kinds will benefit all of them. Sum-
marizing the "measurable progress" of the OEEC "in promoting the integration of specific segments of the European
economies," the ECA said in its third, 1948, report to Congress:[1]

[1] *Third Report to Congress of the Economic Cooperation Administration,*
cited, p. 26.

For example, it [OEEC] has concluded an arrangement under which surplus refining capacity of the French petroleum industry was made available to refine crude oil for the United Kingdom. Arrangements have also been made for the reciprocal supply of electric power between Switzerland and France. Switzerland will furnish electric power during daylight hours in the fall, and France will supply surplus power to Switzerland during slack periods in winter. Similar arrangements are planned between Switzerland and Belgium.

During the OEEC's investigation of the annual program of the countries, certain surpluses available for export were revealed in some participants at a time when others were looking to the Western Hemisphere for similar supplies. As a result of discussions in the OEEC, substantial quantities were moved in intra-European trade.

Other cooperative steps taken by the participating countries include an agreement on the use of Dutch and Belgian ports for German river traffic, and the fuller international use of the Rhine which has released thousands of needed freight cars. . . .

The ERP countries have also agreed to hold regular discussions of their investment plans, and to study the standardization of some of their products, especially railway equipment. The OEEC, for instance, has recommended that the European countries adopt standard designs for certain types of freight cars as well as standardized parts, such as couplings, buffers, wheels, axles and springs, which will make them easily interchangeable when maintenance and repairs are required. The problem of transporting perishable foodstuffs across parts of Europe has been tackled by the formation of an international company by the railway administrations of Belgium, France, Italy, the Netherlands, Luxembourg, and the United Kingdom. This company was expected to start operations in 1949.

In the transportation field the Economic Commission for Europe of the United Nations has been successful in achieving agreements among the countries on a provisional basis for the year 1949 providing for: 1) freedom of international highway transport of commercial vehicles; 2) freedom of transit traffic by bus beginning and ending in the same country; and 3) freedom of transit traffic between seaports and airports.

Some of these economic unity achievements may seem slight to us who are accustomed to moving and trading freely within the borders of a country continental in expanse, but they do indicate a favorable, if modest, trend for Europe, especially in the wake of a devastating war.

In the political sphere five western European nations—Britain, France, the Netherlands, Belgium, and Luxembourg—formed in 1948 at Brussels a Consultative Council composed of their Foreign Ministers. This Council met quarterly, and was assisted by a Permanent Commission in London, a Secretariat, and various other ministerial and technical committees. On January 28, 1949 the Consultative Council reached a compromise agreement for the establishment of a Council of Europe, whose formation was announced on May 5. These official steps had been preceded by unofficial meetings at The Hague, where the Congress of Europe convened in May 1948 and in April 1949 under the leadership of Winston Churchill; at Interlaken, where on September 2, 1948 the European Parliamentary Union adopted a charter calling for an assembly that should proceed to establish a federal Europe with sovereign power vested in a bicameral legislature; and in Rome, where the European Union of Federalists, at its second annual conference, held from November 6 to 11, 1948, expressed itself in favor of a government for Europe as a step toward final world federation. Virtually all schools of thought saw European union as a means to achieve a wide range of objectives, among them solution of the dollar-shortage problem; increase of Europe's military power and assurance of its security against Russian expansion; creation of a third major force to act as a balance between Russia and the United States; and settlement of the German problem by providing a framework within which German industrial capacity could be utilized for co-operation with Europe. A basic conflict, however, soon emerged regarding the methods of achieving these objectives. France and the federalists of various countries urged definitive transfer of sovereignty to a new central authority, while Britain argued that existing agencies, if expanded, would prove adequate, whereas a parliamentary assembly might fail and so weaken the whole movement for unity.

As the "European Movement" growing out of unofficial gatherings gained momentum, these issues were discussed at sessions of an official committee on European unity held on the suggestion of the French government in Paris on November 26, 1948. In the course of these discussions it became clear that the British Labour government believed the OEEC and the Brussels military pact would produce such interlocking mutual obligations and interests that no nation could afford to withdraw from the partnership. This "functional" approach, it was said, would then enable Europe step by step to meet specific problems without the arbitrary limitations of a constitutional apparatus—an approach regarded as desirable by the British, who are traditionally averse to written constitutions. Some non-British observers, however, pointed out that there might be a conflict between Britain's imperial and commonwealth ties, especially as concerns trade-preference arrangements and the continental obligations it would be expected to assume. The British Labour government, moreover, seemed fearful that a European authority might disturb the intricate pattern of national planning now being developed in Britain, and was visibly cool to proposals for European union—clashing on this score with Winston Churchill, one of the leading spirits of the European Movement. Another basic divergence was that the British urged the creation of a committee representing governments, while the French advocated a parliamentary assembly to be composed of representatives elected by the peoples of the participating countries.

The compromise reached by the Consultative Council in January 1949 provided for a European "consultative committee" of severely limited scope. It was to have power to make recommendations only, and its agenda were to be controlled by a ministerial committee. The committee was to hold brief annual public sessions and could appoint preparatory commissions. The national delegations were named by each country as it saw fit, instead of by national parliaments on a proportional-representation basis. This provision, the final point of compromise, grew out of Britain's reluctance to permit its own opposition, led by Churchill, to be represented in an international assembly, and its apprehension that Communist participation—particularly by French delegates—would jeopardize the whole undertaking.

The Council of Europe was established on May 5, 1949, when the representatives of ten nations signed the Council Statute in London. The original signatories were the five Brussels nations—Britain, France, the Netherlands, Luxembourg, and Belgium—plus Norway, Sweden, Denmark, Ireland, and Italy. Invitations to join the Council were extended to Greece and Turkey, and the possibility was discussed that the West German state, when established after the August 14, 1949 elections, might be asked to associate itself with the organization in a limited way. The Statute declares that a member may belong only if it accepts "principles of the rule of law and of the enjoyment of it by all persons within its jurisdiction of human rights and fundamental freedoms." [1] Meetings of the Council, it was decided, would be held at Strasbourg, France, which has long been a bone of contention between France and Germany and was selected specifically to make "a new effort at conciliation and unity," to quote British Foreign Secretary Bevin.

As agreed at Paris in January 1949, the Council of Europe consists of a Committee of Ministers (corresponding to a cabinet), a Consultative Assembly (corresponding to a parliament), and a Secretariat. Each state has one representative on the Committee of Ministers, which will recommend measures to promote the aims of the Council and request mem-

---

[1] *Statute of the Council of Europe*, May 5, 1949. Distributed by the British Embassy, Washington, D.C.

ber governments to report action taken on these recommendations. The Committee, which will meet in secret, has no power to enforce decisions.

When the Consultative Assembly gathered at Strasbourg on August 8, 1949 for its first session, Greece and Turkey, as anticipated in the Statute, were invited to join. Following the West German elections, which resulted in a plurality for the Christian Democrats, led by Dr. Konrad Adenauer, Winston Churchill, the most prominent figure at the Assembly, proposed that the admission of the German Federal Republic should be considered at the next session in December; and one of the first resolutions adopted by the German Parliament that opened at Bonn on September 8 requested admission to the Council on behalf of the West German state.

The Consultative Assembly is at present composed of 101 representatives. Britain, France, and Italy each has 18; Turkey, 8; Belgium, Greece, the Netherlands, and Sweden, 6 each; Denmark, Ireland, and Norway, 4 each; and Luxembourg, 3. This apportionment corresponds roughly to the size of the respective countries' population and offers an interesting possibility for the United Nations, where the one-vote-per-state practice has been adopted. Another suggestive precedent set by the Consultative Assembly was that the seating arrangement was organized alphabetically by individuals and not, as is the custom at international gatherings, by national delegations. This arrangement was reported to have played a significant part in mitigating nationalist friction.

Under the Statute, each participating state decides how its delegation is to be chosen. At the first session Communists were excluded from all delegations; and the Labour Party representatives in the British group were at moments embarrassed by the acclaim given to the Opposition leader, Winston Churchill, as well as by open clashes on policy between Labour and Conservative spokesmen. Although much criticism has been voiced in Europe about the great-power veto in the United Nations Security Council and its overuse by Russia, the Council of Europe Statute provides that all resolutions of the Consultative Assembly will require a unanimous vote (only a two-thirds vote is required in the UN General Assembly for approval of resolutions). Expressions of the Consultative Assembly's "wishes," however, will go through by a two-thirds vote.

Originally it had been expected that, as provided in the Statute, the Assembly, whose debates are open to the public, would make its wishes known to the Council of Ministers, but that the latter would determine the agenda of the Assembly, which was to serve as a sounding-board for "the aspirations of the European peoples." From the outset, however, the Assembly, under the vigorous chairmanship of former Belgian Prime Minister Paul-Henri Spaak, a Socialist, took matters into its own hands. It urged the creation of a European political authority "with limited functions but real powers." It did not go so far as to accept the idea of a European union, but proposed preferential tariff arrangements on the continent, currency convertibility, and negotiations with the United States for American tariff reductions. It discussed the creation of a European economic commission, that would presumably replace the OEEC, which has hitherto served primarily as a clearing-house for channeling to Washington the requests of the Marshall Plan countries. It adopted a code of human rights. Most important of all for its own future, it asserted the right to fix its agenda and to have a permanent steering committee.

The Council of Europe is to discuss economic, social, and cultural matters, but not problems of national defense, which are already being handled by the West Europe Union and the North Atlantic Treaty organization. In the words of the London communiqué of January 1949, there is no question in the Council of Europe "of any military alliance, but rather, as the preamble in the Statute says, of a general desire to achieve peace and bring about a greater unity for the purpose of safeguarding and realizing those ideals which are the common heritage of the members." Russia was not directly denounced at Strasbourg, but a number of references were made to the desirability of setting aside empty seats in the Consultative Assembly for countries of eastern Europe against the time when they might be able to conform with the requirements of the Statute.

The United States began to be seriously interested in projects for western European political and economic union in 1948, when the problem of military assistance to the Marshall Plan countries emerged into the open. The belief then gained ground here that integration of western Europe would be an essential precondition of military co-operation in the North Atlantic area. Washington officially indicated its interest in American-European arrangements for collective defense after British Foreign Secretary Ernest Bevin, speaking in the House of Commons on January 22, 1948, had proposed that Britain, France, and the Benelux countries set up a military-economic-political "Western Union", although Bevin did not then suggest the inclusion of the United States. By that time the growth of Russia's power, together with the demonstrated inability of the UN Security Council to negotiate agreements with member states for the creation of the armed force specified under Article 43 of the UN Charter, had created doubt in some official quarters about the ability of an international organization to safeguard the security of individual nations.

On January 23, 1949 the Department of State declared that "the United States heartily welcomes European initiative in this respect and any proposal looking to a closer material and spiritual link between the Western European nations will serve to reinforce the efforts which our two countries have been making to lay the foundation for a firm peace." Already Senator Leverett Saltonstall, Republican of Massachusetts, had urged that the United States should back the Marshall Plan with arms, and John Foster Dulles, Republican adviser to the administration on foreign policy, had recommended to the Senate Foreign Relations Committee the conclusion of an American-European treaty modeled after the Inter-American defense pact signed at Rio de Janeiro in 1948. The *coup d'état* of the Communist Party in Czechoslovakia at the end of February 1948 intensified official support for the course proposed by Dulles.

The Czech crisis occurred while the administration was concentrating its efforts on obtaining Congressional enactment of the ERP law. When several Republican senators offered an amendment to the recovery program to create a Supreme Council of UN members which would pledge themselves to use their armed forces outside the United Nations to defend a co-member from "aggression or subversion in any form," Senators friendly to the economic program as such defeated the amendment, although it included features later embodied in the North Atlantic Pact. The report on the United Kingdom that the House of Representatives Select Committee on Foreign Aid published on March 6, 1948 said that "only if Western Europe can be given the necessary political and military security will it be willing to rationalize its economy on a continental basis and thereby become economically self-sustaining once again."

The administration associated the United States directly but vaguely with the movement for regional European security in the address President Truman made to Congress on March 17, 1948, the day the Western Union powers signed in Brussels the military mutual-assistance treaty that Bevin had recommended on January 22. President Truman then said: "This development deserves our full support. I am confident that the United States will, by appropriate means, extend to the free nations the support which the situation requires. I am sure that the determination of the free countries of Europe to protect themselves will be matched by an equal determination on our part to help them do so." The Senate, on June 11, 1948, accelerated the development of the regional treaty policy by passing Resolution 239, known as the Vandenberg resolution, by 64 to 4, after debate that consumed only one afternoon.

This resolution, without binding the administration, expressed the sense of the Senate that it was the policy of the United States to "achieve international peace and security through the United Nations." Paragraphs 2, 3, and 4 concerned regional agreements. They proposed that the United States pursue the following objectives:

Progressive development of regional and other collective arrangements for individual and collective self-defense in accordance with the purposes, principles and provisions of the Charter.

Association of the United States, by constitutional process, with such regional and other collective arrangements as are based on continuous and effective self-help and mutual aid, and as affect its national security.

Contributing to the maintenance of peace by making clear its determination to exercise the right of individual or collective self-defense under Article 51 should any armed attack occur affecting its national security.

Encouraged by this resolution, the State Department in July 1948 initiated conversations with the Brussels Pact nations and Canada to explore the possibility of further cooperative efforts in the political and security fields. In the same month military representatives of the United States and Canada began to take part in the consultations of the Permanent Military Committee of the Brussels powers. Canadian officials spoke more freely and more vigorously than Americans about the desirability of an Atlantic pact. "The best guarantee of peace today is the creation and the preservation by the nations of the Free World, under the leadership of Great Britain, the United States, and France, of an overwhelming preponderence of force over any adversary or possible combination of adversaries," then Canadian Secretary of State for External Affairs Louis S. St. Laurent, who since has become Premier of Canada, said on June 11, 1948 in Toronto. Negotiations for the drafting of a North Atlantic security treaty opened in Washington on December 10 after the Brussels nations had chosen officers to command the branches of their combined forces, had approved a common defense policy, and had set up headquarters at Fontaine-bleau, although no actual amalgamation of forces had yet taken place.

When the negotiations were already under way, the United States, in January 1949, expressed its view of the reasons which, in its opinion, made a North Atlantic pact necessary, and of the objectives such a pact was expected to achieve, in a State Department document entitled *Collective Security in the North Atlantic Area*.[1] The thesis presented in this document was that economic rehabilitation of Europe was absolutely necessary to save the continent from a catas-trophe that might well spell the end of Western civilization. Therefore a cardinal point of American foreign policy had been the economic assistance rendered to western Europe under the Marshall Plan. But, said the document, a single country, Russia, had continuously tried to undermine the economic reconstruction of Europe and had endangered world peace. It would be extremely difficult for Europe to reconstruct itself as long as it lived in the shadow of possible aggression. To liberate Europe from fear, the United States had proposed the conclusion of a defense pact for the North Atlantic region, and implementation of this pact by integra-tion of the armed forces of western Europe and the dis-patch of American armaments to countries of this area.

The mere proposal of such a defense pact marked a revolu-tionary step in American policy. Hitherto, the United States, following the advice given by George Washington in his *Farewell Address,* had been opposed to any political or military engagement with other countries, except for tem-porary emergencies such as war. This view had persisted

[1] Department of State, Foreign Affairs Outline, *Building the Peace,* Spring 1949, No. 19.

after World War II, even when Winston Churchill, at Fulton, Missouri, had proposed in March 1946 the formation of a "fraternal association" between the United States and Britain implemented by mutual military aid. At that time Washington still hoped that the United Nations would succeed in effecting military arrangements envisaged in the UN Charter and that these arrangements would be adequate to prevent any act of aggression. Only after the negotiations of the Big Five in the Military Committee, reflecting the overall stalemate in East-West relations, had reached a dead end, did former reluctance to enter military alliances begin to decline in official circles. Thirty-five months after the Fulton speech President Truman, newly elected to office, disclosed the change in the administration's attitude when, in his budget message of January 10, 1949 and in his Inaugural Address of January 20, he proposed that the United States, by treaty, associate itself in a "collective defense arrangement" with "free" European countries in order to "strengthen the North Atlantic Area."

Two postwar precedents were cited by the United States in favor of a regional security pact within the framework of the United Nations. The first was the treaty concluded by the twenty-one nations of the Western Hemisphere at Rio de Janeiro in 1947, which became operative in December 1948. In this treaty the American republics agreed that an attack on any one of them would be considered as an attack on all; that in case of attack, or suspicion of attack, the members of the treaty system will consult at once (action in advance of consultation is contemplated but not required), that the decisions on the listed measures taken by two thirds of the members in consultation will bind them all, except that no state is required to use armed force without its consent; and that the regional security system is subordinate to the UN. An important feature of the Inter-American pact is that it calls for automatic consultation, but not for automatic armed intervention, on the part of the United States or any other signatory. Thus it satisfied the reluctance of Congress to surrender its constitutional authority to declare war, which was expressed by Senator Arthur H. Vandenberg, Republican of Michigan, then chairman of the Foreign Relations Committee, on June 11, 1948, when he said that he favored regional agreements that do not go "outside the final authority of Congress." The second precedent for the North Atlantic Treaty was the Brussels Pact, concluded in 1948, already mentioned, in which Britain, France, the Netherlands, Belgium, and Luxembourg undertook to render each other military assistance in case of armed attack on any one of them, and to set up a permanent council for co-ordination of their military plans and policies. As a result of the Washington negotiations, the Brussels Pact became a part of the larger framework of the North Atlantic Treaty.

This treaty, the text of which was published on March 19 and signed at a solemn ceremony in Washington on April 4, in Article 5—its key article—provides that "the parties agree that an armed attack against one or more of them in Europe or North America shall be considered an attack against them all." The treaty, however, does not require the signatories to go to war when another is attacked, although they agree to consult when one of them believes its territorial integrity, political independence, or security "is threatened." The signatories undertake to "maintain and develop their individual and collective capacity to resist armed attack"; to report any armed attack "and all measures taken as a result thereof . . . immediately . . . to the Security Council" of the United Nations; to leave to the Security Council "the primary responsibility . . . for the maintenance of international peace and security"; to refrain from entering into "any international engagement in conflict with this treaty"; to establish a council which would consider matters concerning the implementation of the treaty and would establish a subsidiary defense committee to work out a Western strategic plan for countering an armed attack; and to "eliminate conflict in their international economic policies." The pact is to run for twenty years, but the signatories will be free to recommend revisions at the end of ten. The initial signatories were twelve nations on both sides of the Atlantic: the United States, Canada, Britain, France, Belgium, the Netherlands, Italy, Norway, Denmark, Iceland, and Portugal.

By 1950 western European union was no longer a mere illusion, the ever elusive dream of many Europeans, from Henry IV to Briand, from Mazzini to Sforza; but neither had it yet become a concrete reality. The economic organization of western Europe, in spite of prodding by the United States, was still in the fetal stage, and political integration remained largely at a governmental level, with little progress toward the whittling down of national sovereignty. Fear of aggression—primarily from Russia, but to a lesser extent from a resurgent Germany—however, was beginning to give form and coherence to the co-ordination of military arrangements based chiefly on expectations of arms aid from the United States. As had often happened in past history, military alliances had proved easier to form than political or economic unions.

But transatlantic debates concerning the pros and cons of unification or, to use the term prefered by Washington, "integration" had revealed a significent trend that is bound to have far-reaching influence on relations between the United States and Europe. While the subject under discussion seemed to be European union, in actuality the Atlantic community was coming to the forefront at the expense of the earlier and narrower concept of a purely European, or even only western European, union. Facts were proving more powerful than theories. The fact that the United States, at midcentury, is the most powerful industrial nation in the world, and thus potentially the most powerful military nation, made it difficult for the Europeans to form a union of their own, a "third force" between America and Russia, without reference to the interest they have in obtaining this country's support in one form or another; but it also made it difficult for the United States to keep its economy and its military establishment completely apart from those of western Europe, on whom we are counting for aid against further thrusts by Russia and communism. Events may show that it was an illusion to expect regional organizations to fulfill functions that, in the highly interdependent world community of the twentieth century, can be effectively fulfilled only through intercontinental ties. The reality is that, no matter how diverse and divergent we may all be, even the Atlantic community cannot thrive and be secure in itself alone, but will be faced by the need to stabilize its relations with the rest of the world.

Chapter X

ARMS AND THE NORTH ATLANTIC TREATY

The negotiation and conclusion of the North Atlantic Treaty were preceded, accompanied, and followed by vigorous discussion both of its provisions and of its implications in Europe as well as in the United States. Among the issues raised in the course of these discussions the following seemed to be at the time most important:

What are the geographic boundaries of the North Atlantic community? The North Atlantic Pact at present embraces not only the countries of western Europe that in 1948 formed the Brussels military pact but also countries that did not join it (Norway, Denmark, Iceland, Portugal, Italy). It does not coincide with the group of countries receiving Marshall Plan aid, since it does not include Greece and Turkey. The group of countries it covers is determined by considerations of strategy rather than by the possible political and economic ties that might develop between the participating countries, throwing the cloak of commitments by the United States and Canada over an arc of nations stretching from Norway and Iceland in the north to Portugal and Italy in the south. Nor is it based entirely on the concept that participating countries should have democratic institutions and free elections, since Portugal, which has neither, is included—persumably not so much because of its own position on the Atlantic and its ancient alliance with Britain as because it controls the strategic islands of the Azores, where the United States during and since the war acquired the right to maintain bases. Italy, obviously not a North Atlantic country, was also included, in spite of the fact that the Italian peace treaty limits to 250,000 men the armed forces of a country that fought against the Allies on the side of Germany. But Franco Spain was finally not brought within the pact, although, in contrast with Italy, it is a North Atlantic country and, in the opinion of some American military leaders, might, at best, play a useful part in any strategic plans evolved by the North Atlantic group or, at worst, should at least be kept out of the Russian orbit by inclusion in the pact. Nor was membership in the United Nations a prerequisite for being invited to sign the pact—in spite of official assurances that the pact was carefully designed to fit into the UN framework—since Italy has not yet been admitted to the United Nations.

Another problem that arose in the course of negotiations was whether countries that might otherwise be regarded as belonging to the North Atlantic community and, at the same time, possess democratic institutions should be accorded the safeguards of the pact unless they were prepared to sign it. When Norway pressed the United States for clarification on this point, Washington made it clear that it would not give arms to any country that did not take the risk of signing the pact. Some observers thought that it was unwise to put pressure on Norway to become a signatory, for it might thereby expose itself to retaliation by the U.S.S.R. at a time when neither the United States nor other North Atlantic countries were in a position to give it effective military assistance. These observers pointed out that the United States, since 1947, had been providing armaments to Greece and Turkey without requiring those two countries to sign any military pact. Ultimately Norway decided to take the risk of signing the treaty, following unsuccessful attempts to establish a limited military alliance with Sweden, but Sweden refused to relinquish its traditional neutrality and therefore remains outside the framework of the pact although it is a democratic nation and a member of the UN.

Another question, to be discussed in the future, is the possible role that might be played in the pact by the West German state, which not only commands the industrial and raw-material resources of the Ruhr, highly useful to a North Atlantic grouping, but also has a larger reservoir of manpower for a potential armed force than any of the European signatories. The Russians, as well as Communist spokesmen in North Atlantic Pact countries, were quick to contend that the United States and its partners in the pact were planning to use German resources and manpower for the purpose of fighting the U.S.S.R., and some Germans expressed fear that their country would again be drawn into war, this time to assist one or other of the great-power groups in Europe. German nationalists of various parties would like to see a unified Germany rearm—but few Germans are enthusiastic about being assigned the role of mercenaries to fight Russia on behalf of the West.

The question whether or not the North Atlantic Pact is really in harmony with the United Nations Charter or violates its terms was hotly discussed both here and in Europe. Before the treaty was signed some American spokesmen expressed grave doubts on this score—notably Hamilton Fish Armstrong, editor of the quarterly *Foreign Affairs,* who stated that while the pact would be "entirely legal under Article 51, and it would be much better for the United States to take it than to do nothing," it was decidedly a second-best choice, and a choice that might eventually hamper, not help, the UN; for "a series of regional pacts might in time overshadow the organization's universal character and aims." [1] A distinguished international-law expert, Hans Kelsen, contended that as long as the Charter's provisions for collective security remained unimplemented it may become inevitable to substitute collective self-defense for collective security; but, he warned, "such substitution would be the

---

[1] Hamilton Fish Armstrong: "Coalition for Peace," *Foreign Affairs,* October 1948, p. 1.

bankruptcy of that political and legal system for which the United Nations was created." [2]

In presenting official American arguments for the pact, the State Department contended that the Charter recognizes "that certain groups of countries have common interests of a strategic, political, economic and social nature and that certain security problems are of a distinctly regional character." Two articles of the Charter were cited in support of the contention that "nations having such common interests" may take "collective action for defense under certain conditions": Article 51, which says: "Nothing in the present Charter shall impair the inherent right of individual or collective self-defense if an armed attack occurs against a Member of the United Nations, until the Security Council has taken the measures necessary to maintain international peace and security"; and Article 52, which provides that "Nothing . . . precludes the existence of regional arrangements or agencies for dealing with such matters relating to the maintenance of international peace and security as are appropriate for regional action . . . consistent with the purposes and principles of the United States."

In answer to this argument, critics of regional defense pacts in general have argued that such pacts would violate the UN Charter and lead to the re-establishment of military alliances incompatible with collective security, the UN. and world peace. The proper relationship of regional arrangements to the system of collective security envisaged in the UN Charter was discussed at length both at Dumbarton Oaks and at San Francisco. In the course of these discussions especial attention was given to the regional arrangements already existing at that time in the Western Hemisphere, and to the problems that might arise if the former enemy states should resort to aggression during the transitional period be-

[2] Hans Kelsen: "Collective Security and Collective Self-Defense under the Charter of the United Nations," *American Journal of International Law,* October 1948, p. 783.

fore peace treaties had been concluded and responsibility for keeping the peace had been transferred to the United Nations Organization. Chapter VIII of the Charter, entitled "Regional Arrangements," was drafted and redrafted at the two conferences primarily with these two problems in mind. It is this chapter that contains Article 52, one of the two articles cited by the State Department in January 1949 in support of the North Atlantic Pact proposal. Article 51, it should be noted, forms no part of the chapter on regional arrangements. It is the last article of Chapter VII, on "Action with Respect to Threat to the Peace, Breaches of the Peace and Acts of Aggression"; and it is this article that appears to have special relevance for the pact. Article 51 recognizes the subordination of the right of self-defense to the collective-security concept of the Charter by explicitly stating that such measures as member nations may take for individual or collective self-defense in case of armed attack are to be reported immediately to the Security Council, and do not "in any way affect the authority and responsibility of the Security Council . . . to take at any time such action as it may deem necessary in order to maintain or restore international peace and security."

Hans Kelsen contended that "the use of force in the exercise of self-defense under Article 51 is intended by the Charter as a provisional and temporary measure, permitted only 'until' the Security Council takes necessary measures to restore peace, especially until collective security comes into action, and not as a substitute for it." In the final text of the North Atlantic Pact, paragraph 2 of Article 5 specifies that any armed attack which brings the pact into operation and all measures taken as a result thereof shall immediately be reported to the UN Security Council. "Such measures shall be terminated when the Security Council has taken the measures necessary to restore and maintain international peace and security."

Still another issue that aroused controversy concerned the

conditions that might bring the North Atlantic Treaty into operation. Was it directed solely against external attacks on any one of the signatories, or might it also be invoked in case of internal unrest that could be interpreted as a threat to security? Would it be limited strictly to situations arising in Europe, or would it be applicable to armed conflicts in colonial areas controlled by European nations that joined the North Atlantic Pact?

Article 6 of the pact states that "for the purpose of Article 5 an armed attack on one or more of the parties is deemed to include an armed attack on the territory of any of the parties in Europe or North America, on the Algerian Department of France, on the occupation forces of any party in Europe, on the islands under the jurisdiction of any part in the North Atlantic area north of the Tropic of Cancer or on the vessels or aircraft in this area of any of the parties." In spite of these specific limitations as to both the categories of acts that might be classified as "armed attack" and the geographic areas where they might occur, many people in Europe expressed apprehension that the fear of instability and disorder understandably generated in the United States by the desire to see the ERP succeed within the time limit of four years might cause some Americans to favor the maintenance of existing regimes and economic and social conditions, and to view any attempt to alter the existing state of affairs as defiance of ERP. The intimate linking of ERP with rearmament, it was said, might then conceivably induce the United States to permit countries benefiting by American aid to use their armaments for suppression of internal disorders. Similar fears had already been expressed by liberals in Latin-American countries, who have asked themselves whether the Rio Treaty might not be invoked by dictatorial regimes in that area to prevent all attempts at internal reform. The fact that the United States has not protested against the establishment, following army coups, of regimes controlled by military and reactionary elements in Venezeuela, Peru, and Bolivia and has not openly objected to the curtailment of liberties there as it has in countries of eastern Europe and the Balkans has further heightened the anxiety of Latin Americans as to the ultimate effects of a regional security pact on prospects for economic and social change.

The question has been asked, too, whether the United States, in underwriting the security and economic recovery of western Europe, would be expected also to underwrite the *status quo* in Indonesia, Indo-China, Malaya, and other colonial areas, whose present condition of unrest has a direct impact on the security and the economic rehabilitation of the Netherlands, France, and Britain. Will the nations of western Europe be free to use the arms they may receive from the United States to subdue native uprising? To this question the State Department, in a special statement to the Senate Foreign Relations Committee on April 27, 1949, gave a categorical no, and it is reported that during the Washington negotiations the Netherlands was informed that American military commitments under the pact would not be extended to cover the colonial areas. It is significant, however, that since conclusion of the pact the colonial nations of western Europe have increasingly pointed out the close economic relationship of colonies in southeast Asia to their economies, and have asked why the United States, which is on record as opposing both Russia and communism in Europe, tolerates Communist movements in Asia.

Other Europeans have gone further and have urged the conclusion of a Pacific pact as a corollary to the North Atlantic Treaty. For example, the London *Economist* said in May 1949:

Britain's first task [in southeast Asia], in cooperation with the Dominions, is to make clear its intention to hold the line against further Communist advance—if necessary, as in Malaya, answering force with force. Whether this determination should take the shape of a formal Pacific Pact is a matter to be decided in consultation with the Pacific Dominions and with India, Pakistan and Ceylon. The inclusion of France and Holland must also wait on the settlement of the internal problems in Indo-China and Indonesia. But the Commonwealth is in itself a nucleus for defense, provided the objective of holding South East Asia is accepted. It need hardly be added that the reinforcement of the proposed defence group by American military and economic aid would strengthen it and consolidate it as nothing else can do.[1]

The *Economist* added, however, that "it is useless to wait for the Americans," pointing to the statement made by Secretary of State Acheson on May 18, 1949 that conditions for such a pact did not exist in Asia. The Indian government of Prime Minister Nehru has expressed its opposition to such a pact, and it seems doubtful that the United States, which since the achievement of Indian independence has looked to New Delhi for leadership in Asian affairs, would seriously advocate a Pacific pact, although it might support a pact urged by Asian nations.

Another problem of concern to both Americans and Europeans is the extent to which military preparations in the United States and in western Europe might interfere with recovery on the continent and consequently foster economic and social unrest that would facilitate the resurgence of communism, thus defeating the main objective of the North Atlantic Treaty. John Foster Dulles, Republican adviser to the administration on foreign policy, in an interview of January 1949 said: "I am inclined to think that we are exaggerating the percentage of our national income that needs to be diverted into the military establishment. I think that there is . . . a risk of war, but I think the risk is not so great that we should seriously jeopardize our own economic health, our ability to demonstrate the great possibilities of a free society, by saddling ourselves with such vast armament." In its official statement of the case for the North Atlantic Treaty the State Department, in the document

---

[1] "South East Asia," *Economist*, May 28, 1949, p. 960.

mentioned above, placed economic recovery ahead of rearmament. "Economic recovery," it declared, "is fundamental and should continue to have priority over rearmament. What is needed is a carefully drawn balance in Europe between recovery and rearmament and a similar balance here between the needs of our own domestic economy, our own defense, our contribution to ERP, and our contribution to European rearmament." Critics of the treaty agreed that such a program, in theory, sounds acceptable. They contended however, that in practice, if past experience is a guide, the very process of rearmament will generate fears that still further rearmament will be needed to allay, creating a mounting spiral of expenditures in which military estimates will prevail over considerations of economic and social recovery, thus bringing about or perpetuating the very conditions of misery, want, and dissatisfaction that the Marshall Plan was intended to combat and alleviate.

Hanson Baldwin, military expert of the *New York Times,* has taken a less pessimistic view. He believes that the maintenance of an alliance—which the North Atlantic Pact is in effect—"as a stabilizing factor in the world rather than as an instrument of aggrandizement must always represent a nice sense of balance of proportion." These negative aims, however, are not impossible of realization. "We must," he said, "keep clearly in mind what the Atlantic pact and the arms-aid program must not become, as well as what they must become. They must not be provocative; they must not sacrifice economic and political and psychological recovery for military strength alone. But on the other hand the positive objective of the Atlantic pact-arms-aid program must be the defense of Western Europe, not its reconquest once overrun, for invasion of Western Europe means the bankruptcy of all our past policies and the mortgaging of the future."

A wise balancing of security and recovery policies becomes of special concern when it is realized that the nations of western Europe, for the present at least, are not in a position to provide out of their own resources an important part either of the manpower or of the armaments that would be required for a major and prolonged conflict. Of the signatories of the North Atlantic Pact, the Netherlands, Belgium, Luxembourg, Norway, Denmark, Iceland, and Portugal are insignificant in terms of the armed forces they possess or might raise in an emergency (until 1950 the Netherlands has 100,000 men in Indonesia). Italy, by the provisions of its peace treaty, is precluded from maintaining substantial armed forces. All of these countries, however, can play an important part as strategic footholds along Europe's Atlantic seaboard and, on the other hand, if occupied by an enemy, would make reoccupation of the continent difficult, if not impossible, and might, in turn, become springboards for attacks by a European aggressor on the British Isles and, at greater remove, on Canada and the United States.

Of the North Atlantic Pact signatories in Europe only Britain and France might conceivably become important military factors. Britain, however, has never maintained a considerable land army and, when left alone on the continent, has been forced by stronger land powers to withdraw across the English Channel, as happened at Dunkirk in 1940. Its Navy and Air Force would be of value again in another war; but if the U.S.S.R is expected to be the aggressor of the future, it is doubtful that such a war would be decided by naval and air power alone, even if implemented by the atomic bomb, whose possible use is feared by our potential allies almost as much as by our potential enemies. France has traditionally relied on its land forces for defense; but today, after its resounding defeat by Germany's heavily armored troops and Air Force and five years of German occupation, the French have at their command so limited a number of trained forces that they would probably be unable to muster more than 500,000 men, or approximately nine divisions—although reliable figures are difficult to obtain from French sources. Moreover, 150,000 of these troops are engaged in highly dangerous and so far fruitless warfare against guerrilla troops in Indo-China, and the French Army is practically devoid of modern weapons, military planes, and armored vehicles. If France were asked by the United States to fill even a portion of its current defense needs, it would have to divert a considerable part of its manpower and material resources to war production. This, the French fear, would be the most direct way to strengthen communism. Thus in France, more than in Britain, the morale factor does not appear to be particularly strong. But the British, too, although less outspoken, and more confident of their ability to defend themselves because of their favorable geographic position, have made clear their reluctance to divert an additional portion of their manpower and resources to military service and armament production at a time when their contention that they must "export or die" is not a slogan but a harsh statement of the terms of survival. Significant, too, is France's fear that the British will in no case fight an aggressor on the continent and will, as in 1940, stage another Dunkirk, take their stand in the British Isles, and leave their European friends to shift for themselves as best they can.

Under these circumstances the United States, with such assistance as it can obtain from Canada, is counted on by western Europe to serve as the principal source both of land forces (military experts contend that forty divisions at least would be needed to withstand the U.S.S.R.) and of modern armaments. From the point of view of the Europeans, therefore, the pledge of American participation in combined resistance to armed attack on any nation in the North Atlantic area, while gratefully welcomed as an indication of this country's peacetime concern in European affairs, would prove of little value unless accompanied by substantial military assistance—and not assistance to be proffered *after* the attack had occurred and western Europe had perhaps been overrun by an aggressor, but available on European soil *in advance* of aggression. In view of these European expectations, it is not surprising that the peoples of western Europe—as distinguished from official laudatory statements by their governments—have been skeptical about the practical significance of the North Atlantic Treaty, especially when they learned, from reports of discussions in Congress, that many of the American legislators who had enthusiastically supported the treaty felt they had not thereby committed themselves to vote for arms-aid measures to implement it. The State Department, following its practice of presenting economic and military aid programs to Congress stage by stage instead of giving an over-all picture of estimated western European needs—presumably to assure periodical Congressional acceptance of relatively small requests for appropriations—had refrained from publicly raising the question of an arms-aid appropriation while the North Atlantic Treaty was in process of negotiation. Once the treaty was concluded, the administration submitted a request for $1,450,000,000, which, in the opinion of experts, is inadequate for furnishing our partners in the pact with the manpower and armaments they need in case of armed attack, even though some armaments will be provided out of this country's war-surplus stocks.

The arms-aid program is intended to bring the 1,500,000 reportedly available for military service in the five Brussels Pact countries—Britain, France, Belgium, the Netherlands, and Luxembourg—up to fighting strength, and to raise the combat effectiveness of relatively small forces in Norway, Denmark, and Italy. The potential 1,500,000 force of the five-nation western European union compares with a reported Russian military strength of 150 divisions, totaling more than 4,000,000 land troops. The United States, in addition, has a total of 1,600,000 men under arms in the Army, Air Force, Navy, and Marines. The Soviet air fleet has been estimated variously at from 14,000 to 16,000 planes of all types, of which forty-two per cent are thought to be fighters; and some experts believe that the U.S.S.R. may be turn-

ing out 200 jet fighters a month and about 1,000 bombers of
the B-29 type a year. The continental countries of western
Europe lack planes, but Britain has continued to produce
planes since the war and has done intensive work on jet
fighters. In addition to B-29 bombers, a number of which
are stationed in Britain, the United States Air Force has an
improved superfortress, the B-50, and a limited number of
the still longer-range bombers, the B-36, on which it has
been concentrating production in spite of controversy concerning its qualities.

Until the gap between the promise of substantial military
aid implicit in the North Atlantic Treaty and the performance thus far made by the United States has been closed, or
at least narrowed, the danger will remain that, by inviting
the nations of western Europe to sign the pact, we have irrevocably lined them up on our side and have thereby ex-
posed them to possible hostile measures by the U.S.S.R.,
without, at the same time, placing at their disposal the resources they require to defend themselves—and this country
as well—in case of emergency.

The existence of this gap makes another question about
the pact less important in the immediate future for Europeans than for American legislators: and that is whether or
not it will go into operation automatically or must wait on a
decision by Congress. True, European spokesmen have repeatedly complained that under the American system of
government any pledges of aid given by the executive are
always subject to final decision by Congress, which conceivably might repudiate such pledges, as the Senate did in the
case of the Versailles Treaty in 1919—a vote that has been
indelibly imprinted on the memories of Europeans. In view of
this recent experience, however, and of considerable subsequent study of American constitutional and political practices, few responsible Europeans expect automatic action by
the United States on any issue, no matter how many treaties
may be drafted by the Secretary of State, signed by the Presi-

dent, and ratified by the Senate. They do count, however, on the growing community of interests, and especially on considerations of American security, to bring about a quick decision by Congress on setting the North Atlantic Treaty in operation—although under conditions of modern warfare, with France defeated within ten days in 1940, and the Low countries conquered in a matter of hours, even a brief delay for consideration of the matter might prove fatal to western Europe and, presumably, also to the United States.

The American Congress, for its part, remains determined both to retain freedom of action for the United States and to make sure that such action as the executive may have to take in an emergency will not infringe on the recognized authority of the legislature. It was this issue that created the most extended discussion in the Senate Foreign Relations Committee before it unanimously recommended, on June 7, 1949, that the Senate ratify the North Atlantic Pact as a way "greatly to increase" the prospect of averting a third world war. In its article-by-article report on the pact the Committee presented an extended analysis of its understanding of the provisions of the pact's key article, Article 5. Referring to the phrase: "such action as it deems necessary," it stated that each party remains free to exercise its honest judgment in deciding upon the measures it will take to help restore and maintain the security of the North Atlantic area. Freedom of decision, however, "in no way reduces the importance of the commitment undertaken." The Committee further declared: "Obviously Article 5 carries with it in important and far-reaching commitment for the United States; what we may do to carry out that commitment, however, will depend upon our own independent decision in each particular instance reached in accordance with our constitutional processes." The Committee also made a distinction between an armed attack on the United States, which "by its very nature would require the immediate application of all force necessary to repel the attack," and armed attack on other countries.

Nevertheless, in the opinion of the Committee, "an armed attack within the meaning of the treaty would in the present-day world constitute an attack upon the entire community comprising the parties to the treaty, including the United States. Accordingly, the President and the Congress, within their sphere of assigned Constitutional responsibilities, would be expected to take all action necessary and appropriate to the United States against the consequences and dangers of an armed attack committed against any party to the treaty." [1]

In commenting on the division of powers between the executive and the legislature the Committee then added, largely to meet objections that had been raised by Senator Walter F. George of Georgia: "The committee does not believe it appropriate in this report to undertake to define the authority of the President to use the armed forces. Nothing in the treaty, however, including the provision that an attack against one shall be considered an attack against all, increases or decreases the Constitutional powers of either the President or the Congress to change the relationship between them."

The North Atlantic Treaty, ratified by the Senate on July 21, 1949 by a vote of 82 to 13, was implemented after prolonged controversy by the Mutual Defense Assistance Act, which President Truman signed on October 6, 1949. This act authorized military assistance to foreign countries, principally our North Atlantic partners, to the amount of $1,314,000,000 by June 30, 1950. Once the appropriations have been approved by Congress, only the first $100,000,000 can be spent prior to a Presidential finding that an "inte-

---

[1] Senate Committee on Foreign Relations Report, *North Atlantic Treaty*, 81st Congress, 1st Session, Executive Report, No. 8 (Washington: United States Government Printing Office; June 6, 1949), p. 14.

grated defense" is being planned by the treaty signatories, and the President must approve plans for such "integrated defense" before the last $900,000,000 of the projected supplies can be shipped across the ocean. At the time the Brussels Pact countries—Britain, France, the Netherlands, Belgium, and Luxembourg—had not yet gone beyond the stage of appointing leaders of their armed forces to examine possibilities of military co-operation. Under the chairmanship of Field-Marshal Viscount Montgomery of Britain, the military committee of the Brussels Pact countries, with headquarters at Fontainebleau, had set up skeleton agencies for co-ordination of the three principal armed services—land, sea, and air—under the suggestive titles of *Uniter, Unimer,* and *Uniair.* The appointment of Viscount Montgomery to the key position in the Brussels Pact military setup had alarmed the French, who feared that Britain's strategic concept would be based on abandonment of the continent, and defense of Europe, or its liberation, from the British Isles.

These fears were somewhat allayed by the creation in October, at a Washington conference of the twelve North Atlantic Defense Ministers, of the Defense Committee of the North Atlantic Treaty organization. This Committee, in turn, appointed a Military Committee composed of the chiefs of staff of ten of the participating countries (Iceland and Luxembourg elected not to appoint members), under the chairmanship of General Omar N. Bradley, chairman of the United States Joint Chiefs of Staff, who was expected to take the direction of plans for "integrated defense" of the North Atlantic area. The Military Committee is to have a sort of executive committee, the Standing Group—composed of General Bradley, Sir William Morgan, chairman of the British Joint Services Mission, and Lieutenant General Paul Ely of France—which will function continuously in Washington.

Among the first tasks of the Standing Group was to decide, with the aid of a staff of experts, the frontiers of the area to be defended in case of attack—this promises to be the thorniest question on the agenda—and to assign roles to the participating nations. If defense is to be genuinely "integrated," it will be necessary for each of the nations to concentrate on development of the military functions it is best prepared to perform, and not seek to build up for itself ground, sea, and air forces according to national calculations of defense needs. It is expected that France would be invited to concentrate on ground forces, and not undertake a naval construction program, while the United States and Britain, which together command the greatest naval strength in the world, would concentrate on naval and air power. Strategic bombardment would probably be assigned to this country, which has developed long-range bombers, notably the much disputed B-36, while Britain might perfect medium, or tactical, bombardment in direct support of ground forces, and the use of jet planes, in the construction of which it has excelled the United States. For the time being, this country retains control both of its stockpile of atomic bombs and of the discoveries it has made in the process of manufacturing the bomb since 1947, when the MacMahon Act prohibited the giving of atomic information to other countries. However, Britain and Canada, our partners in the original discovery of the secret of bomb manufacture, requested in the summer of 1949 the right to share our post-1947 knowledge, and proposed that we pay a higher price for uranium, which is found in Canada as well as in the Belgian Congo, whose uranium resources are controlled primarily by the British.

President Truman's announcement in September 1949 that "an atomic explosion" had occurred in the U.S.S.R., although long expected, precipitated reconsideration of the defense strategy that should be adopted by the North Atlantic countries. If the atomic bomb is as decisive a weapon as has been contended by some of our military leaders, then Russia is now in a position to wreak destruction on our western European allies with no possibility for genuine defense

on their part—a prospect that has haunted European statesmen since Hiroshima. Then, it has been asked, of what value
will prove our present plans for building up the ground
forces of France, or even the naval strength of Britain and
the United States? If, however, as argued by Admiral Arthur
W. Radford and other of our naval leaders, an atomic blitz
not only is technically impracticable, but would also be un-
desirable from the point of view of over-all policy, for it
would leave Europe devastated beyond hope of reconstruction and give us, at best, a Pyrrhic victory—then is not the
first step of the North Atlantic Defense Committee to make
another attempt at international control of atomic energy, or
at least propose outlawry of the bomb? Thus no sooner had
the North Atlantic Pact machinery been created than the
knowledge that Russia could retaliate against atomic-bomb
warfare, on which our strategists had placed their principal
reliance, and our decision to develop the hydrogen bomb, appeared to make this machinery obsolete. Yet, President Truman having approved the Atlantic Defense Committee's strategic plans, and the United States having completed in January 1950 bilateral arms agreements with eight North Atlantic nations, American equipment began to move to western
Europe.

At midcentury many observers, studying the still flimsy
structure of western European union, linked to the United
States and Canada through the North Atlantic Pact, wondered whether economic and security arrangements on a
regional basis would prove effective, or whether they had
already been outdistanced by events, such as the rise to
power of new, non-Western nations like India and Communist China, and the development of global political, economic, and social links within the framework of the United
Nations and other international agencies.

Chapter XI

THE UNITED STATES, EUROPE,
AND THE UNITED NATIONS

When we discuss the United Nations organization with our friends in Europe, we are often taken aback by the question: "Do Americans *still* believe in the United Nations?" The automatic response is apt to be: "Why, we have just *begun* to believe in it." And only after prolonged and frank exploration of the subject do we realize with what high expectations the United States, as compared with Europe, has been viewing the UN.

This difference is due to a time-lag that it will take a real effort on our part to overcome. Between 1919 and 1939 some sixty nations—one more than the number now belonging to the UN—participated more or less actively and wholeheartedly in the League of Nations. Even the U.S.S.R., which had remained aloof from most of the League's activities except in the field of health, had joined it in 1934 following the departure of Germany and Japan; and Soviet Foreign Commissar Litvinov made Geneva resound with eloquent pleas for collective security until Russia was expelled in 1939, following its invasion of Finland.

Of the great powers the United States alone remained outside, steadfastly holding to its 1919 decision not to become a member of the League, although many Americans were intensely interested in various phases of the League's work and a few held office in the League Secretariat. Yet even in that period of American isolation from international organization there was probably more written and said about the League in this country than in nations that convened at Geneva. And a significant number of idealistic men and women worked unremittingly here to inform public opinion about the plans and achievements of the Geneva institution and to convince Americans that they should give it full aid and support.

Thus paradoxically it came about that the nations which had been in the League from the outset, when high hopes were held for the future of international organization, had by 1939 become doubtful about the League's capacity to solve conflicts between nations and had developed a kind of resigned cynicism, while the United States, the principal outsider, was reaching a pitch of fervent belief in the efficacy of international co-operation as the only alternative to isolation.

It is therefore not surprising that it was the United States, under the leadership of President Roosevelt, that gave the impetus to discussions about the establishment of a new world organization dedicated to the prevention of war and the creation of conditions of stable peace through timely adjustment of economic, social, and political issues that might otherwise lead to war. Nor did Roosevelt forget the tragic experience of Woodrow Wilson, who had failed to win the backing of the Senate and the public for the League Covenant. Great efforts were made to inform the American people during World War II about the need for and the proposed structure of the United Nations organization, and public discussion of the preliminary negotiations at Dumbarton Oaks was warmly encouraged. It was also decided that the United Nations would in no sense be linked to the peace treaties, and in fact would not even be asked to consider any of the problems directly resulting from the war, these problems being left for settlement by the victors. President Roosevelt and his advisers regarded it as a great achievement of American foreign policy that, at the Yalta conference of 1945, Stalin, who during the war had displayed no enthusiasm for an international organization, agreed to have the great powers summon a conference at San Francisco to draft a charter of the United Nations.

In this attempt to create a climate of opinion favorable to Senate ratification of the United Nations Charter, the potentialities of the world organization were so highly extolled that the American people came to expect far more from it than it could in reality achieve—and certainly far more than was expected by other nations, which had had twenty years of experience with the limitations, as well as the potentialities, of the League of Nations. With the best of intentions, the UN was oversold in the United States.

Then, when events showed that an international organization is not a universal panacea and cannot overnight solve problems deeply rooted in world history, a reaction set in that proved just as exaggerated as the earlier hopes. People in the United States began to shrug their shoulders, to say that the UN was impotent, and to suggest a wide range of substitutes—from various regional arrangements outside the UN to the immediate proclamation of world government. There was also a strong tendency among us to believe that Russia alone was responsible for the deficiencies of the UN, and that if Russia were excluded, it would prove possible to undertake effective international action and solve most of the outstanding problems.

In spite of doubts voiced here about the efficacy of the United Nations, American officials have been at pains to reiterate that support of the UN is a foundation stone of this country's foreign policy, and that the United States is determined to strengthen the UN. On March 17, 1949, in transmitting to President Truman a report on United States participation in the United Nations during 1948, Secretary of State Acheson, after analyzing the many difficulties faced by the UN, concluded: "Nevertheless, there is no sound reason for Americans to lose confidence in the United Nations. Responsible collective judgment on matters of international concern is better than the interested and sometimes irresponsible judgments of individual nations. The future of America is closely related to the extension of democratic principles and practices in other areas; we believe the United Nations is the proper agency for promoting that extension by peaceful and proper means. Much remains to be done; the present need is to reaffirm our belief in the Charter of the United Nations and to strengthen our support for its processes of peace." [1] Speaking at the dedication of the World War Memorial Park in Little Rock, Arkansas, on June 11, 1949, President Truman declared that the United Nations is "a valuable instrument," adding: "It has already achieved the peaceful settlement of difficult issues. It has stopped hostilities in the Near East and in Indonesia. It has done a great deal to explore and find solutions for many of the economic and social problems which afflict the world." At the same time he said: "Much remains to be done, however, to carry out the principles of the United Nations"—and then described the North Atlantic Pact as an attempt by this country and by other nations to provide greater assurance within the terms of the UN Charter against the danger of armed conflict.

The avowed determination of the United States to base its policy on the United Nations has been tempered by two factors: the belief that the U.S.S.R. has consistently sought to block operation of the UN and to undermine its decisions; and an almost automatic reflex on the part of American leaders, when dealing with measures regarded as of major importance for national interests, to take unilateral action outside the framework of the UN, on some occasions because of reluctance to have such measures subject to discussion or veto by the U.S.S.R., on others because of a disposition on the part of Congress to work directly through national

---

[1] *United States Participation in the United Nations:* Report by the President to the Congress for the year 1948 on the Activities of the United Nations and the Participation of the United States therein. Department of State Publication 3437 (Washington: Government Printing Office; 1949), p. vii.

rather than international agencies—a disposition that may be regarded as a contemporary form of what was once isolationism.

American conviction that the U.S.S.R. is the principal if not the only stumbling-block to effective operation of the United Nations runs like a leitmotiv through official reports on the work of the UN. For example, the 1948 report already referred to contains the following statements:

Consideration of these questions [in the General Assembly]—particularly those of atomic energy, reduction of conventional armaments, and the Greek question—led to debates on foreign policies generally and on the broad issues separating the Soviet Union from other countries. . . . The decisions on all of the specific political matters were, with isolated exceptions, opposed only by the Soviet group. The Assembly did not automatically adopt the proposals made by any one Member, as often alleged by Soviet spokesmen. On the contrary, national proposals were, in practically all instances, modified through the process of discussion. They expressed the views of a large majority, and they emerged with the support of practically the entire Assembly except the Soviet bloc. This fact reflects clearly the extent of the divergence of Soviet aims and policies from those of practically all other Members. Unfortunately, no tendency was seen on the part of the Soviet group to reconcile its views with those of the rest of the membership. . . . The Security Council's work, naturally reflected the political instability and division that prevailed in 1948. In part, these conditions were incidental to the process of achievement of full independence and political unification by a number of nations. In part, they resulted from the continued inability of the major powers to reconcile their world policies, because—in the view of practically the entire non-Soviet world—the Soviet Union was engaged in varied efforts to expand its power and influence and extend its system. Such circumstances gave rise to disputes and situations which engaged the attention of the Security Council and some of its subsidiary bodies almost constantly throughout the year. . . . Although the Interim Committee of the General Assembly made a useful study of the [veto]

problem and its *Ad Hoc* Political Committee adopted its conclusions in large part, the U.S.S.R. stubbornly opposed any
liberalization of the voting procedure. . . . In the report to
Congress for the year 1947 attention was called to the danger in
which the [Economic and Social] Council found itself of being
diverted to essentially political debates arising from ideological
differences between the Soiet Union and most of the other Members of the United Nations. Unfortunately the tendency to intro-
duce into the deliberations of the Council political arguments
not relevant to the matters at hand continued during 1948 in even
more pronounced form and materially hindered the constructive
work of the Council. . . . The effect of Soviet participation in
the Trusteeship Council was to disrupt the cooperative spirit
which had characterized the sessions of the Council during its
formative period.[1]

Thus, from the point of view of the United States, the
United Nations has been continuously hamstrung by the attitude of the U.S.S.R. In American opinion, the conflict
within the UN is not between the two superpowers, but between the U.S.S.R. and practically all other members of the
UN. No official Russian document comparable to the reports
of the Department of State on United States participation in
the United Nations is available, but, judging by the violent
diatribes of Soviet spokesmen at UN meetings, notably those
of Foreign Minister Andrei Vishinsky, the Kremlin is convinced that the United States, not Russia, is the villain in the
drama enacted at Flushing Meadow and at Lake Success.

In the four years of its existence the United Nations has
had relatively few occasions to act or recommend actions on
strictly European problems. In the political field it has devoted considerable attention to extra-European problems—
Iran, Palestine, Indonesia, Korea, Kashmir, Hyderabad—all
of which were closely linked to European and American interests and in most cases represented facets of the East-West
struggle, but did not directly spring from situations on the

[1] Ibid., pp. 8–19.

continent of Europe. In the economic field the United Nations has some solid accomplishments to its credit in Europe, chiefly through the work of the UN Commission for Europe (ECE) in Geneva, which under the leadership of its secretary-general, the Swedish economist Gunnar Myrdal, has served as a valuable clearing house for East-West economic contacts. The NU Economic and Social Council as a whole, however, has studied the entire gamut of world economic problems and through its economic commissions for Asia, Latin America, and the Middle East has ranged far beyond exclusively European and American interests. The Trusteeship Council has been preoccupied with the problems of non-self-governing territories, but in setting standards for the progress of the fifteen million inhabitants of the trust territories it has influenced the administration by European colonial powers of other non-self-governing peoples who are not under its supervision.

Thus in the United Nations both western Europe and the United States have had to set their sights for wider horizons than those of their respective civilizations and of the relations they have forged with each other since World War II. The resulting discussions, even if often unpalatable to Americans and western Europeans, especially when the West has been subjected to denunciation by the U.S.S.R., have caused the West to reappraise its own position in the modern world and to redefine its objectives and policies with respect to non-Western peoples. The opposite, of course, has also proved true, as the U.S.S.R., Asia, the Middle East, Latin America, and Africa have been drawn more and more closely into the problems of the international community and, in their turn, have been affected, even if against their will, by Western views and practices. This interaction between the Western World and the rest of humanity, however, is a subject for another book.

Looking solely at relations between Europe and the United States within the framework of the United Nations,

the most important issues—aside from the perasive controversy with the U.S.S.R.—have been the Greek question; the
disposal of Italian colonies; the Berlin crisis; the veto; international control of atomic energy; and American economic
assistance, both directly to European nations under the ERP,
and indirectly to underdeveloped nations, some of which are
colonies of western European countries, under President
Truman's Point Four program.

The problem of Greece came before the United Nations
in 1946, when the Security Council appointed a commission
which, following an on-the-spot investigation, reported to the
Council on May 23, 1947. Eight of the eleven members of the
commission found that Greece's three northern neighbors—
Albania, Bulgaria, and Yugoslavia—were supporting guerilla
warfare in Greece. When the U.S.S.R. vetoed implementation by the Security Council of its commission's majority
recommendations, the Greek case in September 1947 was
transferred from the agenda of the Security Council to that
of the General Assembly under the heading "Threats to the
Political Independence and Territorial Integrity of Greece."
Six months earlier, in March 1947, the United States, having proclaimed the Truman Doctrine, had extended economic and military aid to Greece in an emergency atmosphere that, according to Washington, had been created by
Britain's decision to remove its small armed force from
Greece.

The second UN General Assembly, on October 21, 1947,
established an eleven-member Special Committee on the
Balkans (UNSCOB) to keep the Balkan situation under
continuous observation, to make available its assistance to
the four states concerned in the implementation of Assembly
recommendations, and to keep the United Nations informed
of developments. UNSCOB, composed of the representatives
of nine of the eleven governments originally named—Australia, Brazil, China, France, Mexico, the Netherlands, Pakistan, the United Kingdom, and the United States, with "seats

being held open" for Poland and the U.S.S.R., which refused to participate—established its headquarters at Salonika, in northern Greece, in December 1947. The Special Committee posted observers at various vantage points in Greece, but was denied access to the territory of Albania, Bulgaria, and Yugoslavia. During 1948 it submitted three reports to the General Assembly, in which it stated that large-scale aid continued to be furnished to the Greek guerrillas from Greece's northern neighbors, that the guerrillas in the frontier zones depended largely on external supplies and had been able to take refuge in the northern states, returning at will to Greece; that as long as these conditions prevailed, the UN should maintain an appropriate body to watch in the Balkans and work for eventual peaceful settlement of disputes; and that continuation of such a situation should be considered a threat to the independence and integrity of Greece and to peace in the Balkans, while the conduct of Albania, Bulgaria, and Yugoslavia should be regarded as "inconsistent with the purposes and principles of the Charter of the United Nations."

The Greek problem was discussed at length in the third session of the UN General Assembly at Paris in the autumn of 1948, when John Foster Dulles, for the United States, declared that the violent effort on the part of the Greek guerrillas assisted by Albania, Bulgaria, and Yogoslavia to overthrow the Greek government "is but part of a general effort to extend the power of Soviet Communism throughout the world." Conciliation talks initiated under the sponsorship of Herbert V. Evatt of Australia, president of the General Assembly, failed to bear fruit, and a proposal by the U.S.S.R., which would have exonerated the northern countries and abolished UNSCOB, was overwhelmingly defeated. The Assembly adopted a resolution calling on Albania, Bulgaria, and Yugoslavia to cease any further assistance to the guerrillas "in any form" and to co-operate with the Special Committee, particularly in the exercise of its conciliatory functions.

All members of the United Nations "and all other states" were asked to refrain from any action designed to assist any armed group fighting against the Greek government.

Following the third session of the General Assembly, it became increasingly apparent that such aid as Yugoslavia had previously rendered to the Greek guerrillas before Marshal Tito's break with the Kremlin in July 1948 was rapidly falling away, and by the spring of 1949 it was reported from various sources that Yugoslav aid had been reduced to "a mere trickle." Meanwhile in the United States it became known in March that Soviet representatives had informally approached American officials concerning the possibility of reaching a settlement about Greece which called for free elections with the participation of guerrilla representatives, and withdrawal of American aid and advisers. Secretary Acheson answered these overtures by declaring on May 20, 1949 that any negotiations about Greece would have to take place within the United Nations. Shortly after the opening of the fourth General Assembly on September 20, 1949 its president, General Carlos P. Romulo, initiated conferences with the United States, Britain, the U.S.S.R., and the Balkan countries on the Greek question, but without success. When the Truman administration decided in 1947 that it was urgently necessary to give the Greek government economic and military aid, the American aid program was not submitted to the United Nations, nor does the UN have jurisdiction over American operations in Greece. Official American reports on the Greek case in the United Nations have not dwelt either on the ancient frontier quarrels between Balkan countries and Greece which plagued that area on the eve of World War I and are now emerging once more into the open with the demand of Greek nationalists for northern Epirus, an area of Albania otherwise known as southern Albania, or on the character of the Greek government receiving American aid, which, in the opinion of many non-Russian observers, has been neither democratic nor representative.

Although the United Nations originally was to remain aloof from problems involved in the making of the peace, the disposal of Italy's colonies in North Africa—Libya, Eritrea, and Italian Somaliland—came before the General Assembly in 1948. Under the Italian peace treaty Italy had renounced all right and title to its African colonies, and it then became necessary to make arrangements for their administration. The treaty provided that final disposition of these possessions was to be determined jointly by the United States, Britain, France, and the U.S.S.R. within one year of the treaty's coming into force on September 15, 1947. A four-power commission of investigation visited all of Italy's former colonies, and the deputies of the Big Four Foreign Ministers considered the question until August 31, 1948. Having failed to reach an agreement at Paris in September 1948, the Council of Foreign Ministers, in accordance with the peace treaty, referred the matter to the General Assembly for its recommendation. Although the recommendations of the General Assembly have no binding force, the peace treaty provided that the Big Four would accept whatever recommendation the General Assembly might make and take appropriate measures to put it into effect—a decision that set an important precedent for direct Assembly action.

The conflicts that developed over Italy's former colonies among the great powers, and between some of the great powers and the Arabs, have already been mentioned in Chapter 7. Pending final disposal, Italy's former colonies in Africa remained under their postwar administration, which was British for all the territories except Fezzan in Libya, a strategic territory adjoining the French Chad, which has been under French control. The agenda of the third session of the General Assembly at Paris in 1948 was so crowded that consideration of the Italian colonies was postponed to a special session held at Flushing Meadow in April 1949. At that time the controversy grew sharper and more extensive as Latin-American countries urged the return of the colon to Italy, while the Arab nations and the Soviet bloc voted against such a move, being joined in this position by the newly admitted state of Israel. An arrangement for return of the colonies to Italy worked out by London and Rome without prior consultation with the United States, France, and Russia failed of adoption, and the mere rumor of this arrangement provoked riots in Arab countries. In June 1949, after the special session of the UN General Assembly had adjourned, it was suddenly announced in London that Britain had unilaterally recognized a new native regime in Cyrenaica, a part of Italian Libya that has strategic value and might replace the base in North Africa that Britain lost in Egypt after World War II, on termination of the Anglo-Egyptian treaty. This move, so far as is known, came as a complete surprise to Italy, and had not been submitted to the United Nations, in spite of the fact that disposal of the Italian colonies was still on the agenda of the General Assembly.

Shortly after the opening of the fourth session of the Assembly in September 1949, the Soviet government proposed immediate independence for Libya, accompanied by the withdrawal of all foreign troops, which would mean both termination of British administration and surrender of the airfields in Tripolitania used during and since the war by Britain and the United States. Italy's Foreign Minister, Count Carlo Sforza, then urged independence for both Libya and Eritrea. (Russia had proposed that Ethiopia be given an outlet to the Red Sea through Eritrea, while Britain and the United States had suggested that Eritrea be divided between Ethiopia and the Anglo-Egyptian Sudan.) Under Count Sforza's plan the three areas of Libya—Cyrenaica, Fezzan, and Tripolitania—would receive immediate independence (the United States set the date at 1952, Britain at 1955), with a "unitary structure" in federal form; genuine free elections would be held within six months under the supervision of a control commission including an Italian representative; and Britain would give up its administration as soon as the constituent assembly elected had formed a government for the new state. For Italian Somaliland Count Sforza requested a United Nations trusteeship—also proposed by the United States—to be administered by Italy, which would promote independence. It was expected at Lake Success that if Libya did become an independent state, Britain and the United States would seek to retain the right to use airfields in Tripolitania. The controversy about the Italian colonies revealed that the Western powers, in spite of frequent charges that Russia alone was following an old-fashioned policy of trying to obtain strategic bases, had not yet divested themselves of similar considerations.

The most important European political issue to come before the United Nations was the crisis that arose over Berlin in 1948, after the U.S.S.R. had imposed a blockade on the German capital. On September 29, 1948 the United States, Britain, and France drew the attention of the Security Council to the situation that had arisen as the result of the Russian blockade. In their letter to the Secretary-General of the UN, the three governments stated that Soviet restrictions on transport and communications were contrary to the obligations of the U.S.S.R. under Article 2 of the UN Charter and created a threat to the peace within the meaning of Chapter VII. After hearing the views of the Big Four, the president of the Council, Juan Bramuglia, Argentine Foreign Minister, adjourned the Council subject to further call by him, and then the Council members not directly involved—Argentina, Belgium, Canada, China, Colombia, and Syria—began exploratory talks under his leadership to clarify the issues. Efforts by the neutrals to reconcile the U.S.S.R. and the Western powers proved futile, and the United States placed the blame for failure squarely on Moscow. Following other attempts to bring about a narrower agreement on currency and trade, and further deterioration of the situation in Berlin, talks on the Berlin crisis came to a standstill. In April 1949, however, it became known that Dr. Phillip C. Jessup, United States "roving ambassador" who represented this country in the United Nations, had held talks with Jacob Malik, the U.S.S.R. delegate to the UN, and that an agreement had been reached whereby the Soviet government would lift the blockade, and Big Four conversations on Germany would be resumed. These negotiations led to the conference of the Council of Foreign Ministers in Paris, which, following four weeks of conversations, ended without accord on any of the basic issues presented concerning Germany. The Western powers, however, felt that something had been gained by relaxation of East-West tension, and all four powers planned to continue their discussion of German problems. Meanwhile, Secretary-General Trygve Lie declared that the United Nations could take credit for facilitating talks about the Berlin crisis. "Many people," he told the annual convention of the Rotary International in New York on June 14, 1949, "thought this crisis would lead to the breakup of the United Nations and even to the ultimate disaster of a third world war. Neither of these things happened and one of the main reasons why they did not happen was that the United Nations set in motion forces of mediation and conciliation which at first did not succeed, but which persisted and eventually prevailed."

Over and above all political questions debated in the United Nations has hung the shadow of the atomic bomb, the new weapon that might pulverize our world. It is interesting, if fruitless, to speculate as to what might have happened if World War II had ended without this lethal invention—the secret of whose manufacture had been mastered by American scientists with the aid of British and Canadian colleagues, as well as of scientists of other nations—if the curtain raised on the postwar period had revealed at least moderate expectations of peace rather than forebodings of another and far more devastating global conflict that might spell the end of human civilization. Ever since Hiroshima the Russians have been working with feverish determination to discover the secret of the bomb and to master the industrial processes of its manufacture; while many Americans have put such blind faith in the decisive efficacy of the new weapon as to create the danger that the bomb in another war might prove to be the Maginot Line of the United States.

At the same time, mutual suspicions that had existed between this country and the U.S.S.R. since the Bolshevik Revolution of 1917, but had been somewhat abated while the two powers fought a common enemy, burst forth with new virulence in the post-war period. Charges of spying and counter-spying were hurled about; each of the great powers accused the other of warmongering and expansionist designs; the Soviet government, which during the interwar years had displayed keen interest in learning American techniques, reverted to frenzied xenophobia, seeing a spy in every foreigner and a deleterious influence in all contacts with other nations; and many among us, falling into the much denounced Russian pattern, began to suspect "red" propensities in all aspects of life, but especially in scientific activities connected with the manufacture of atomic bombs, and advocated restrictions on freedom of expression that, if adopted, would cumulatively result in the introduction here of totalitarian thought-control.

The United States has justifiably taken credit for its decision, reached shortly after the end of the war, to advocate international control of atomic energy instead of insisting on perpetuation of a unilateral monopoly of the manufacture of fissionable materials that can be used both for the destructive purposes of making atomic bombs and for constructive peacetime purposes. At the same time American representatives, in discussing at UN meetings Washington's proposal for atomic-energy control, have tended to take a "holier than thou" attitude and have appeared indifferent to the repercussions that our possession of a stockpile of atomic bombs might have in the U.S.S.R. To complicate matters further discussion of the bomb became inextricably linked with discussion of the veto enjoyed by the Big Five in the UN Security Council, to such an extent that it was no longer possible to consider one without the other.

The problem of the veto was raised from the outset by the United States, when Bernard M. Baruch, American member of the UN Atomic Energy Commission, in introducing the Acheson-Lilienthal plan for international control on June 14, 1946 declared that punishment of violations of the proposed control convention lies at the very heart of the system of security against atom bombing, and that "there must be no veto to protect those who violate their solemn agreement not to develop or use atomic energy for destructive purposes." The American plan, which became associated with the name of Baruch, was adopted in expanded form by the United Nations General Assembly at its Paris session on November 4, 1948 by a vote of 40 to 6. The majority plan provided for the conclusion of a convention establishing an international atomic development authority, which would regulate the production and use of atomic energy. The authority would own and operate all mines and production facilities connected with atomic energy throughout the world and would have effective powers of inspection in all member nations, as well as the power to punish violations of the control convention by both governments and individuals. The use of atomic energy for "dangerous purposes" would be prohibited. The authority would be an independent agency, and its operations would not be subject to the veto possessed by the Big Five in the UN Security Council. The convention would specify a series of stages for the transfer to the international authority of atomic materials, scientific knowledge, and already manufactured bombs. The United States indicated that it was unwilling to take the final step of handing over its stockpile of bombs to the UN, or otherwise "disposing" of them, until it was satisfied that the control authority would really prove effective.

In the course of two years of arduous discussion in the AEC, the U.S.S.R. agreed to the establishment of an international authority—but only provided it had power to control and inspect, not to own and operate, atomic installations and facilities. It flatly disagreed, however, with the step-by-step timetable of the United States, and insisted that exising bomb stockpiles should be destroyed at the time that international control was created. The Kremlin agreed that the use of atomic energy for war purposes should be prohibited and, in fact, from the beginning of the atomic discussions demanded outlawry of the bomb on the same basis that poisoned gas had been outlawed under the Hague convention of 1911. It contended, however that, aside from this prohibition, every country should be free to carry out its own atomic production program, subject only to periodic inspection of the atomic installations it had reported to the international authority. Under the Soviet plan, as contrasted with the Baruch plan adopted by the AEC majority, the international authority would operate not independently but within the framework of the Security Council. The U.S.S.R. agreed that the veto would not apply to its day-to-day operations, but decisions concerning punishment of violations—regarded by the West as the core of the control convention— would be made by the Security Council, where the Big Five could invoke the veto. The Russians indicated that, in their opinion, Baruch's suggestion for waiver of the veto in case of violations was a backdoor attempt to evade the veto, on which the U.S.S.R. set great store. The United States, for its part, made it plain that it would not give up manufacture of atomic bombs, or destroy existing stockpiles, or sign an international control convention, until the two principles of international inspection and waiver of the veto had been accepted.

With the same persistence that has marked all their activities in international affairs the Russians, when they had failed to achieve their objective in the AEC, returned to the charge in the Political and Security Committee of the General Assembly in November 1946, when they tried to have information about atomic weapons included in the reports on armed forces that member nations, at Foreign Minister Molotov's original suggestion, were to submit to the UN. The U.S.S.R. has consistently sought to have all armaments considered together, and has advocated across-the-board arms reduction, while the United States has taken the position that the atomic bomb, as the most devastating weapon hitherto known, should be considered apart from other armaments, and that the production of atomic energy, which can be used for both war and peace purposes, should be subjected to international control. When the Russian proposal was defeated, Molotov, who at the opening of the 1946 General Assembly had urged general disarmament, announced that Russia would be ready to accept international inspection for disarmament in general and for atomic weapons in particular, and would agree to waive the veto for day-to-day operations of the atomic control authority. At the same time he pressed for progressive reduction of armaments, by which he meant, as Vishinsky, then Foreign Vice-Minister, soon made clear, abolition first of all of the atomic bomb, which, said Vishinsky, hangs over the world like "a sword of Damocles." The core of Molotov's proposal was the creation of two new commissions "within the framework of the Security Council" to control fulfillment of UN measures about general disarmament and about war use of atomic energy respectively. This proposal, in the opinion of Australia and Canada, as well as of the United States and Britain, would make decisions of the UN not only on atomic energy, but also on disarmament in general, subject to the veto in the Security Council. It would thus undo the work as far accomplished by the Atomic Energy Commission, whose establishment as an independent organ responsible to the Security Council had been approved by Russia during the first session of the General Assembly in January 1946.

When the AEC, following conclusion of the General Assembly's session, resumed its work in December 1946, the United States insisted that first priority should be given by the Security Council to the Commission's proposal for atomic-energy control, while Russia insisted that first priority should be given to the Assembly's resolution on general disarmament, contending that control of the atomic bomb was only one of the aspects of a disarmament program. Baruch himself had intimated in June 1946, when presenting the United States proposal, that control of the atomic bomb was but one step, important as it is in the context of presenday events, toward the objective that for centuries has been eluding mankind: abolition of war itself. The U.S.S.R. steadfastly resisted all proposals for international inspection and punishment of violations by individual citizens, contending that they constituted an infringement of national sovereignty, a point freely conceded by the United States.

The fundamental issue, as revealed in the debate on disarmament in the Political and Security Committee of the General Assembly, is not whether the veto power in the Security Council should be abandoned (the United States has no intention of giving up the veto over measures for enforcing the Council's decisions), but whether certain questions can be excluded from the area covered by the veto, notably the use of atomic energy for war purposes. Warren R. Austin, permanent United States delegate to the UN, who in January 1947 succeeded Bernard Baruch as American member of the Atomic Energy Commission, indicated that this country favored the establishment of another body in the United Nations organization in which the veto would not apply, thus by-passing the Security Council, which is just what the Russians had feared when they first learned the contents of Baruch's proposal.

Commenting on the Austin proposal, Henry P. Fletcher, former Under Secretary of State and member of the United States delegation at Dumbarton Oaks, who had had an opportunity to learn at first hand Russia's views on the veto, stated in a letter to the *New York Times* on January 17, 1947 that there was very slight chance "of acceptance of this expedient." He then went on to say:

Assuming, however, that this scheme could be adopted, it seems clear that it never could be effective without the support of Russia. And if Russian support were forthcoming, why divest the Security Council of its functions by an attempt to circumvent its powers and responsibilities? If, on the other hand, Russia or any of the other great powers should object to measures adopted by the proposed Atomic Control Commission, it is idle to suppose any action, individually or collectively, by members of the United Nations could be effective over such objection, and any attempt to enforce the decrees of this proposed commission would—unless there was unanimity among the three powers—almost certainly result in the destruction of the United Nations and lead very possibly to war.

Following exhaustive discussion of the American proposal, and of Soviet counterproposals presented in June 1947, the majority members of the Atomic Energy Commission in 1948, to quote the American report on United States participation in the United Nations, "were forced to recognize that the Soviet Union was unwilling to accept any of the basic elements of control considered necessary by the majority." In its third report to the General Assembly the AEC stated "that agreement on effective measures for control of atomic energy is itself dependent on co-operation in broader fields of policy." The Commission recommended that, until the situation had altered, or a basis for agreement on international control of atomic energy acceptable to the majority was found to exist, negotiations in the AEC be suspended. The General Assembly in 1948 found no evidence that the Soviet Union was prepared to accept any effective international controls, and rejected a Russian proposal that the AEC draft a convention for the prohibition of atomic weapons and a convention for the establishment of effective control of atomic energy, "both conventions to be signed and brought into operation simultaneously." The Assembly, in a resolution adopted over Soviet opposition, approved the AEC control plan, based on the Baruch proposal; expressed "deep concern at the impasse which had been reached in the work" of the AEC; called on the six permanent members of the AEC, including the U.S.S.R., which in 1946 had approved creation of the Commission, to consult "in order to determine if there exists a basis for agreement on the international control of atomic energy to ensure its use only for peaceful purposes and for the elimination from national armaments of atomic weapons," and report to the next regular session of the Assembly in September 1949. Meanwhile the Assembly called on the AEC "to resume its sessions, to survey its program of work, and to proceed to the further study of such of the subjects remaining in the programme of work as it considered to be practicable and useful." [1]

The United States declared itself satisfied with the resolution of the General Assembly, which, in its opinion, "constitutes a worldwide judgment that the Soviet proposals are inadequate and thus unacceptable." The resolution, says the United States report on the United Nations for 1948, "confirms what the Atomic Energy Commission had already determined—that there can be no effective control of atomic energy as long as the Soviet Union refuses to take an open and cooperative part in the world community." [2] In August 1949 Frederick H. Osborn, American member of the AEC, proposed abandonment of negotiations because of the non-co-operative attitude of the U.S.S.R.

This country, as well as other members of the AEC, took the view that Moscow's control scheme would leave each country free to develop its atomic-energy facilities as it saw fit and would be worse than no control at all, for it would create a dangerous illusion of security. Russia's refusal to ac-

[1] *United States Participation in the United Nations,* cited.
[2] Ibid.

cept the Baruch plan has been vigorously criticized in the West as another example of its unwillingness to work harmoniously with the United Nations; and there can be no doubt that our policy-makers—Acheson, Baruch, and Lilienthal—were completely sincere in believing that their proposals should have been acceptable to the Russians. The situation might have appeared to us in a somewhat different light if we had tried to imagine how we would have reacted had the roles been reversed—had Russia, instead of the West, emerged from the war with a new weapon whose destructive power has been described by our experts as surpassing that of all other known engines of destruction, and had Russia then insisted on the right to inspect our atomic installations before turning over its own supply of this weapon to an international authority. Would we have welcomed Russian inspection, even though it took place under the auspices of the United Nations, if we knew, as the Russians did in 1946 about themselves, that we were considerably behind Russia in atomic development? Or would we have regarded proposals for such inspection as another form of spying on our production—possibly as a prelude to preventive attack on us if it was discovered we were not yet capable of retaliation? Even more important, if Russia were to agree right now to the establishment of an international authority with effective powers of inspection and enforcement, would we be ready to have Soviet representatives on such an authority scrutinize our installations, and would we waive the veto we now have in the UN Security Council?

To such questions two answers are usually given. First, it is said that we demonstrated our goodwill by offering to surrender national sovereignty to the extent of accepting an international authority, while Russia continues to cling to an old-fashioned concept of unlimited sovereignty. The United States unquestionably blazed a trail toward abandonment of national sovereignty, but we have not yet traveled very far along that trail. As late as October 1949, after we had helped to create the North Atlantic Treaty organization, members of the Congressional Joint Committee on Atomic Energy were sharply divided along party lines concerning the advisability of sharing information about atomic-energy production with our wartime bomb-discovery partners, Britain and Canada.

The second answer, which goes to the heart of the matter, is that we do not and cannot trust Russia while it remains a police state, but that Russia can and should trust us. But does it, jaundiced though its point of view may seem to us? Stripped of technicalities, the issue of international atomic control boils down to mutual confidence; and the obvious fact is that adequate confidence does not exist on either side. This dilemma became all the more apparent after President Truman, on September 23, 1949, three days after the opening of the fourth session of the UN General Assembly, announced that an atomic explosion had occurred in the U.S.S.R. The immediate reaction of administration spokesmen in Washington was that this news, which had long been expected, would cause no change in our foreign policy. This may have been true in the sense that our policy-makers had taken such an eventuality into consideration. But up to that time most discussions of atomic warfare appeared to be based on the assumption that the United States had the initiative to use the bomb as it saw fit—either in a "quickie" war (the "let's drop a few bombs on Russia and get it over with" school of thought, which has had spokesmen in both military and political circles), or to deter the Russians by the mere threat of such a war.

Now the psychological atmosphere had undergone a marked change. For the knowledge, or even the presumption, that Russia would be in a position to retaliate—either directly by an attack on this country, or indirectly by an attack on one or more of our North Atlantic partners—weakened the assurance given us by control of the bomb. In fact, fear on the part of western European nations, particularly

France, that they might be the first targets of Russian atomic warfare, had made them far more reserved about the North Atlantic Pact in the spring of 1949 than we generally realized here. After September 23 the question was promptly raised on both sides of the Atlantic whether, given Russia's possession of the atomic-bomb secret, the administration's provisions for military aid to western Europe, which envisaged primarily the building up of land forces, might not have become obsolete.

Once the danger of atomic destruction threatened us as well as a potential enemy, Washington for the first time heard a frank public discussion of the technical practicability as well as the moral advisability of atomic bombing, during the House Armed Service Committee hearings on the Navy's protests against the Air Force thesis that victory could be easily won by long-range B-36 bombers delivering atomic bombs. Navy spokesmen argued that the atomic-blitz theory of war was militarily unsound, as well as politically and morally wrong; that it would not guarantee a quick and easy victory and, on the contrary, might lead to defeat; and that in any case the atomic bombing of targets from forty thousand feet could only result in the destruction of enemy cities, not just military targets, and the killing of thousands of noncombatants. Such bombing, according to the Navy, would create devastation so widespread that, regardless of who won the war, everyone would lose the peace.

Yet, in spite of these warnings and forebodings, the news that the U.S.S.R. might offer a proposal for atomic-bomb control was received coolly in Washington, officials from President Truman down indicating that the United States would have to be "shown" that the Kremlin really meant business this time. When Soviet Foreign Minister Vishinsky on September 23 called in the UN General Assembly for "the establishment of an adequate and rigid international control" of the atomic weapon, American spokesmen asked what kind of control Russia now had in mind, and revealed again mistrust of Russia's aims, which was reciprocated in Moscow. Without mutual confidence it was difficult to see how any kind of agreement could be reached about atomic control.

For the time being, the problem of the veto, like that of control of atomic energy, remains unsolved. The veto is a symptom of the disease, which is the continuing struggle of great nations for power—not the disease itself. Consequently efforts to curtail use of the veto, or to abolish it altogether, are bound to prove ineffective. Britain, France, and China—three of the five permanent members of the UN Security Council which enjoy the right of veto under the UN Charter—have indicated willingness to surrender the veto, although there is reason to doubt their desire to act on this premise. But neither the United States nor the U.S.S.R. has been ready to follow suit. Some American commentators have given the impression that the veto was included in the Charter at San Francisco solely at the insistence of Russia. The United States, however, was just as insistent as Russia on retention of the veto by the great powers, believing that otherwise the Charter did not stand a chance of being ratified by the Senate; and debates in the Senate Foreign Relations Committee on the North Atlantic Pact indicate that Congress is not willing to relinquish the right of final unilateral decision about use of American armed force against aggression even under an agreement that not merely excludes the U.S.S.R. but presumably has the U.S.S.R. primarily in mind as the potential aggressor. Russia's concept of the veto is based on its conviction that unanimity among the Big Five, and especially among the Big Three—the United States, the U.S.S.R., and Britain—is essential in time of peace as it was in time of war, and that the veto is necessary to assure such unanimity. The United States agrees that without accord by the great powers the work of the UN will come to a standstill, and has given no indication that it intends to abandon or curtail the veto in the Security Council, no matter what pressure is brought to bear on it by leading small nations like Australia and Cuba. To this extent the United States, like the U.S.S.R., accepts limitations on the sovereignty of small states as compared with the great, or, to put it another way, accepts the attribution of special rights, as well as special responsibilities, to the great powers.

Where Russia has differed from the United States is that, contrary to an understanding reached in San Francisco, it made frequent, not sparing, use of the veto, and has taken the view that the veto can be used to prevent discussion of a question brought before the Security Council as well as of action by the Council against an alleged aggressor. The United States, by contrast, has taken the view that the veto should be used sparingly, that it should not be invoked during discussion of a question, and can be used only when the time has come for the Council to reach a decision concerning application of military force. The controversy over the veto has clearly revealed some important differences between the United States and Russia in ways of thinking. The Russians, who brook no political dissension or even discussion at home, want to be free, by virtue of the veto, to cut short any debate in the Security Council that may appear to threaten their interests. They contend that if the Security Council starts discussing a question—for instance, trouble in the Balkans—it will by "chain of circumstances" reach a decision concerning the use of force; therefore the veto must operate from beginning to end of any discussion of a threat to peace. Americans, accustomed to untrammeled and often vituperative political discussion at home, find nothing objectionable in discussion of any given issue before the Security Council, but, having historically preferred to play a lone hand in world affairs, want to make sure that this country retains the right not to become involved in any punitive action against an alleged aggressor that the Council may recommend.

The United States has charged the U.S.S.R. with "over-use" of the veto. The record shows that the U.S.S.R. has invoked the veto on forty-one occasions, as compared with none by the United States. Twenty-three of the Russian vetoes, however, concerned the same subject: the admission of new members to the United Nations. There appears to be a definite link in the mind of the Russians between voting rights in general in the United Nations and the use of the veto. In the General Assembly, where no nation has the veto, the U.S.S.R. has so far been easily outvoted by the other members, each of which has one vote, irrespective of size or strength. From the Russian point of view, therefore, it becomes an important question whether additional votes are brought against it through admission of new members known to be hostile to the Kremlin. Thus the U.S.S.R. has vetoed the admission of Portugal (an old ally of Britain), Eire, Jordan (closely connected with Britain), Ceylon (a former British colony, which achieved independence in 1948), Italy, Korea, Austria, and Finland unless all the former Axis satellites are admitted as a single package. The United States, for similar reasons, has opposed the admission of Albania, Bulgaria, Hungary, Rumania, and Outer Mongolia and has won majority support for its position in the Council, obviating the need to invoke the veto. This deadlock has kept thirteen countries out of the UN. In 1949, however, both the United States and the U.S.S.R. supported the admission of Israel.

It will be recalled that Russia was preoccupied by the vote question as early as the Yalta conference, where Stalin first asked that votes should be given to the sixteen republics composing the U.S.S.R., but finally settled for American support of two votes—the Ukraine and Byelorussia—after President Roosevelt jokingly intimated that the United States might lay claim to votes for each of its forty-eight states. Britain was the first to accept the Russian proposal for two additional votes, as it was then considering the possibility that an independent India would apply for membership in the United Nations. President Roosevelt, at Secretary

Byrnes's suggestion, asked whether Stalin would agree to two additional votes for the United States, and the marshal readily acquiesced in this proposal. When, contrary to Byrnes's expectations, however, announcement of votes for the Ukraine and Byelorussia occasioned no outcry in the United States, the idea of asking for two extra votes for the United States at the San Francisco Conference was abandoned in Washington.

Discussion of the voting procedure in the United Nations has strengthened the impression that the United States, not the U.S.S.R., is a champion of the rights of small states, as contrasted with Russia's aspirations to great-power dictatorship. There are, in fact, important differences of opinion between the two great powers on this question. The United States, in accordance with its concept at home that all individuals, no matter whether strong or weak, rich or poor, are equal before the law, holds the view that all sovereign states, whether great or small, are equal in the UN and must receive a hearing. Russia, in accordance with its concept that the rights and duties of individuals are determined by the state, which, in effect, is the political dictatorship of a small group of self-appointed leaders, holds the view that the activities of the UN, especially with respect to security, should be directed by a limited inner group of great powers, not elected by the international community, but self-appointed by reason of their military and industrial strength; and that the small nations must accept the decisions of the great, on the ground that these decisions are intended to assure the general welfare. The United States certainly cannot be accused of using toward other nations the ruthless methods of the U.S.S.R. Yet its influence on smaller countries, if less direct, has nevertheless been far-reaching.

The countries of eastern Europe and the Balkans have been described as "satellites" of the U.S.S.R.—a term the Poles and Czechs strongly resent. Moscow has countered by calling Italy and Greece "satellites" of the United States.

Italy and Greece obviously enjoy a latitude of action at home and abroad that does not exist for Russia's neighbors. It cannot be denied, however, that they have become dependent on American aid, both military and economic, especially Greece. Whether or not it is possible to avoid subordinate, if not subservient, relationships between small and great nations, or whether the best that can be achieved is to try to make such relationships as pleasant and mutually tolerable as one can, remains an unanswered question. Some spokesmen of small nations, no matter how grateful for American aid or fearful of Russian encroachments, are inclined to feel that the authority and influence of all great powers should be limited. At present the outlook for this is dim; for both the United States and Russia, although committed to international action through the United Nations, have shown on many occasions that they still want to hold on to the attributes, vestigial as they may seem, of national sovereignty.

This situation has been obscured for us by Washington's contention that this country, unlike Russia, is ready to abandon national sovereignty with respect to control of atomic energy. When Soviet delegates in the United Nations repeatedly argued that such control would constitute a derogation of sovereignty, the United States readily admitted this, saying that such derogation is inherent in the solution of the problem. The third report of the Atomic Energy Commission to the General Assembly in 1948 contained the following clause, suggested by Canada: "In face of the realities of the problem it [the Commission] sees no alternative to the voluntary sharing by nations of their sovereignty in this field to the extent required by its proposals." This history-making statement, however, appears to be restricted to a single field —atomic-energy control—if we are to judge by our own official actions in fields where American interests are regarded as seriously at stake, notably in the sphere of international economic policy.

It is important to bear in mind that, although the American government had come to the conclusion in 1946, steadfastly adhering to it since, that the United Nations was sufficiently strong to administer international control of the most lethal weapon thus far invented by man, it decided in 1947 that the United Nations did not have the strength to administer Marshall Plan aid to Europe, or economic and military assistance to Greece and Turkey. Both programs, although admittedly going to the roots of the major problems of Europe and the world, have been carried on outside the framework of the United Nations and without being subject to its supervision or criticism. When President Truman announced his Point Four proposal for technical assistance to underdeveloped countries, however, he indicated that this proposal would be presented in the United Nations. This was done in the UN Economic and Social Council in March 1949. It would have been in this Council, where no member nation has the veto, and not in the Security Council, as is often erroneously assumed, that the Marshall Plan and economic aid to Greece and Turkey would have been introduced under normal circumstances.

The United Nations was requested by Washington to make a study of the character and cost of a Point Four program; and in accordance with this request Secretary-General Trygve Lie announced in June 1949 that 85 million dollars would be needed for a program of technical assistance. Shortly after, it became known that the Truman administration had been thinking in terms of a 45-million-dollar outlay on technical aid; and that a marked trend had developed in both House and Senate against proposals for expenditure of American funds through the United Nations or other international agencies. Whatever financial aid might be given under Point Four, it was said, would probably have to come from the International Bank for Reconstruction and Development, in which the United States, a major shareholder, and Britain exercise dominant influence.

The most promising development in the four years of the United Nations' existence was the little publicized decision of the General Assembly's Economic and Social Committee on October 14, 1949, adopted unanimously and without any substantial amendment, to accept two programs devised by the Economic and Social Council (where no nation has a veto) for technical assistance, through the UN, to underdeveloped countries. This unwonted unanimity, achieved in spite of the fact that the United States had initiated the discussion of the technical assistance programs by presenting Point Four for consideration in the ECOSOC, was widely hailed as an indication that the gulf between the United States and the U.S.S.R. might be partly bridged by common efforts to improve the productivity of the economies of retarded countries.

In the United Nations the European countries have played a relatively modest role, and the initiative for introducing policies or rejecting them has been largely in the hands of the two superpowers, the United States and the U.S.S.R. The best hope for Europe would seem to be the possibility of strengthening the United Nations through more active participation by the smaller nations—the potential international "third force"—which might ultimately act as a buffer between the superpowers, as the committee of neutrals succeeded in doing during discussion of the Berlin crisis in 1948. It is therefore of paramount concern for Europe to know the attitude the United States will take in the future toward the United Nations.

Today we are in the process of reassessing the strengths and weaknesses of the United Nations. Most of us no longer view it through the rosy spectacles of "great expectations." We can see that membership in the UN does not automatically transform nations into saints or eliminate national ambitions and suspicions. Nor do UN members check sovereignty or considerations of "face" at the door of the Security Council or the General Assembly. Russia, being one of the two superpowers left in the world, and at the same time the standard-bearer of communism, often appears to be the villain of the piece because of its insistence that it must have its way or at least prevent others from having theirs. But experience has shown that less powerful nations, and nations not particularly swayed by ideological fervor, can be just as determined as the U.S.S.R. in opposing UN action that they consider inimical to their interests—for example, Britain on Palestine and on the Italian colonies, France on Indo-China, the Netherlands on Indonesia, India and Pakistan on Kashmir, the Union of South Africa on the status of Indians and on the Southwest Africa mandate. Nor are lobby maneuvers and deals on votes limited to any one nation or group of nations.

Some critics of the UN are particularly disheartened because, they say, the UN has not "solved" many problems that have been placed on its agenda. It is wise to bear in mind, however, that in domestic politics, where we have the advantages of a common language, common traditions, and common objectives, we do not "solve" our economic, labor, racial, or political problems. What we do is to re-examine these problems from time to time, make adjustments here and there, but always with the knowledge that there can be no permanent solutions and that a settlement made today will have to be reviewed tomorrow.

It certainly seems unrealistic to expect more from ourselves, and other peoples, in international organization than we are able to accomplish in domestic affairs. Nor must we forget that it has not proved easy, through the centuries, to reconcile fundamental differences within nations, and that even the most advanced Western countries, like Britain France, and the United States, have gone through civil wars and revolutions before achieving a measure of stability. Therefore it is not surprising that the international organization should pass through comparable crises in the brief period of its existence.

These aspects of the UN discourage only those who had assumed that an international organization would act from higher motives and on a loftier plane than political assemblies in Washington or Kansas City, in Paris or Rome. We are quite tolerant about logrolling and pork-barrel operations in the nation's capital, but are deeply disappointed when we discover that similar methods are used in international agencies. Some of us believe that a world government would correct this situation. What we need to change, however, are not the institutions themselves, but the men and women of nations that compose the international organization.

For, in the final analysis, there is no such thing as "the UN" which achieves this or fails to accomplish that—any more than there is a single entity that achieves or fails on the national scene. ("Congress," after all, is composed of Congressmen.) If we want to see improved relations between nations, or within nations, if we want less self-seeking and more social responsibility, we have to find some way of imbuing human beings with these ideals. Neither the United Nations, nor world government, nor any system the fertile imagination of man might devise is a self-operating machine. We must train enough people who have the skill and understanding to make such machinery as we have on hand work, and then they will have ample opportunity to tinker with it and perfect it, as Henry Ford tinkered with and perfected the first automobile once he had learned how to put it together and make it run.

It is in this respect that the United Nations performs its most valuable work—as the League of Nations had also done during the interwar years. For in the various committees of the UN, and in the international agencies clustered around it, men and women of widely differing political, economic, and social outlook and traditions learn through actual experience to fuse their thoughts and actions into practical international co-operation. This is not an easy process.

It means that everyone concerned must learn to hear opposing opinions, to see the point of view of other nations, to adjust conflicting interests, to find a middle course between extreme positions. This is in essence the process of democracy, which is already a great test of human capacities for adjustment on a local or national scale, but is even harder to practice on the international scale. Yet, as President Roosevelt said, the only way to learn how to work together is to work together.

Just as the peoples of dependent areas can become familiar with the institutions of self-government not by reading about them in books but only if they are entrusted with more and more responsibility, so nations cannot continue merely to discuss international co-operation. They must have more and more opportunities to co-operate, not merely in diplomatic or political fields, but on the innumerable problems of daily life—health, food, population, eradication of racial discriminations, and so on—which may seem lacking in glamour, but which are the stuff and substance of human existence.

This, in turn, means that all members of the UN should bring more and more of their business into the international organization, rather than try to limit the UN to perfunctory tasks. Each nation has something to contribute, as well as something to gain, from work in the UN; and not the least we all gain is the very valuable experience of reappraising our own activities by seeing them through the eyes of other peoples.

It is through this process, which often seems tedious and barren of dramatic moments, that world government will gradually be forged. The greatest accomplishment of the United Nations would, in fact, be to keep newspaper headlines permanently in lower case. Men and women who have just gone through grueling years of war and civil strife are not hungry for crises and sensational verbal victories by one nation over another. What they crave is the opportunity to live and to obtain adequate food, housing, clothing, education, and leisure for themselves and their families. The test of any government, whether local, national, or world-wide, is the extent to which it can fulfill the modest needs of mankind while furthering human liberties.

We might all do well to bear in mind the words of Ralph J. Bunche, UN Acting Mediator in Palestine, who, after the successful completion of his task, said on May 9, 1949:

I am confident that the United Nations, with all its imperfections and weaknesses, is the sole force in the world today which can issue reliable peace and freedom insurance. The United Nations, by dint of ever-persistent effort, is slowly moulding the kind of peaceful and free world that you and I wish to live in and wish to hand down to our children and grandchildren. The United Nations is the only bridge over which nations can come together to settle their differences. . . . This United Nations bridge will be no weaker and no stronger than we, the people make it. Let us thank God that in these parlous times we have it. And let us build it ever stronger.

Chapter XII

THE FUTURE SEEN THROUGH
THE PRESENT

Soothsaying has always been both sought and feared by mankind; and soothsayers are usually careful to utter predictions in terms sufficiently obscure to bear any interpretation events may ultimately place on them. When the present, as in our times, seems particularly grim, the past is looked back to with nostalgia, and the future is awaited with a mixture of hope and apprehension. History is useful as a record, however distorted or incomplete, of the road already traveled. It offers only fragmentary clues to what lies ahead.

Yet such clues are worth examining. So far as European-American relations are concerned, they show that by the end of the nineteenth century Europe had reached its zenith. Henceforth it was to undergo not so much an absolute decline as a marked diminution relative to the rise of newly developed continents. No longer, as it had been for centuries, the political and cultural center of the known universe, Europe was also no longer the sole source of the material benefits made available by the Industrial Revolution. Power and influence had begun to shift to areas hitherto regarded as peripheral—the United States, later the U.S.S.R., most recently India. Midway in the twentieth century Europe and America are still in the process of readjustment to these seismic changes.

As Walt Whitman prophetically wrote in *Years of the Modern:*

The perform'd America and Europe grow dim, retiring
  in shadow behind me,
The unperform'd, more gigantic than ever, advance,
  advance upon me.

Once the readjustment has been made, it may prove possible to strike a new balance of power within the framework of the United Nations. In such a balance, however, Europe, which once tipped the world's scales, will be but one factor —not, as in the past, a dominant source of intellectual inspiration and propulsion to action. As Europe settles down to a less influential position, the United States will have to acknowledge, and learn to exercise, the responsibilities of our immensely enhanced power, which places us, whether we like it or not, squarely in the center of the world stage. In the spheres of both commerce and defense this country will find itself increasingly forced to take the place once occupied by Britain. Unless commerce is allowed to dwindle into primitive barter, the United States will have to become both a large-scale exporter of investment capital and a large-scale importer of goods produced by other industrial nations. And while we urge the Marshall Plan countries to integrate their economies and abandon trade restrictions, we ourselves must re-examine the possibility of further lowering or altogether abolishing our tariffs and of integrating our own economy with that of the rest of the world.

Not that nationalism will vanish overnight, any more than feudalism did at the close of the Middle Ages. Ideas and practices that have become obsolete linger on long after life has proved them to be inadequate, and sometimes they become all the more virulent as they approach extinction. Nationalism will continue to exert a potent influence, particularly among peoples but lately arrived at nationhood; and in Europe it will defy attempts by either the United States or the U.S.S.R. to determine the destiny of long-established nations. But nationalism is being gradually eroded by economic necessity and the desire for security against aggression, by a wide range of endeavors for mutual aid undertaken through concerted efforts. Someday, perhaps before the end of this century, when the thick fog of national recriminations has been dispelled, we shall suddenly see with amazement the extent of this erosion and shall find it possible to look with clearer vision at the greatly altered international landscape.

Then we shall also realize the extent to which all peoples, irrespective of political ideologies and practices, have come to agree on the need to use the resources of modern science and industry to improve the welfare of human beings. As Assistant Secretary of State W. W. Butterworth said in New Orleans on October 10, 1949, atomic power in itself is a "feeble agent" compared with the element of hope that science has given to mankind. "The outstanding fact remains," he declared, "that men are convinced by what they have seen or heard that sickness, drudgery and want are no longer the inevitable lot of humanity. The tides of discontent are running, and by so much as men are discontented, they look to their governments to bring about an improvement in these circumstances."

Yet, in spite of the promises of science, most of the world's inhabitants—except for North America, which possesses a peculiarly fortunate combination of geography, resources, population and political traditions—continue to live in, or on the very verge of, poverty, even in some of the more advanced nations of Europe. This obvious discrepancy between what is said to be attainable and what has actually been attained cannot persist indefinitely without provoking friction and turmoil. The Communists, dogmatically convinced that capitalism is on the point of collapse and determined to speed its demise by all the means at their disposal, have unquestionably contributed to this state of ferment, but they did not in the first place create it. Nor shall we bring it to an end merely by containing the Russian national state or international communism, or by insisting, with a dogmatism not unlike that of the Communists, that our own way of life, developed out of the special conditions of our sector of the New World, offers the only way of life to all nations.

So far as outward signs are concerned, communism in Europe, which seemed to be in the ascendant immediately after the war, is now on the wane. The prestige and power Communists had won after the Nazi invasion of Russia in 1941, when they placed their tightly knit and disciplined cadres at the disposal of resistance movements in German-conquered countries, have to a large extent been dissipated.

This change is due in part, but in part only, to the economic aid given by the United States to the sixteen Marshall Plan countries. For although American aid has unquestionably speeded postwar reconstruction and has thereby acted as a brake on political extremism, it has clearly not gone to the roots of western Europe's economic problems. Nor has it affected the situation east of Berlin, where international communism has met its greatest challenge since 1917—a challenge delivered neither by the socialist democracies of the Atlantic seaboard nor by the free-enterprise democracy of the United States, but by the national communism of Marshal Tito, which has found echoes among Russia's neighbors from the Baltic to the Black Sea.

Disillusionment with Russia and with the actions of local Communist parties has whittled down Communist ranks throughout western Europe and has sundered the labor unions—some of which continue to adhere to the Communist-dominated World Federation of Trade Unions, while others are supporting the democratic labor international organization formed at London on November 28, 1949. Yet in Yugoslavia, which has defied the Kremlin with greater vigor than any Western nation, the injection of nationalism into communism appears to have strengthened a Communist regime instead of weakening it.

These developments raise two fundamental questions con-

cerning the political future of Europe. If communism is actually declining in the West or at least has reached its high-
water mark there, does this represent a victory for democracy? And if communism in Yugoslavia can thrive after a
break with the U.S.S.R., is it accurate to say, as some observers have long said in this country, that communism is due
solely to Russian influence and would disappear once the
power of the Soviet government had been broken?

Except for Britain and the Scandinavian countries, where
the general acceptance of socialist regimes that preserve
political liberties has assured stability, the decline of communism in western Europe cannot yet be hailed as a clear-cut
victory for democracy. In France, Italy, and the West German state, socialism continues to vie for power not only with
communism but also with what is called liberalism—the
desire of some groups to abandon all controls and planning
and return to laissez-faire—by which is often meant nothing
more than the protection of reactionary vested interests.

Europe is still in a state of flux, still groping for political
formulas that can prove workable in modern societies shattered by war and economic dislocations. But it is already
clear that no European government can long survive that
does not attempt to respond, either freely or under pressure,
to the bare subsistence needs of the workers and peasants
who, for better or worse, form the majority of the population
of the continental countries. In making this response, even
governments that are ideologically opposed to socialism find
it impossible to evade the problems of human welfare which
today are in the foreground of their peoples' preoccupations and discussions.

The basic issue is not whether, in theory, socialist nationalization or communism or laissez-faire is in itself wholly good
or wholly bad. Frustrated and discontented people, many of
whom are still illiterate or barely educated to political responsibilities, are far less interested in questions of doctrine
than the leaders of clashing groups assume. Even in police

states governments cannot entirely overlook popular discontent, as shown by Moscow's postwar efforts to meet consumers' demands. The real test of socialism, communism, and liberalism in Europe, as in the case of the proverbial pudding, will come in the eating—in their practical capacity to satisfy at least the minimum needs of millions who have been aroused by the promises of nineteenth-century democracy and of the Industrial Revolution to expect promptly a modest improvement in their living-standards and in their opportunities for personal development through education.

Quite apart from humanitarian considerations, it is to our self-interest that the peoples of Europe—not to speak of the rest of the world—should have a tolerable standard of living. Every time we oppose European efforts in that direction on the ground that they spell "socialism" or "cost too much," we actually work against our own long-term benefit. Every time we take the initiative in helping to improve living-conditions in Europe, as we have done under ERP, we make a sound investment for our own future. We know full well that we are not callous to human suffering, and that we are deeply concerned with improvement of life for all in our own communities. Yet too often bitter denunciations here of "statism" and "the welfare state" in Europe give the impression abroad that as a nation we still cling to nineteenth-century concepts of "everyone for himself, and the devil take the hindmost"—thus causing not only our Communist opponents but also our potential friends among Socialists and social-minded Catholics to condemn what they regard as the heartlessness and crass materialism of the American "capitalist" system. We speak to Europe not merely in one "Voice of America," but in many voices, whose contradictions often confuse our listeners. And in spite of our matchless facilities for propaganda we have not yet succeeded in conveying to Europeans the conviction that the United States is out front in the unending struggle for human progress, not lagging behind in a vanished era of laissez-faire, which in

Europe is not synonymous with genuine liberty for all.

When President Truman on September 23, 1949 announced that "an atomic explosion" had occurred in the U.S.S.R., one phase of United States postwar policy came to a close and a new phase began, fraught with as yet unforeseeable eventualities. During the four years from the time when the first atomic bomb was dropped on Hiroshima to the moment when it became known that Russia had discovered the secret of manufacturing the bomb at least two years earlier than had been anticipated in the West, relations between the world's two remaining great powers had been dominated by expectations of atomic warfare. For four years Western "containment" of Russia was thought to be relatively free of risk, although fear of Russian attack existed both here and in western Europe. But it was generally believed, first, that the United States would retain at least until 1951 or 1952 a monopoly of the atomic bomb, which Winston Churchill has described as the greatest deterrent to aggression; and, second, that in case of conflict the atomic weapon would assure a quick and decisive victory, without the necessity of exhausting our own economic and manpower resources through large-scale prewar preparations and prolonged fighting. These two suppositions are no longer tenable. While no one in the West can say with assurance just how far Russia has advanced in its atomic-bomb production, the mere fact that it can manufacture the atomic bomb has ended our monopoly of this weapon. And Dr. Vannevar Bush has emphatically told us that "the atomic bomb is for the immediate future a very important but by no means an absolute weapon, that is, one so overpowering as to make all other methods of waging war obsolete."

Even assuming, with the majority of well-informed observers, that neither this country nor the U.S.S.R. wants war, it is no longer possible to think of the "cold war" now in progress as involving only limited risks, which, if they materialized, would always be met by resort to the atomic bomb, with little or no danger to ourselves or our allies in Europe. Moreover, as the United States undertakes increasing responsibilities all over the globe, it is by no means so certain as it seemed to many Americans during the past four years that all of the world's problems are attributable solely to Russia and communism, and that once Russia and communism have been obliterated, peace would reign throughout the world.

An indication that the international situation is far more complex than had been admitted in the past was given by Secretary of State Acheson when he said in Berlin on November 14, 1949 that there are two categories of problems: those created by Russia's "thrusts," and those that we would face today even if Russia and communism did not exist. Among the problems in the second category are the economic decline of western Europe as compared with the rise of the United States and the U.S.S.R.; the culmination in this century of nationalist movements in nonindustrialized nations, whether politically independent or still in the status of colonies; the determination of retarded peoples to achieve economic and social improvement; and the struggle, of which we are witnessing the early stages, on the part of all national states still jealous of their sovereignty to form an effectively functioning international community. While the conquests of militant Nazism and Fascism and the "thrusts" of Russia and world communism have aggravated these problems and have increased the urgency of alleviating them, they did not in the first instance create situations that have been maturing for decades and cannot be exorcised overnight by declarations of good intentions or even by practical efforts.

Few today can share the faith of the Victorians that mankind can advance uninterruptedly from one achievement to another without frequent setbacks and occasional retreats. We no longer think of human progress as a steadily ascending line, but as a jagged line dipping from peaks into valleys and rising to peaks again. Nor can we, who have known

Belsen and Dachau, and Stalingrad and Hiroshima, measure progress solely by the yardstick of material accomplishment. We are growing aware that material development must be guided and accompanied by a spirit of dedication to larger objectives than mere satisfaction of our own needs, or the needs of our family, our community, even our nation.

The craving of human beings for something outside themselves to which they can devote their energies and aspirations, once satisfied by religious beliefs, led many of our contemporaries to seek sustenance in fascism, nazism, or communism. Russia's influence in our times has been due not to its industrial power, vastly inferior to that of the United States and even of Germany and Britain, nor to its military might, but to the fact that Moscow was the headquarters of international communism, which exerted a powerful attraction over the minds of millions of men and women throughout the world who felt not only materially but also spiritually disinherited. Subsequent disillusionment has turned many of them into violent anti-Communists; but this does not mean that they have automatically become convinced adherents of Western democracy. The West, seedbed in the past of many religious and political beliefs, is now groping to arouse new loyalties outside the orbit of the Atlantic community. The U.S.S.R. has as yet had neither the political experience nor the technical skills to translate the promises of communism into reality for the Russian people, let alone the peoples of still more backward nations. But it has acted, to use Professor Arnold Toynbee's phrase, like "a catfish in a herring-pond," stirring the Western democracies, which were in imminent danger of becoming stagnant, into renewed efforts to fulfill the promises they had been holding out for over a century to their own as yet underprivileged citizens and to the nonindustrialized areas of the world. Under the goad of communism we have become aware as we had not been for years that mankind, as always, needs both something to live *on* and something to live *for*.

It is not surprising that in the midst of these fresh stirrings we feel fearful of the future, and often blindly fight the very ideas to which we are struggling to give birth. The crumbling of a long-accepted social order, the confusion of thought and the self-questioning unleashed by the decline of formerly authoritative ideas and the emergence of new ones, cause many to regard the very process of change as dangerous and all proponents of unfamiliar concepts as evil or even endowed with sinister power. It is not in periods when men have faith that they turn to witch-hunting, but in periods when, their faith profoundly shaken, they seek scapegoats for their inner unrest and anxiety. Lewis Mumford has wisely pointed out that from the fifteenth century to the seventeenth the world seemed empty, and was daily growing emptier, of spiritual content. Men "said their prayers, they repeated their formulas; they even sought to retrieve the holiness they had lost by resurrecting superstitions they had long abandoned; hence the fierceness and hollow fanaticism of the Counter-Reformation, its burning of heretics, its persecution of witches, precisely in the midst of the growing 'enlightenment.' " [1]

Soon, we must hope, we shall emerge from the dark tunnel through which we have been arduously digging our way into an "enlightenment" period of the twentieth century. We may then find that all peoples, like sandhogs working from different places of departure toward the same end, will meet at approximately the same point, intent on integrating modern technology with those spiritual values that Western man in modern times either had lost or had failed to infuse into his material achievements. But whenever and by whatever process of mutual accommodation the meeting-point is ultimately reached, it will, like other such points in history, be but a starting-place for further journeying. In Hart Crane's phrase, we shall continue to witness "New thresholds, new amazements!"

[1] Mumford: *Technics and Civilization*, cited, p. 44.

SUGGESTED READING

A comprehensive list of books on Europe, and Europe's relations with the United States, would constitute another volume. The scholar requires no selected bibliography or, rather, would prefer to draw up his own. For the general reader who might wish to explore further the subject matter of this book, I offer here suggestions that reflect my personal preferences—or, some might say, idiosyncrasies.

For a bird's-eye view of Europe from the Roman Empire to the end of the nineteenth century, *Europe: a Personal and Political Survey of 3,000 Years of European History* (New York, Scribner, 1948) by C. A. Alington, an English historian, can be recommended.

The British skill for historical synthesis without unpalatable popularization is also exemplified in J. J. Saunders's *The Age of Revolution: The Rise and Decline of Europe since 1815* (New York, Roy, 1949) which paints in broad strokes the interplay of liberal romanticism and industrial revolution, of democracy and nationalism, of scientific materialism and irrational racialism, and closes with a litany on "the passing of liberalism" at the close of World War II. By contrast, Professor J. Salwyn Schapiro, formerly of City College in New York, in *Liberalism and the Challenge of Fascism; Social Forces in England and France (1815–1870)* (New York, McGraw-Hill, 1949) strikes a positive note, viewing twentieth-century socialism as a natural outgrowth of nineteenth-century liberalism. Essential to an understanding of the impact of the Industrial Revolution on Western Europe and, through European transmission, on underdeveloped areas of the world, is *The Rise of Modern Industry* by J. L. and Barbara Hammond (New York, Harcourt Brace, 1926), a classic in its field. Everyone concerned with the forces and ideas that have shaped Western society will want to read, and

345

reread, Lewis Mumford's *Technics and Civilization* (New York, Harcourt Brace, 1934). On current economic problems the most stimulating volume is Peter F. Drucker's *The New Society: the Anatomy of the Industrial Order* (New York, Harper, 1950).

Volumes have been published on the influence of the West on colonial peoples. The quintessence of informed thought on this subject is imaginatively distilled by Cora du Bois, now a member of the State Department staff, in her slim volume, *Social Forces in Southeast Asia* (Minneapolis, University of Minnesota Press, 1949).

An excellent succinct summary of the development and operation of European socialist institutions is found in "Socialism in Western Europe," by Professor Herbert Heaton of the University of Minnesota (Foreign Policy Association, *Headline Series* #71, September–October 1948). For texts and analyses of the economic plans of European countries, the best source is Seymour Harris's, *Economic Planning* (New York, Knopf, 1949). Of Europe's centuries-old struggle to achieve unity Stringfellow Barr, president of the Foundation for World Government, gives an eloquent account in *The Pilgrimage of Western Man* (New York, Harcourt Brace, 1949).

For an over-all picture of post-war Europe, *The State of Europe* by Howard K. Smith (New York, Knopf, 1949), CBS European correspondent, is the most up-to-date, as well as the most even-handed in its appraisal of the East-West conflict. On individual countries the following are definitely worth reading: on *Britain*—Francis Williams's *Fifty Years March* (London, Odhams Press, 1949), a Laborite writer's appraisal of post-war Britain; Virginia Cowles's *No Cause for Alarm* (New York, Harpers, 1949), presents Britain as viewed by an American correspondent frankly partial to Labor; and Ivor Thomas's *The Socialist Tragedy* (London, Latimer House, 1949), registers a dissenting opinion for the Opposition; and on *Anglo-American* relations—*The United States and Britain* by Professor Crane Brinton (Cambridge, Harvard University Press, 1947); on *France*—Pierre Maillaud's *France* (London, Oxford University Press, 1943), is brief but penetrating; on the *Mediterranean*—William Reitzel, *The Mediterranean: Its Role in America's Foreign Policy* (New York, Harcourt, Brace, 1948); on *Germany*—two *New York Times* correspondents present widely differing conclusions as to the extent to which Germany has recovered from Nazism, in Drew Middleton's *The Struggle for Germany,* (Indianapolis and New York, Bobbs-Merrill, 1949), and Delbert Clark's *Again the Goose Step: The Lost Fruits of Victory* (Indianapolis and New York, Bobbs-Merrill, 1949). Mr. Clark turned out to be more correct in his diagnosis than Mr. Middleton—but Mr. Middleton, in subsequent dispatches to *The New York Times,* considerably modified his own estimate of the situation; on the *U.S.S.R.*—Edward Crankshaw, an English authority on Joseph Conrad, was attached to the British military mission in Moscow during the war and has contributed a discerning and well-written study of the Russian character in *Russia and the Russians* (New York, Viking, 1948); *Russia Is No Riddle* (New York, Greenberg, 1945), the thoughtful book of Edmund Stevens, for many years *Christian Science Monitor* correspondent in Moscow, should be reread now in conjunction with his series of 1949–50 articles on post-war Russia in the *Monitor; Russia in Flux,* edited and abridged by S. Haden Guest (New York, Macmillan, 1948) from two works by the British expert on Russia, Sir John Maynard, and *Russia* by Sir Bernard Pares (New York, Penguin, 1943), remain the most valuable guides to an understanding of modern Russia in the perspective of history. For an analysis of Russo-American relations the reader may want to consult Vera Micheles Dean, *The United States and the U.S.S.R.* (Cambridge, Harvard University Press, 1948, third printing), and the chapters on Stalin's foreign policy in Isaac Deutsher's *Stalin* (New York, Oxford University Press, 1949).

Among authors who have presented informed criticisms of the Soviet system are William Henry Chamberlin, American correspondent in Moscow, who records his profound disillusionment in *The Confessions of an Individualist* (New York, Macmillan, 1940) which should be read along with his *The European Cockpit* (New York, Macmillan, 1947); Louis Fischer, also an American correspondent in Moscow during the twenties and early thirties, long known for his admiration of Soviet ideas and practices, who explains why he became critical of the Soviet system in *The Great Challenge* (New York, Duell, Sloan and Pearce, 1946); David J. Dallin, Russian Socialist in exile since 1922, who has written a number of works on Russia, notably *The Real Soviet Russia* (New Haven, Yale University Press, 1947), and (with Boris I. Nicolayevsky) *Forced Labor in Soviet Russia* (New Haven, Yale University Press, 1947); and Nicholas S. Timasheff, Russian-born member of the sociology department of Fordham University, in *The Great Retreat* (New York, Dutton, 1946).

In a period of fast-moving developments fiction and essays frequently offer a far more illuminating picture than the most elaborate political and economic analyses. Among works which no one interested in post-war Europe should miss are Albert Camus' *The Plague* (New York, Knopf, 1948); the plays and novels of Jean-Paul Sartre and Jean Giraudoux; Anouilh's tragedy, *Antigone* (Paris, Table Ronde); Carlo Levi's *Christ Stopped at Eboli* (New York, Farrar, Straus, 1947); Konstantin Simonov, *Days and Nights* (New York, Simon and Schuster, 1945); Theodore Plievier's *Stalingrad* (New York, Appleton, 1948); the novels and essays of Simone de Beauvoir; George Orwell's *Animal Farm* (New York, Harcourt, 1946) and *Nineteen Eighty-Four* (New York, Harcourt Brace, 1949); Alexander Baron (pseud.), *From the City, From the Plough* (New York, Washburn, 1949); John Hersey, *The Wall* (New York, Knopf, 1950); the novels of Joyce Cary and Henry Green, rich in allusions to our times.

In appraising the interaction of Europe and the United States, the reader will want to consult *The American Spirit in Europe* by the Norwegian historian Halvdan Koht (Philadelphia, University of Pennsylvania Press, 1949), and a journalist's analysis of European attitudes toward America by André Visson in *As Others See Us* (New York, Doubleday, 1948).

Among the few works so far published on the European Recovery Program, Western union and the Atlantic community, the most valuable are Walter Lippmann's prophetic *U.S. War Aims* (Boston, Little Brown, 1944); *The West at Bay* (New York, Norton 1948), a plea for Western unity by Barbara Ward, foreign editor of the London *Economist; Last Chance for Common Sense* by James P. Warburg (New York, Harcourt Brace, 1949), wartime Deputy Director (Overseas Branch) of the Office of War Information; and Professor Seymour Harris of Harvard, *The European Recovery Program* (Cambridge, Harvard University Press, 1948). On the overshadowing armaments problem, Dr. Vannevar Bush in *Modern Arms and Free Men* (New York, Simon & Schuster, 1949) and Marshall Andrews, military analyst of the *Washington Post,* in *Disaster through Air Power* (New York, Rinehart, 1950), state, with varying degrees of emphasis, their doubts about the "absolute" character of the atomic bomb and the decisiveness of air warfare.

The many memoirs published by former American Cabinet officers and diplomats provide valuable material for analysis of relations between Europe and the United States during and since World War II. Notable among them are, by Henry L. Stimson and McGeorge Bundy, *On Active Service in Peace and War* (New York, Harper, 1947); Cordell Hull, *Memoirs* (New York, Macmillan, two volumes, 1948); James F. Byrnes, *Speaking Frankly* (New York, Harper, 1947); Robert Sherwood, *Roosevelt and Hopkins* (New York, Harper, 1948; Edward Stettinius, *Roosevelt and the Russians* (New York, Doubleday, 1949); Lt. Gen. Walter Bedell Smith, *My Three Years in Moscow* (New York, Lippincott, 1950); and Gen. Lucius D. Clay, *Decision in Germany* (Garden City, Doubleday, 1950). To this growing shelf of American reminiscences should, of course, be added Winston Churchill's war memoirs: *Their Finest Hour* (New York, Houghton Mifflin, 1948), *The Gathering Storm* (1949), *The Grand Alliance* and *Europe, Unite* (to be published in 1950).

The reader interested in following current developments in Europe will find useful material in the quarterly, *Foreign Affairs* (New York); the weekly *Foreign Policy Bulletin* and the bimonthly *Foreign Policy Reports* published by the Foreign Policy Association; *The Economist* (London) and *L'Economie* (Paris); *L'Esprit,* a distinguished Catholic monthly published in Paris; and leading European newpapers, notably *The Times* (London), *The Manchester Guardian,* and *Le Monde* (Paris).

For official texts, the reader should turn to the *Bulletin* and other publications of the Department of State, and the reports of the Economic Cooperation Administration, the Organization for European Economic Cooperation (OEEC), and the United Nations agencies, notably the United Nations Economic Commission for Europe.

INDEX

i

Index

Organization *(cont.)*
amples of European co-operation, 267
Orwell, George, 124
Osborn, Frederick H., 319
Osservatore Romano, 66

Pacciardi, Randolfo, 141-2
Pacific Pact, 287-8
Paderewski, Ignace, 19
Paine, Thomas, 197
Pakistan, 32, 43, 191; imperialism abandoned, 32
Palacky, František, 19
Palestine, 14, 238
Pan-Americanism, 21
Pan-Slavism, 16, 21
Paris, 6
Pearl Harbor, 42
Perón, Juan D., 51, 229
Petkov, Nikola, 234
Philip, André, 205
Philippines, 32, 34, 192
Pilsudski, Marshal Joseph, 135, 159, 160
Pius XII, Pope, 55
Planned economy, 72
Poincaré, Raymond, 200
Point Four program, 328
Poland, 87, 135, 154-6, 160; Communist Party, 161-2; conflict between church and state, 167-9; eastern border problem, 159; fear of German irredentism, 160; industrial recovery, 165-6; manufacture of cotton goods, 49; nationalists rebel against U.S.S.R. dictates, 18; natural resources, 101; no reparation obligations, 102; peasant resistance to co-operatives, 164-5; population, 30, 158-9; possession of German territories, 158; Roman Catholic Church challenged, 54; six-year plan, 119; state control, 116
Poles, 7-8, 16; attitude toward Russia, 161; challenged by Nazis, 160
Politbureau, 64, 169
Political power, from monarch to people, 48
Polo, Marco, 33
Popular will, 14

Port Arthur, 40, 42, 216, 217
Portugal, 33, 52, 106
Postal service, 113-14
Poverty, world-wide, 336
Prague, 154
Private enterprise, 59, 70, 95, 96, 258; abandonment in England, 71; anti-social results of, 60; criticism of socialization, 121; Germany, 151; social control of, 71-2
Profits, 58, 60; tax on, 108
Proletarian revolution, 64
Propaganda versus war, 171
Public utilities, state control, 114

Queuille, Henri, 138-9, 140, 141

Racial-superiority doctrine, 32
Radford, Arthur R., 298
Radio broadcasting, state control, 114
Railroads, state-operated, 113
Rapallo Agreement, 147
Rathenau, Walther, 147
Rationalism, 53, 54
Red Shirts, march on Rome, 19
Reed, John, 218
Reformation, 10, 47
Reformers, nineteenth-century, 60, 61, 62
Regional grouping of countries, 28
Regional Security Pact, 277
Religion: and science, 54-5; "opium of people," 55
Religious groups, wrestling with economic justice, 66
Renaissance, 10, 47
Renan, Ernest, 7
Renault autmobile and airplane factory, 117-18
Reparations, 83, 102
Rerum novarum, encyclical, 55, 132
Revolutionary movements, 13
Reynaud, Paul, 137, 139
Rice, 38
Roman Catholic Church: attacks on, 54; attitude on heretics, 9; attitude toward social-economic issues, 55; conflict with Social Democrats, 137; dogmas, 53; excommunication of Communists, 56, 143-4; free thought discouraged, 47; influence

A NOTE ON THE TYPE

The text of this book was set on the Linotype in Baskerville. Linotype Baskerville is a facsimile cutting from type cast from the original matrices of a face designed by John Baskerville. The original face was the forerunner of the "modern" group of type faces.

John Baskerville (1706–75), of Birmingham, England, a writing-master, with a special renown for cutting inscriptions in stone, began experimenting about 1750 with punch-cutting and making typographical material. It was not until 1757 that he published his first work, a Virgil in royal quarto, with great-primer letters. This was followed by his famous editions of Milton, the Bible, the Book of Common Prayer, and several Latin classic authors. His types, at first criticized as unnecessarily slender, delicate, and feminine, in time were recognized as both distinct and elegant, and his types as well as his printing were greatly admired. Four years after his death Baskerville's widow sold all his punches and matrices to the Société Littéraire-typographique, which used some of the types for the sumptuous Kehl edition of Voltaire's works in seventy volumes.

COMPOSED, PRINTED, AND BOUND BY H. WOLFF, NEW YORK